PERFECT GRACE!

It's All About Jesus

Thomas M. Hughes, MA

The author assumes full responsibility for the accuracy of all facts and quotations as cited in this book. The opinions expressed in this book are the author's personal views and interpretations, and do not necessarily reflect those of the publisher.

This book is provided with the understanding that the publisher is not engaged in giving spiritual, legal, medical, or other professional advice. If authoritative advice is needed, the reader should seek the counsel of a competent professional.

ISBN-13: 978-1-4796-0873-7 (Paperback)
ISBN-13: 978-1-4796-0874-4 (ePub)
Library of Congress Control Number: 2018946719

www.PastorTomHughes.com
www.BibleBiker.com

Unless otherwise indicated, all Scripture quotations are from the King James Version. Italics in the text have been added by the author. Other versions used include:

New King James Version® (NKJV), copyright © 1982 by Thomas Nelson. Used by permission. All rights reserved. *The Holy Bible, English Standard Version®* (ESV). © 2001 by Crossway Bibles, a publishing ministry of Good News Publishers. All rights reserved. *The New American Standard Bible* (NASB), copyright © 1960, 1962, 1963, 1968, 1971, 1972, 1973, 1975, 1977, 1995, by The Lockman Foundation; *The Holy Bible, New Living Translation* (NLT). ©1996, 2004, 2007. Used by permission of Tyndale House Publishers, Inc., Carol Stream, Illinois 60188. All Rights Reserved.

Quotations from the writings of Ellen G. White are used with permission from the Ellen G. White Estate, www.whiteestate.org

All emphasis in this book is by the author.

Published by

DEDICATION

This book is dedicated to the people of the world who understand that God's last day message is *all about Jesus!*—to the people of the world who walk in the perfect grace of God rather than trying to earn their way to heaven by their own achievements. I hope that you like Paul will say with me, "'For I am not ashamed of the Gospel of Christ, for it is the power of God to salvation for everyone who believes' (Rom. 1:16). It is a free gift, and it is the power of God unto salvation."

A loving God has given us perfect grace. God's last-day church is to proclaim the messages of the three angels of Revelation 14. The first of those messages includes the true everlasting gospel, the final message of judgment, and heaven-directed worship. Why is it that the church has not fulfilled its mission to warn the world by proclaiming the three angels' messages? Why is it that the church has been wandering in the wilderness for over a century? What is delaying Christ's return?

God's plan of salvation provides perfect grace that cannot be improved upon. Let's not miss the true first angel's message that contains the elements to arrest the world's attention and complete our mission.

This book is also dedicated with my deepest love and respect to my wife Debbie, whom I had the privilege of leading to Christ and baptizing, whose encouragement and love made this book possible.

TABLE OF CONTENTS

INTRODUCTION

For over a century the Seventh-day Adventist Church has been proclaiming what they call "the three angels' messages" of Revelation 14. The first angel's message, according to Adventist theology, is the final message of warning to a world that is soon to end when Jesus returns to earth. Seventh-day Adventists claim that they are the only church that is warning the world of its impending doom from the last-day message in the book of Revelation. In spite of the church's claim, many—though certainly not all—Seventh-day Adventists have missed the significance, the timelessness, and the eternal truths contained in the first angel's message. Revelation 14:6, 7 proclaims that message:

> And I saw another angel fly in the midst of heaven, having the everlasting gospel to preach unto them that dwell on the earth, and to every nation, and kindred, and tongue, and people, saying with a loud voice, Fear God, and give glory to him; for the hour of his judgment is come: and worship Him that made heaven, and earth, and the sea, and the fountains of waters."

These verses have an ominous tone that certainly grabs a person's attention. This first angel is flying in the middle of heaven like a satellite circling the earth, an indication that the message comes from God and that it is to be broadcast to all people on the planet.

We could say that the angel is "preaching," or proclaiming, God's message to all people—no matter where they live—in every country of the world and in every language. His message is proclaimed so loudly that everyone in the entire world can hear it. It is a message that commands everyone to fear God and challenges all human beings to glorify God. It is a message that *demands* that people worship the Creator who made the heavens and the earth, the sea, and the waters that spring up from the earth. This means that a worldwide movement of people must be confidently and vigorously preaching in all the world. And what are they preaching? They are preaching *GOD'S PERFECT GRACE*, which is the everlasting gospel, the arrival of God's judgment hour, and the worship of the Creator. Many Adventists embrace God's perfect grace and share a Christ-centered, worshipful message of judgment. Some, however—and not an insignificant number—are preaching a false message because, however well-intentioned they may be, they are missing the key point of the first angel—God's plan of salvation has provided PERFECT GRACE that is sufficient to redeem every person willing to accept it. Christ's perfect grace is our only hope!

The Adventist message is sometimes presented under the influence of "mythologies," which may sound right, but end up preventing us from understanding the message of the first angel. These "mythologies" will be addressed throughout this book, though we will always aim to do so with a positive focus. When the FBI trains its agents how to spot counterfeit currency, they spend hundreds of hours studying real bills and almost no time studying counterfeit ones. When you know what the genuine looks like, the counterfeit will be easy to spot. That is why we will spend most of our time on the truth of God's Word, which is the antithesis of the seven mythologies of Adventism we will briefly mention below.

1. **The first mythology, which has done terrible harm to the Adventist Movement, is the heresy of perfectionism.**

   Far too often, when Adventists are asked, "Are we saved by faith *and* works?" they will answer, "Yes, we are." Their answer reveals that they have a Roman Catholic understanding of the gospel. Large segments of Adventists believe that works done by the Holy Spirit are meritorious and have an influence on our acceptance with God. They say, "It's not my works; it's the Spirit's works." However, this is the same understanding that Roman Catholics have when they assert that their works count towards their salvation. To respond to this assertion, we will have an in-depth study of true perfection and how human beings can acquire it. Our church's official position in the twenty-eight fundamentals is that God's grace is perfect and cannot be improved upon. Unfortunately, too many of us are "achievers" rather than "receivers." Even though an entire Sabbath school quarterly was devoted to the gospel as proclaimed in Galatians, the church has struggled, ever since 1888, to grasp the concept that "by no works of the law shall any man be saved." Sadly, the heresy of meritorious works *through* us is still alive and well in our midst. In a church where no Adventist has even kept a single Sabbath perfectly, some proclaim to the world that, unless they keep the Sabbath, their soul will be in peril. But, only Christ's perfect Sabbath-keeping has merit with God.

Unfortunately, too many of us are "achievers" rather than "receivers."

2. **The second mythology is "Harvest Theology."**
   Many leading Adventists, including church officers and editors of denominational periodicals and publications have, for over fifty years, taught what was first espoused by M. L. Andreasen, an Adventist minister who was once disfellowshipped and then reinstated. Many have accepted this teaching and have failed to see that it is built on a system of worship that leads to an erroneous view of righteousness by faith. The basic premise that Andreasen taught is that, before Jesus can return, Seventh-day Adventists must reach a state of sinless perfection through character development so that, by the time Jesus steps out of the sanctuary in heaven, they will be so perfect that they can

stand before God without a mediator and will live sinlessly until Jesus comes. In this teaching, the world will only be "harvested" when the church has achieved this state of perfection.[1]

A corollary teaching is that Adventists must develop a perfect character that will "vindicate the character of God" by achieving sinless perfection and developing a perfect character that will vindicate God's character by living sinless lives before probation closes, and through the time of trouble. When Ellen White states that God's people "vindicate the character of God," she is not talking about their achieving a sinless character.[2] She is talking about "sustaining grace." She refers in the same statement to "the matchless grace shown in the plan of redemption," in the context of "great salvation" for God's people. She is encouraging us to praise God for His redeeming, saving grace, and vindicating Him by revealing His grace in our lives *by faith*. She says this to encourage us to study the science of gospel salvation and to praise God with our whole heart and soul.

She does not mean that we must achieve sinless perfection so we can "vindicate" God's character. She is encouraging God's people to be faithful, and, by their example, strive to be found faithful to the gospel by bearing the fruit of praise, gratitude, and the obedience of faith. She is not teaching "Harvest Theology" because our characters are "as filthy rags" and our good works are sinful. We can hardly vindicate ourselves by our sinful characters, let alone vindicate God. She is simply encouraging us to take God's side in the great controversy and demonstrate our faith by our works, imperfect though they may be. Walking by faith and trusting only in Christ's righteousness is the only way our characters in a relative sense vindicate God's character. Since the noblest and gentlest among men are but a faint reflection of the character of Christ, no human other than Jesus Christ vindicates God's character in the fullest sense.

In our limited sphere, doing our best, we can imitate the pattern, though never equaling it. In this relative sense we can vindicate God's point of view. However, if we define vindicating God's character as achieving sinless perfection, we are mis-characterizing the meaning of Ellen White's statement. Her statement was an admonishment to accept and study the gospel of Jesus Christ and, by grace through faith alone, vindicate God's plan of salvation by taking His side, accepting His redemption and walking in the obedience of faith, receiving a righteous character, *not* achieving it. The doctrine of "Harvest Theology" relies on a Roman Catholic version of the gospel, which is far from perfect, and which is not grace (which means "a gift") at all!

3. **The third mythology is a Roman church understanding of worship and reverence.**
   For centuries, reverence was defined in the Roman Church as "silence before God."[3] Only the priests and higher officials of the church were allowed to speak. This view has persisted into modern times. Many Adventists hold this strict view of reverence. They believe that we should not speak out in church services. They believe that we should not praise God in a loud voice saying, "Amen!" or "Praise the Lord!" They believe that we should not raise our hands in the sanctuary or to applaud when a brother or sister sings or plays an instrument that gives glory to God. They believe that we should not shake hands or hug a fellow worshipper in the pew beside us. They have forgotten that Jesus taught, "It is lawful to do good on the sabbath days" (Mark 3:4). They embrace a formal, Christless, joyless, silent religion in which, if there is any hand raising, it better be to ask a question! No wonder our children find our services so dull and uninspiring. We will explore in God's Word what true reverence is and discover that our God is pleased by and how He inhabits the praise of His people (Ps. 22:3)!

4. **The fourth mythology is the concept of Puritan—or Adventist—separatism.**
   Some of the early founders of the church came from Puritan separatist roots. They had a very strict view of the world to the point of accepting "extra-biblical" elements into their belief system. In the area of dress,

they believed that merely having buttons on one's clothing was showy, that wedding rings and jewelry of all sorts were worldly, and that the church is a fortress to protect believers from the world rather than a hospital for sinners and a rescue station for the lost. Under that strict view, Adventists sometimes wore extreme fashions that demonstrated "separation from the world." Some modern Adventists have mistakenly taken the position that does not encourage members to be joyful and exuberant in their worship, music, and praise. Surprisingly, the Adventist pioneers were often exuberant in their worship practices. Though many are unaware of it, the Seventh-day Adventist Church has a heritage of enthusiastic prayer and praise meetings. Adventists have come to believe they have to be extreme in their diet and lifestyle, even though Ellen White was a "shouting Methodist" who wrote many times that shouting would beat the devil back[4] and that we should be exuberant in our worship and praise of God, and that we should not make dress a test.[5] "Adventist separatism" contradicts all this and more. It leaves people believing that they are following her counsels as a prophetess while exceeding her standards because of a hyper-conservative ideology. If Adventism as a whole continues to embrace this theology, they will soon be as marginalized and culturally irrelevant as "Adventist Separatists."

5. **The fifth mythology is the false theology of a condemnatory judgment.** Even though the Bible repeatedly teaches that Jesus did not come into the world to condemn the world, "but that the world through him might be saved," many Adventists teach that the primary purpose of the judgment is to expose those who are still imperfect because they have failed to achieve the necessary character perfection through the work of the Holy Spirit. This message of sinless perfectionism has driven off whole generations of Adventist youth who are observant enough to realize that neither they nor their parents could ever achieve the expected "righteousness." For decades, Adventists have emphasized what we must do for God more than they have emphasized what God has done for us. The judgment is all about what Jesus did—not about

what we accomplish in our own works! These Adventists teach that they have to achieve a perfect character because they must vindicate God's character by their achievements. Yet, God's grace is perfect, and so is Christ's character as no other. Those of this mindset somehow overlook the truth that "No one is perfect but Jesus" (Ms. 24, 1892, in *That I May Know Him*, p. 136). We cannot add to perfect grace. We can only receive it.[6]

6. **The sixth mythology is the doctrine that we will have to live sinlessly without a Mediator during the time of trouble.**
   Some among us preach the time of trouble so much that they become "troublemakers." They teach that one day Jesus will throw down the golden censer and that, when he does, all God's people who remain alive on earth will have to live a perfect life without a mediator or they won't be saved. Absolute sinless perfection must be achieved with a sinless life because, if anyone sins after Jesus steps out of the most holy place in heaven, he or she will be lost. This heresy has been taught in our churches and Sabbath schools for over fifty years. Many have become so fearful of having to stand without a mediator that they have either left the church, lost their minds, or become perfectionists who are constantly striving to become holy enough that they won't need Christ anymore when He steps out of the heavenly sanctuary. They define sin to be about specific controllable acts and fail to see that their sinful nature will remain until Jesus comes. Confusing sanctification and glorification, they misinterpret both. As we continue, we will see how that, when Christ has left the sanctuary above, we won't need a mediator, for we will have already been mediated, and whoever is righteous will be righteous *still!*

7. **The seventh mythology that has caused some to miss the meaning of the first angel's message is failing to share a judgment message that declares saints "not guilty" and delivers them from sin and all its consequences.**

By missing the good news of the judgment, we can make judgment something to be feared and dreaded rather than embraced and celebrated. The gospel gives us the right to worship the Creator and secures us freedom from the consequences of our sins, declaring us "not guilty" and making us joint heirs with Christ. How have we failed? By preaching that the second coming of Jesus is a moment of condemnation, a judgment that will condemn those who have insufficiently achieved perfection, which is taken as a guarantee of salvation. We have also failed by preaching that those who remain imperfect will be punished and those who still eat meat will not make it through the time of trouble.[7] This dark message of condemnation offers zero hope. There is no way out except to get on the treadmill of earning our own salvation. By not preaching the "hour of his judgment has come" as an hour to "receive" salvation as a free gift rather than as a lifetime of futile "achieving," we rob the gospel of its power and the judgment of its hope. Could it be that a church that emphasizes the "Revelation of hope" has missed the very message it claims to be proclaiming? These messages are often very condemning of Roman Catholicism and emphasize that the majority of the Christian community is "keeping the wrong day" and eating "unclean foods" and that we have to "glorify God in our bodies" by preaching the health message! We sadly leave out the fact that righteousness by works, even in keeping the correct day, gains us nothing, and that it is God who makes us holy, not our Sabbath keeping, for such works cannot save us. Neither can "righteousness by mouth" save us. Our only perfection, our only law keeping, our only Sabbath keeping, our only way of glorifying God is found in the *righteousness of Jesus Christ!*

So what we are going to do in this book is to present the true first angel's message, which is the foundation and heart of the three angels' messages. This book will be divided into three major sections: The Everlasting Gospel, the Judgment in Heaven, and True Worship. The first angel's message is the heart and soul of Seventh-day Adventism. Without a firm understanding of this message, the movement becomes a Christless, legalistic, perfectionistic religion that damages its children and fails in its mission. Without it, where is the hope? Where is the joy? Where is the power? Where is the freedom? Where is the eternal life? Where indeed! What have we missed? All the above, and much more! Let's start learning, embracing, and proclaiming the most powerful, hope-filled, joyful message of freedom and deliverance ever given! It is *GOD'S PERFECT GRACE!* It's all about Jesus! Let's get it right this time and preach it when we do!

PERFECT GRACE!

PART I

THE TRUE EVERLASTING GOSPEL

Seventh-day Adventists have preached the three angels' messages for over a hundred and fifty years. The first of those angels flying in the midst of heaven is a worldwide message that must be proclaimed before the second and third angel's messages can be proclaimed. While there is no doubt that this is God's last message to a dying world and that Adventists have been entrusted with delivering it, there are truths in that message that have been missed by a large part of God's church.

Perfect grace needs no improvement from us! We just need to get it and proclaim it! It is God's perfect eternal *plan of grace!*

> *The purpose and plan of grace existed from all eternity. Before the foundation of the world it was according to the determinate counsel of God* that man should be created and endowed with power to do the divine will. The fall of man, with all its consequences, was not hidden from the Omnipotent. Redemption was not an afterthought, a plan formulated after the fall of Adam, but an *eternal purpose*, suffered to be wrought out for the blessing, not only of this atom of a world, but for the good of all the worlds that God had created. (*Signs of the Times*, Feb. 13, 1893)

The everlasting gospel must be preached first and foremost. Even though many in the church understand the true gospel, many others have forsaken the true gospel and have proclaimed a gospel of righteousness by mouth, placing diet above Jesus. Others have proclaimed righteousness by "character development." Still others believe that they are working their way to heaven by overcoming their sins, and they truly believe that they will soon be perfect through their strivings. Throughout the history of the church, fanatics have taken a good thing—striving for holiness—to an extreme. And the result has been pietism, perfectionism, legalism, extreme monasticism, and, of course, Pharisaism. These extreme forms of righteousness by works have even reared their ugly heads from time to time in Adventism. Only an absolutely perfect person's obedience is acceptable to God. What is your basis for righteousness? Some tend to place more emphasis on sanctification than justification, defining the atonement in terms of God's work to cleanse our character from sin in addition to payment of the penalty for sin. "*Eschatological perfectionism*" is the teaching that a final generation of believers must achieve a state of complete sinlessness in the final period just before the second coming of Jesus. Accordingly, the cleansing of the heavenly sanctuary, or investigative judgment, is thought to also involve the complete cleansing of the lives of believers from sin on earth. Those who promote M. L. Andreasen's "Last Generation Theory" are spreading the seeds of this heresy.[8] This heresy teaches that a group will vindicate God's character before Jesus comes by achieving sinless perfection.[9] This belief is fostered and promoted by those who teach the so-called "Last Generation Harvest Theology."[10] Their teaching, that sinners somehow vindicate God by achieving a sinless, perfect character, is blasphemous. Christ alone is sinless and only He vindicates God's character through His character development, *not* sinful man! His righteousness is the only true basis of acceptance with God. Apart from Christ, even our prayers are an abomination to God. Therefore, the true everlasting gospel rejects any claims of perfection or good works apart from those of Jesus Christ. Sinless perfectionism, the teaching that people can somehow "achieve" a form of perfection by their obedience is a common heresy. God's perfect grace alone can meet the demands of the law, and human beings can add nothing to it. God's perfect grace is sufficient to provide all our needs through Christ.

Sinless perfectionism is taught by:

1. **Roman Catholics.** "Justification is not only the remission of sins, but also the sanctification and renewal of the interior man."[11] You are justified by your Spirit-enabled obedience. You in fact *become* holy.
2. **The "Holiness Movement" of Wesleyan Methodists.** Through the experience of the "second blessing," these Christians believe that the Holy Spirit enables sinless perfection (though Wesley did not like the term since it was unbiblical). Wesley combined some aspects of the Catholic emphasis on perfection with the Protestant emphasis on grace.[12]
3. **Pentecostals.** Coming out of the Wesleyan movement, they have also taught that the "second blessing" of the Holy Spirit enables sinless perfection.
4. **Adventist sinless perfectionists.** Self-described "historic" Adventists share the Roman Catholic belief that works done through the Holy Spirit are "not our works" and that Spirit-enabled obedience *justifies* us through the development of a holy character.[13] (This view is not a teaching of the Seventh-day Adventist Church.[14])

The belief that you must achieve holiness and *become* holy for God to accept you is rampant throughout Christianity. Luther's concept (which was shared by Ellen White) was that "the Christian man" is "*simultaneously sinful and righteous, a sinner in fact and a righteous man in hope, i.e., as a repentant sinner or as a forgiven sinner*" (*Luther: Lectures on Romans*, Wilhelm Pauck, translator, p. xliv). This concept is often overlooked. Our carnal nature is not removed, so, though we are considered righteous, yet we will remain sinners with a sinful nature until Jesus' second coming. (*Acts of the Apostles*, p. 560, says: "Sanctification is not the work of a moment, an hour, a day, but of a lifetime. It is not gained by a happy flight of feeling, but is the result of constantly dying to sin, and constantly living for Christ.")

The similarities are startling. All four groups—Roman Catholics, Wesleyan Methodists, Pentecostals, and Adventist perfectionists—are all teaching salvation by works. In all four groups, people are justified by faith, but must do a second work of Christian perfection through the sanctification of the Holy Spirit for their justification to remain valid. All four groups insist that it is not one's works, but the Holy Spirit's works that save a person. Yet, the end result is exactly the same—we are forgiven for our past sins, but, to *remain* justified, we must "overcome" our present sins by living a "perfect and sinless" life. Each group gives justification with one hand while taking it away with the other if we don't perform by achieving sinless perfection now. How can God ever accept us if it is based on achieving perfection? Only Jesus is perfect. Perfection in this life is only found in the righteousness of Jesus Christ. The true everlasting gospel is the message that only Jesus Christ is perfect; only His righteousness is acceptable to God, for He alone is holy, perfect, and acceptable to God. The gospel proclaims that He is our only hope and our only perfection. The gospel is to help the people of God to come to Jesus by faith in His righteousness. Worshipping the Father in spirit and truth is the very purpose for which this book was written. Let no man enslave you in the bondage of salvation by works! Live free in Jesus—*by faith!* Saved by grace … through faith … to work! The obedience of faith works by love! Walk in the Spirit! Let us demonstrate that the gospel of *perfect grace* results in holier, more sanctified lives than perfectionism ever could! By beholding we become changed! As we spend time with Jesus through Bible study and prayer, we will be changed into His image. By faith through the righteousness of Christ, God gives us a new nature that is renewed by a daily dying to self, surrendering to God, and renewal of our minds through a study of God's word and prayer. We have a very important part to play in our daily transformation and renewal. We don't read and pray for its own sake in order to achieve something FOR GOD. We read and pray to RECEIVE something FROM GOD—a transformation of our carnal nature, putting off the old and RECEIVING the new by renewal of our minds through the daily baptism of the Holy Spirit. We will be inspired by His example to live godly lives. He will accomplish the work that He has begun in us through faith! We must worship God in spirit and in truth! We need to get our eyes off of ourselves and our own performance. Looking unto Jesus, our faith will be brought to completion (Heb. 12:1, 2)!

Notice the following commentary:

> *Your hope is not in yourself; it is in Christ.* Your weakness is united to His strength, your ignorance to His wisdom, your frailty to His enduring might. So you are not to look to yourself, not to let the mind dwell upon self, but look to Christ. Let the mind dwell upon His love, upon the beauty, the perfection, of His character.... When the mind dwells upon self, it is turned away from Christ, the source of strength and life. Hence it is Satan's constant effort to keep the attention diverted from the Saviour and thus prevent the union and communion of the soul with Christ. The pleasures of the world, life's cares and perplexities and sorrows, the *faults of others*, or *your own faults and imperfections*—to any or all of these he will seek to divert the mind. Do not be misled by his devices. Many who are really conscientious, and who desire to live for God, he too often leads to *dwell upon their own faults and weaknesses, and thus by separating them from Christ he hopes to gain the victory. We should not make self the center and indulge anxiety and fear as to whether we shall be saved.* All this turns the soul away from the Source of our strength. Commit the keeping of your soul to God, and trust in Him. *Talk and think of Jesus.* Let self be lost in Him. Put away all doubt; dismiss your fears. Say with the apostle Paul, "I live; yet not I, but Christ liveth in me: and the

> life which I now live in the flesh I live by the faith of the Son of God, who loved me, and gave Himself for me." Galatians 2:20. Rest in God. He is able to keep that which you have committed to Him. *If you will leave yourself in His hands, He will bring you off more than conqueror through Him that has loved you.* (*Steps to Christ*, pp. 70–72)

We must emphasize what God has done for us and not what we have to do for God. When we overemphasize the latter, we become legalistic and miss the mark. Jesus said, "Go home to your friends, and tell them how much *the Lord has done for you*" (Mark 5:19, ESV). The first angel's message calls men and women back to God's perfect grace—with the true everlasting gospel and judgment taking place in heaven, while men and women live as if nothing is taking place. It calls people back to the biblical worship of their Creator. We must awaken the world to the judgment in heaven and their need to worship God in spirit and truth, clothed in Christ's beautiful white robe of righteousness.

Christ is our only perfection, our only righteousness, our only hope!

CHAPTER 1

PERFECT GRACE! THE TRUE EVERLASTING GOSPEL

And I saw another angel fly in the midst of heaven, having the everlasting gospel to preach unto them that dwell on the earth, and to every nation, and kindred, and tongue, and people, saying with a loud voice, Fear God, and give glory to him; for the hour of his judgment is come: and worship him that made heaven, and earth, and the sea, and the fountains of waters.
—Revelation 14:6, 7

The Seventh-day Adventist Church has been entrusted with the task of preaching the everlasting gospel to the whole world. There is no doubt that, through our missionaries, we have gone into the vast majority of countries in the world and have preached a gospel. But have we preached the *true* everlasting gospel? Have we emphasized God's perfect grace? Many among us have. But there are also those among us who have preached a gospel based more on Roman Catholic tradition than on the Bible message of Christ's righteousness. Some among us have preached a gospel of faith *and* works, or of faith *and* character development, or of faith *and* vegetarianism. All good things—works, character development, and vegetarianism—but none is the gospel. As a result, for many among us, our faith has become a treadmill that never ends. It is the endless effort to work our way to heaven by developing our characters, eating the right foods, wearing (or not wearing) the right fashion accessories. It is the endless effort of an achiever rather than a receiver of Christ's precious gift. When will we learn that we have nothing to contribute that is of value? It is not Christ *and* anything else! When will we learn that we cannot add anything to Christ's completed work? Our only Righteousness is sitting at the right hand of God and is holier than any mere mortal can ever achieve. The first angel's message must be proclaimed in its biblical purity. We must preach the true everlasting gospel or we will have missed the most important truth in the first angel's message! *IT'S ALL ABOUT JESUS!* Either we proclaim the everlasting gospel of Christ's righteousness alone or we aren't proclaiming the gospel at all! Christ's righteousness is our only righteousness. We have no righteousness apart from Him. He is our only hope of salvation. Our works cannot justify us with God. And, as sinners, we cannot become sinless until Christ comes and removes our sinful flesh. As long as we are in this body, we will have to fight with our sinful, carnal nature. Only when our sinful nature is removed and we receive our glorified bodies can we claim any type of sinless perfection. All of our righteousness comes from Jesus Christ alone. He alone is worthy of praise. He alone is perfect. He alone is sinless. He alone is perfection personified.

Only Jesus is sinless. Do you agree with that? Not one person—not one except Jesus Christ—is perfect. Not one person apart from Jesus is good. Not one person is holy. Every single person except Jesus Christ has sinned and is sinful. We are sinners, and we will be sinners until Jesus returns. All our sins, whether they are conscious sins or unconscious sins, *are punishable by death*. There is no free pass on unconscious sin. In an effort to justify perfectionism, some minimize any sin that is not conscious or deliberate. Any such "perfection" is worthless, and it is vile in God's sight. Christ's perfection is the only perfection acceptable to God for salvation. That is why Jesus said, "Except your righteousness exceed the righteousness of the scribes and Pharisees, you will by no means enter the kingdom of heaven" (Matt. 5:20). The scribes and Pharisees were the most meticulous, careful sinners that ever lived on earth, and more meticulous, I believe, than anyone who would ever live after them. Yet, Jesus said that their righteousness wasn't good enough—and neither is ours. On the other hand, if Jesus is your Savior, your righteousness *exceeds* that of the Pharisees because His righteousness becomes your righteousness and you are credited with *Christ's perfect life*. H. M. S. Richards put it this way when I once spoke with him about this subject. I said, "Elder Richards, I've got a question about righteousness by faith." He said, "Good, Tom, because that's the only kind there is! It's by faith. There is no other kind. Our only righteousness sits at the right hand of God." That was a really wise answer. Isaiah 64:6 says, "all our righteousnesses are like *filthy* rags" (NKJV). What does the little word "all" mean in the phrase, "*all* our righteousnesses [plural]"? The word is in the phrase just in case somebody might think, *Well, it may be true that some kinds of righteousness are not okay, but mine certainly is!* Remember that the passage is referring to our *good deeds—not* to our sins! The Hebrew is using an illustration from a woman's time of the month, when she was considered "unclean." It is a very graphic way of telling us that even our best works are unclean. And the reason the prophet used the term "filthy rags" is because he wanted us to understand just how foul our own works are.

Ecclesiastes 7:20 says that not only have all sinned, but there is not a person on the earth who "does good and does not sin" (NKJV). In Isaiah 55, verses 8 and 9, God declares that His thoughts—His ideal *for His children*—are higher than the highest human thought can reach. News flash: That means you will never reach them—they are too high. This was God's plan for Adam, and for all who followed. Sadly, Adam's sin changed and corrupted his nature, and reaching God's ideal became impossible. So, if God's thoughts are higher than the highest human thought can reach and they are His ideal, then only Jesus' perfect character can reach God's ideal and is acceptable for salvation. That we can't reach the ideal, I would think, is obvious, but some people still miss it. And they say, "Oh, I have to work really hard to develop a perfect character, or I won't be saved." Well, you can work all you want, but the harder you work, the less saved you will be. You need to accept the free gift of Christ's perfect character. In the book, *Steps to Christ*, Ellen White wrote that, when we accept Him as our Savior, we receive His perfect character credited to our account.

> If you give yourself to Him, and accept Him as your Saviour, then, sinful as your life may have been, for His sake you are accounted righteous. *Christ's character stands in place of your character, and you are accepted before God just as if you had not sinned*. (*Steps to Christ*, p. 62)

Christ's character stands in place of your character, and you are accepted before God just as if you had not sinned. (*Steps to Christ*, p. 62)

That's how you get His character. The matter of trying to work to get more perfect gets worse when we consider the following scriptures. David described, in Psalm 14, how human beings are lost and unrighteous and not a single one is sinless. He also wrote: "Do not enter into judgment with Your servant, for in Your sight no one living is righteous" (Psalm 143:2, NKJV). Paul wrote in his gospel epistle to the Romans: "For the wages of sin is death, but the gift of God is eternal life in Christ Jesus our Lord" (Romans 6:23, NKJV). Before this he quoted Psalm 14 to make this same point: "As it is written: '*There is none righteous, no, not one; There is none who understands; There is none who seeks after God. They have all turned aside; they have together become unprofitable; there is none who does good, no, not one*'" (Rom. 3:10–12, NKJV). Jesus asked the man who addressed Him as "Good Master," "'Why do you call Me good? No one *is* good but One, *that is*, God'" (Mark 10:18; Luke 18:19, NKJV).

The whole of Revelation, chapter 5, is glorious, especially verse 9. So is chapter 15, in which it says that only the Lord is holy. Is that true? Does that leave us out? It is tough for human beings to admit that they are sinful and that there is nothing they can do to save themselves. That admission is the hardest thing for us proud humans to make. Even if we accept Christ, we want to say, "Can't I add just a little bit? Can't I work really hard and maybe develop a really good character so I can be proud of my accomplishments and maybe get a little bit of self-worth out of them?" No, it does not—and should not—work that way.

Our self-worth should come from the fact that Jesus loved us so much that He died to save us. We measure our worth in the fact that God gave His only Son to save us, and we find our only righteousness in the perfection of Jesus. We are not sinless, and we won't be until Jesus comes again. "We cannot say, 'I am sinless' till this vile body is fashioned like unto his glorious body" (E. G. White, *Signs of the Times*, March 23, 1888). We cannot say, "I am sinless" until Jesus transforms our sinful flesh. Here is another very interesting statement for "those who would be true to God." "Their only hope is in the mercy of God … They are fully conscious of the *sinfulness of their lives*, they see their weaknesses and unworthiness" (*Prophets and Kings*, p. 588). Do you know who she is talking about when she describes those who are alive just before Jesus comes? "But while the followers of Christ have sinned, they have not given themselves up to be controlled by the satanic agencies. They have repented of their sins and have sought the Lord in humility and contrition, and the divine Advocate pleads in their behalf. He who has been most abused by their ingratitude … who knows their sin … declares: '… They may have imperfections of character; they may have failed in their endeavors; but they have repented, and I have forgiven and accepted them'" (*Prophets and Kings*, p. 589). Notice her words, "they may have imperfections of character … but they have repented, and I have forgiven them." So they still have imperfections of character, do they? It gets more interesting when we read what she wrote in *Steps to Christ*, p. 64, about true children of God realizing "that their character is imperfect, their life faulty." Then she added, "Even if we are overcome by the enemy, we are not cast off, not forsaken and rejected of God. No; Christ is at the right hand of God, who also maketh intercession for us." Then, she delivers the blow that takes us to our knees: "The closer you come to Jesus, the more faulty you will appear in your own eyes; for your vision will be clearer, and your imperfections will be seen in broad and distinct contrast to His perfect nature. This is evidence that Satan's delusions have lost their power; that the vivifying influence of the Spirit of God is arousing you.… No deep-seated love for Jesus can dwell in the heart that does not realize its own sinfulness.…" (*Steps to Christ*, p. 64, 65). The people who claim that they are getting closer and closer to God and feeling better and better about how perfect they are becoming, cannot be coming closer to Him. They are on the devil's highway, and they have believed a lie! The closer you come to Christ the more you see your own sinfulness, the more obvious it becomes! This is a word of warning to any self-righteous, sanctimonious Pharisee who goes around telling people that they have to become perfect and holy by stopping eating this and wearing that and checking off an endless list of things to win his approval. The truth is, the closer you get to Jesus, the worse you look in your own eyes. I pity the people who have listened to this sanctimonious, self-focused gospel of having to achieve a perfect character before Jesus comes, for they will surely get discouraged and give up. What do you think Jesus will say when you get to heaven? Do you actually think that Jesus will say, "My! You're almost too good to enter My kingdom! O great one, we are so fortunate that you showed up, for you have developed such a flawless character that you have almost surpassed the Son of God!"

What blasphemy it is to even suggest that we could ever equal the Son of God! And to teach people that they have to be as absolutely perfect as Jesus is perfect is an assertion that makes the angels shudder. Anybody who gets to heaven will fall down on his or her knees and say, "I am unworthy! It is a gift of grace that you are letting me in!" Remember—the closer you get to Christ, the more you will see your own faults and imperfections! So, dear saint, as you read your Bible more and as you pray more, and it feels as if you are just getting worse, you are not. You have always been that sinful! But God, in His mercy, just hid it from you. He didn't want to break your heart and discourage you. Yet, now that you are reading the Bible and praying and getting close to Him, and the Holy Spirit is in you, He believes that you can handle the truth, and He gives you a good look at yourself! And then you go away, saying, "I'm getting even worse! I pray; I read my Bible, and I thought I was getting closer to You, but look at me!" And Jesus probably just thinks to Himself: *How do you think I feel? It is even worse than you realize, but, in mercy, I won't give you more than you can bear*. The followers of Christ have sinned. He who has been the most abused, who knows our sin best says, "They have repented and I have forgiven them." "If we do not see our own moral deformity, it is unmistakable evidence that we have not had a view of the beauty and excellence of Christ.... and when the soul, realizing its helplessness, reaches out after Christ, He will reveal Himself in power. The more our sense of need drives us to Him and to the word of God, the more exalted views we shall have of His character, and the more fully we shall reflect His image" (*Steps to Christ*, p. 65).

Do you feel helpless? Do you feel unworthy? Do you feel like a sinner? Do you feel like you cannot control your life and the sinful nature inside of you? Do you look at yourself and feel like a wretch? If you do, then you sound like the apostle Paul in Romans 7, when He cried out, "O wretched man that I am!" (Rom. 7:24, NKJV). Notice, he didn't say, "O wretched man that I *used to be*." Paul knew exactly what he was. He was a sinner and a pretty unrelenting one at that. I don't know how many deaths of believers he was responsible for. And he said that he believed that he had been doing God's will when he did it. Though he may not have done the deed, he was responsible for taking them outside and watching as others stoned them to death, and he held the people's coats while they were doing it. "O wretched man that I am! Who will deliver me from this body of death?" (Rom. 7:24, NKJV). And then, in Romans 8:1, Paul added: "There is therefore no condemnation to those who are in Christ Jesus." Yes, with Paul I can admit that I am a wretch. However, I'm a *saved* wretch. I'm a *born-again* wretch. I'm a *Christian* wretch. Romans 7 describes the carnal nature; Romans 8 describes the spiritual nature. They exist simultaneously in all who are Christians. As John Wesley used to say: The carnal nature *remains* but it does not *reign*.[15] And Luther said, "We are righteous (in Christ) and sinful (in ourselves) at one and the same time."[16]

"The sinner may err but he is not cast off without mercy" (E. G. White, Ms. 21, 1891). The next statement I am going to quote is a hard saying for me. It says that, even when I am in church, in my best clothes and praying—wouldn't you think that would be my holiest moment in the week—I am still totally unworthy. You know, if you were going to depend on a time when, if a big boulder fell on you that you would be assured of going to heaven, wouldn't that probably be the time you would want it to happen—when you're in church and praying and feeling very pious and holy? Now consider the statement:

The carnal nature remains _but it does not_ reign.

> The religious services, the prayers, the praise, the penitent confession of sin, ascend from true believers as incense to the heavenly sanctuary, but passing through the corrupt channels of humanity, they are so defiled that unless purified by blood, they can never be of value with God. They ascend not in spotless purity, and unless the intercessor who is at God's right hand presents and purifies all by His righteousness, it is not acceptable

> to God.... He gathers into this censer the prayers, the praise, and the confessions of His people, and with these He puts His own spotless righteousness. (E. G. White, Ms. 50, 1900)

That's what makes any of us acceptable—Christ's achievements. Even our prayers are an abomination to God apart from Christ's righteousness. Now that is kind of shocking, isn't it? I have always thought, when I was praying, that maybe the things I was saying were good. But the Bible says that the Holy Spirit has to take what I say in prayer and has to clean it up (Rom. 8) and make it what it should be because it is going up to the King. Isn't it great how God has sent the Holy Spirit to take our prayers and reinterpret them, making them pure by His righteousness before delivering them to God as if Jesus had uttered them to His Father? The Father is pleased, and He blesses us just as if Jesus Himself had been praying to the Father! Isn't God good to us! When we pray and praise Him, even though we are corrupt human beings, our praise ascends, purified by the righteousness of Christ, as interpreted by the Holy Spirit, and presented to God as a beautiful thing. Such perfect grace! in transforming a sinful thing into a beautiful thing because God loves us so much that He gave us Jesus and His Holy Spirit! Paul declared: "We are saved by grace through faith ..." Did He add anything to that? No. That is how we are saved—*by* grace alone, *through* faith, *to* work. That is what Ephesians 2:8–10 says:

> For by grace you have been saved through faith; and that not of yourselves, it is the gift of God; not as a result of works, so that no one may boast. For we are His workmanship, created in Christ Jesus for good works, which God prepared beforehand so that we would walk in them. (Eph. 2:8–10)

The verse states: HAVE BEEN SAVED. It has already taken place. It's past tense! Only the finished work of Christ, completed 2,000 years ago on Calvary, is sufficient to save us. We cannot add to it in any way. Jesus does *not* make up the difference, as I've heard people say. It is not true that, when we do the best we can, Jesus makes up the difference. Oh, no! We have nothing to contribute. Otherwise, we can get holier and holier and finally end up with nothing to make up and with no need for Jesus at all. Say it isn't so! *It's all Jesus!* He doesn't "make up the difference" in that sense. *It's all Jesus*. Salvation is a gift from Christ. What we do comes as we walk in the good works of His making (see Eph. 2:10). Based on our forgiveness and our acceptance of His loving gift, we respond in love by being obedient. Yet, it earns us nothing. There is no merit in it! The only thing that our works can do is show God that we love Him as we serve others out of that same love. God does take notice of what we do, and He does command us to render unto Him the obedience of faith—but not for salvation. "A man is not justified by the works of the law but by faith in Christ" (Gal. 2:16). "For by grace you have been saved through faith" (Eph. 2:8). "Therefore by the deeds of the law there shall no flesh be justified in his sight: for by the law is the knowledge of sin. But now the righteousness of God without the law is manifested, being witnessed by the law and the prophets; Even the righteousness of God which is by faith of Jesus Christ unto all and upon all them that believe: for there is no difference: for all have sinned, and come short of the glory of God" (Rom. 3:20–22). "Yet indeed I also count all things loss for the excellence of the knowledge of Christ Jesus my Lord, for whom I have suffered the loss of all things, and count them as rubbish, that I may gain Christ and be found in Him, not having my own righteousness …" (Phil. 3:8, 9, NKJV). Paul says, *Get my righteousness as far away from me as you can! I don't want to be found in it.* Then he continues:

> Not having my own righteousness, which is from the law, but that which is through faith in Christ, the righteousness which is from God by faith; that I may know Him and the power of His resurrection, and the fellowship of His sufferings, being conformed to His death, if, by any means, I may attain to the resurrection from

> the dead. Not that I have attained, or am already perfected; but I press on, that I may lay hold of that for which Christ Jesus has also laid hold of me. Brethren, I do not count myself to have apprehended; but one thing I do, forgetting those things which are behind and reaching forward to those things which are ahead. I press toward the goal for the prize of the upward call of God in Christ Jesus. (Phil. 3:9–14, NKJV)

Ellen White also weighed in on the subject.

> Those who are really seeking to perfect Christian character will never indulge the thought that they are sinless … These professedly sanctified persons are not only deluding their own souls by their pretensions, but are exerting an influence to lead astray many who earnestly desire to conform to the will of God. They may be heard to reiterate again and again, "God leads me! God teaches me! I am living without sin!" Many who come in contact with this spirit encounter a dark, mysterious something, which they cannot comprehend. But it is that which is altogether unlike Christ, the only true pattern. (*The Sanctified Life*, pp. 7, 10)

Anyone who says that he is perfecting himself or that he is almost perfect is deceiving himself. I had one dear Seventh-day Adventist brother tell me, "Pastor Hughes, I have not sinned in three weeks." I said, "Brother, you just blew it because you just bragged to me about not sinning. Sorry about that. You're going to have to start over."

Only Christ's character is perfect. We cannot attain it by works. It can only be received by faith. It is a gift. You do not need to despair about what a wretch you are. We are all wretches. Some people just won't admit it. We are all lost sinners. We are saved by grace through faith, and I know that that wounds our pride. It is a gift by God's perfect grace alone. The only character worthy of entrance into heaven is Jesus' character. Our best efforts have no merit for salvation. They are valuable only as an outward demonstration of our inward acceptance of God's free gift and as an act of love and devotion to God. Even the good works that we do are a gift from God, which He prepared for us before the foundation of the world. It's all about Jesus. Amen? "It is a gift of God lest anyone should boast." One day, a group of people asked Jesus, " 'What shall we do, that we may work the works of God?' Jesus answered and said to them, 'This is the work of God, that you believe in Him who He has sent' " (John 6:28, 29, NKJV). Our work is to *believe*. We need to be Christ-centered and allow Him to do the perfecting, bringing it to completion when He comes again and not before. The work of believing—with God's gift of faith (Eph. 2:8)—is our work. Our challenge is to continue to believe, even though we are so unworthy, even though we so often fail, even though we see nothing good within ourselves. That's the challenge—to know how far short we fall and yet *still believe* that Jesus will complete the work that He has begun in us. That is where we need to put our focus and our will. We need to read our Bible every morning. We need to pray. We need to keep our eyes on Jesus. We need to get our eyes off ourselves. Jesus works on transforming us through His Spirit, and He will complete the work in us when we ascend to meet Him in the air! That carnal nature that makes you so depressed and so weak, that knocks you down and makes you feel like you're never going to make it—that carnal nature is going to be removed when Jesus comes!

You need to put on the armor of God. As a good soldier of Jesus Christ, you need to fight those feelings, fight that nature, by keeping your eyes fixed on Jesus! The more you look at yourself, the more discouraged you will get because you are not achieving what you think you should. When you look at yourself, what do you see? You see that you are a sinner. The principle is: "By beholding we become changed." So, if you look at yourself, you will become a bigger and better sinner. You know the internal dialogue—*Oh, no! I'm not doing this; I'm not doing that. I should be doing this; I should be doing that. I, I, I, I, I.* No wonder you're depressed! Get your eyes off yourself and get them on Christ! "Turn your eyes upon Jesus ... and the things of earth will grow strangely dim"—even that carnal nature of yours that is driving you crazy! Keeping your eyes on Jesus nails your carnal nature to the wall! Self is a killer! Self will kill me and drag me—and anybody else he can get—down to hell. And the kicker is that he lives inside of me, and your carnal nature lives inside of you. You know what I'm talking about. The first day that you quit reading the Bible, the first day that you don't have your worship, the first day you stop praying—that is the first day you are on the road to hell as your carnal nature begins to drag you down. When Jesus was asked, "What shall we do that we might work the works of God?" He said, "Believe on Him whom God has sent." And Paul said, "For I bear them record that they have a zeal for God, but not according to knowledge. For they being ignorant of God's righteousness" seek "to establish their own righteousness" and "have not submitted" to "the righteousness of God.... *For Christ is the end of the law for righteousness to every one that believeth*" (Rom. 10:2–4). This means that Christ is the great goal of the law to bring righteousness to all who believe.

Speaking of the law, Jesus said, "I am not come to destroy, but to fulfill." Here He uses the word "fulfill" in the same sense as when He declared to John the Baptist His purpose to "fulfill all righteousness" (Matt. 3:15), that is, to fill up the measure of the law's requirement, to give an example of perfect conformity to the will of God. His mission was to "magnify the law, and make it honorable" (Isa. 42:21). He was to show the spiritual nature of the law, to present its far-reaching principles, and to make plain its eternal obligation.

When I accept Christ, He pays the price of my redemption set by the law, and the law can no longer condemn me. When I stumble and when I fall, I need to ask forgiveness and I need to pray. Then, whenever I fall, I choose to fall toward God and not away from Him. The Bible says that the righteous man falleth seven times, but he rises again. It's not a question of *when* we're going to fall, or *if* we're going to fall. It's *how* we're going to fall. Are we going to fall, fighting for all we're worth? Sometimes, the carnal nature is going to sabotage you. It is going to catch you by surprise. Sometimes people of the world will catch you by surprise. Sometimes the old devil will fool you and knock you down flat. We're all going to fall sometimes. We're all going to struggle sometimes.

Some people think we need reformation. The carnal nature cannot be reformed. It is not subject to the law of God, neither indeed can it be (Rom 8:7). Instead of reformation we need transformation! We need a new nature to make us new creatures in Christ. Colossians 3:10 exhorts us to "put on the new man" through knowledge of the nature of Jesus Christ. We need a Romans 8 experience! We don't need to reform the old nature—we need to kill it! We need to nail it to the cross so that it won't control us anymore. No more old deeds of the flesh, driven by our carnal nature's lusts! Romans 12 gives us a glimpse into this process: "And be not conformed to this world: but be ye transformed by the renewing of your mind, that ye may prove what is that good, and acceptable, and perfect, will of God" (Rom. 12:2). "Through the merits of Christ you may part with that which scars and deforms the soul, and which develops a misshapen character. You must put away the old man with his errors and take the new man, Christ Jesus" (*Testimonies for the Church*, vol. 4, p. 92).

So we don't have to live in sin and degradation any longer. We can be free of the sins of the flesh as well as the sins of self-righteousness, pride, and false religious beliefs, which make us feel superior to others. We can, through the merits of Jesus Christ, be transformed into a NEW CREATURE. Paul writes in 2nd Corinthians 5:17: "Therefore if any man be in Christ, he is a new creature: old things are passed away; behold, all things are become new." The carnal nature, the sin nature, REMAINS until Jesus comes. Even though we cannot have that total transformation and perfection until Jesus comes and removes our carnal nature, we can nail it to the cross and begin a new life with Jesus Christ when we PUT ON THE NEW NATURE given to us through the Spirit of God.

Paul encourages us to "put on the new man which is renewed in knowledge." Romans 12:1–2 reads, "Be transformed by the renewing of our mind." So, the "New Nature" of Romans 8 is found residing in our mind, and renewed by knowledge. The carnal mind is not subject to the law of God. Our new mind, or nature, must be able to be subject to, and obedient to, the law of God. This new nature is capable of things our carnal nature is not capable of. Through a transformation of our mind, and a knowledge of scripture, we can become a "New Creature" in Christ! Galatians 6:15 tells us, "For in Christ Jesus neither circumcision availeth any thing, nor uncircumcision, but a new creature." That's good news! We are something new and different! God makes us into new creatures. Ezekiel wrote it like this: "And I will give them one heart, and I will put a new spirit within you; and I will take the stony heart out of their flesh, and will give them an heart of flesh" (Ezek._11:19). And, "Cast away from you all your transgressions, whereby ye have transgressed; and make you a new heart and a new spirit: for why will ye die, O house of Israel?" (Ezek._18:31). He goes on to say, "A new heart also will I give you, and a new spirit will I put within you: and I will take away the stony heart out of your flesh, and I will give you an heart of flesh" (Ezek._36:26). You become a New Creature, with a New Heart, and a NEW LIFE! HOW? Through divine transformation of your nature and renewing your mind through the Holy Spirit who communicates with your new spirit that God puts inside you. The struggle is the experience of a perfectly normal Christian, fighting the fight of FAITH!

Falling down in the mud isn't failure; it's lying in the mud and wallowing in it! Get up! Run back to Jesus. He'll wash you off. He'll cleanse you with His blood, and He'll put His beautiful white robe on you. "Therefore, having been justified by faith, we have peace with God" (Rom. 5:1, NKJV). Do you want to have peace while in your carnal nature? Get justified by faith. Quit trying to work your way to heaven, do everything right, earn God's approval, and just admit that you can't. Christ is God's heir, and you are joint heirs with Him. Just say, "Look, He did it right. I can't do it right. However, everything He did I want. Can I have what He has?" And God will say, "Through my Son, whatever I give My Son, I will give to you as well."

"Righteousness is love" (*Thoughts from the Mount of Blessing*, p. 18), and we receive righteousness by receiving Him. How was that? We receive righteousness by receiving Jesus, and righteousness is love. *Love* is what is important. If you're as mean as a snake, but you keep the right day, what good is that? If you can't love your neighbor or your brothers and sisters or your family, who will care whether you keep the right day or not? "Not by painful struggles or wearisome toil, not by gift or sacrifice, is righteousness obtained; but it is freely given to every soul who hungers or thirsts to receive it ..." (*Thoughts from the Mount of Blessing*, p. 18). "Their righteousness is of Me, saith the Lord" (Isa. 54:17). "This is His name whereby He shall be called: THE LORD OUR RIGHTEOUSNESS" (Jer. 23:6). Regarding the "divine beauty of the character of Christ," Ellen White declared, "the noblest and most gentle among men are but a faint reflection" (*Thoughts from the Mount of Blessing*, p. 49). This is because "He is altogether lovely" (Song of Solomon 5:16).

No one has ever equaled Christ's divine beauty—not John the Baptist, not Enoch, not Elijah, not Moses, not any of the apostles. Their lives were all "but a faint reflection." No one has even come close to His holy, glorious, righteous character, and no one ever will! He alone was and is and always will be worthy! Glory—all glory—to Jesus alone"[17] *Thoughts from the Mount of Blessing*, p. 49, reveals that the theology of acceptance with God through character development or righteousness by works, which has been preached in this church for eighty-five years, is a lie. Hear me now! Perfectionist teachings like Andreasen's "harvest theology," which have been preached for years, are not the truth. It does not matter who has promoted them, be it M. L. Andreasen, Herbert E. Douglass, author of *How to Survive in the 21st Century*, or any other author. The teaching that, unless you develop a perfect character, you can't be saved or you won't be able to stand in the time of trouble, is *not* what the Bible teaches.

"The noblest and most gentle among men are but a faint reflection." Think about that! So, if preachers are telling you that, unless you achieve a perfect character, you can't be saved, what does that mean? It means that they are setting you up to be lost! It means that no one can be saved, for no one but Christ has ever or could ever have developed a perfect character! I'll tell you what—they're not going to teach and preach that unchallenged on my watch! Oh, no, my brothers and sisters! I've got the Bible! And the Bible tells me that Christ is our only righteousness and that He *towers* above Moses and Elijah and Enoch and all the great prophets of old. Christ is the "Mt. Everest of righteousness," and any and every human being is but a molehill compared to Him! Bow before the righteousness of Jesus Christ and accept His "Mt. Everest" righteousness as a free gift. You don't have to work for it. I've had people say to me, "But don't you want to be perfect? Don't you want to have a perfect character?" And I have said, "Why are you working so hard for something that I already have? And why are you looking at me? I'm a wretch—miserable, poor, blind, and naked. But I am wearing Christ's beautiful white robe. That means that I have *His* perfect character, and up in heaven, God has written it down in His 'book of remembrance.' I am perfect in Him! Do you understand? His grace is sufficient; His grace is perfect! His plan of salvation is what I need!"

Do you see why this message breaks the devil's hold on you? How many years have you worked and struggled to become what you thought you were supposed to be and yet you failed and thought that, because you were failing, God would never accept you? Just admit it! *O God, I have failed! I cannot do it! Please do it for me! I accept Jesus. Give me Your salvation! I receive it! I can't do it. I'm a miserable failure. I'm a miserable wretch!* But there is "now no condemnation to those who are in Christ Jesus" (Rom. 8:1, NKJV). Oh yes! Now I'm on my way to heaven! Now I'm on the right path, not because of anything *I've* done, but because of what Christ has done on my behalf. This takes place during the time of the end. Let's read what Ellen White wrote about it. *Pay close attention.* "While those who are self-confident, and trust in their own perfection of character, lose their false robe of righteousness when subjected to the storms of trial, the truly righteous, who sincerely love and fear God, wear the robe of Christ's righteousness in prosperity and adversity alike" (*The Sanctified Life*, p. 11). Isn't that beautiful? Don't be one of those who are self-confident and trust in your own perfection of character. Oh, no. Trust only in the love and mercy of God by accepting by faith the free gift of eternal life!

Occasionally we hear a story that we can't forget. One such story is about a father who was heartbroken because a man on the street mugged his only son, stabbing him to death. At the trial, the father listened as the criminal described killing the man's son. The man was sentenced to life in prison, and, after about a month, the father went to visit him, began studying the Bible with him, and, in time, the man was converted. The two became close friends. After about 15 years, the man was paroled and let out of prison. And do you know why officials decided to let him out of prison? The father of the son who was murdered legally adopted his son's killer as his son and vouched for his safety to society. Amazingly, the man invited the man who had murdered his son to come live in his own home; he gave him his son's old room, and adopted him into his family. Now isn't that bizarre! The young man had never had a home and never had a father. He was converted and later became a preacher, proclaiming the Word of God.

Now, isn't that exactly what God has done for us? Didn't we murder His only Son? And doesn't He give to us everything that Jesus gets? He gives us eternal life. He gives us a home in heaven. He treats us as if we are His only Son and loves us just like we never murdered His. Aren't we joint heirs with Christ (Rom. 8:17)? Have not the Scriptures declared that Christ alone is our righteousness, that Christ is our only hope, our only perfection? When the time of trouble arrives and Christ's priestly ministry comes to an end as He finally throws down His censer, do you not believe that He will be with us even to the end of the world and that His righteousness is the only kind there is? Do you not believe that God's grace makes perfect provision for your salvation? We can say with Paul, "I am crucified with Christ: nevertheless I live; yet not I, but Christ liveth in me: and the life which I now live in the flesh I live by the faith of the Son of God, who loved me, and gave himself for me. I do not frustrate the grace of God: for if righteousness *come* by the law, then Christ is dead in vain" (Gal. 2:20, 21).

God's standard is the same for all mankind, including those living in the last days. God's perfect grace is sufficient! There is one righteousness, one plan of salvation, one Savior—Christ our righteousness! Which gospel are you preaching, sharing, and embracing? The true first angel's message contains the true everlasting gospel! The true gospel is *ALL ABOUT JESUS!*

Jesus saves us by His perfect grace alone! He is our only perfection, our only righteousness, our only hope!

CHAPTER 2

ONE MAN'S OBEDIENCE

For as by one man's disobedience many were made sinners, so by the obedience of one shall many be made righteous.
—Romans 5:19

My challenge to every person reading this book is to step away from the endless wrangling that has divided our churches for so long and humbly admit your own sinfulness, submit yourself to God, and claim the righteousness of Christ as your only perfection. It is my hope that we will all come together in the unity of the faith regarding God's perfect grace and plan of salvation. Adventists must proclaim the true everlasting gospel or none at all! Part of the everlasting gospel is to magnify the law as Jesus did and not dilute or diminish its requirements. What the law demands is a lifetime of perfect obedience. Absolute perfection, by definition, is a lifetime of perfect obedience. When Adam and Eve sinned, they only had to commit one sin to lose their home and their souls. They would have died the day they sinned had Jesus not stepped in and literally saved them. They would have perished that very day except for the perfect grace of God:

> The law requires us to present to God a holy character. It demands of men today just what it demanded of Adam in

> Eden—perfect obedience, and perfect harmony with *all* its precepts in all relations of life, under *all* circumstances and conditions. No unholy thought can be tolerated, no unlovely action can be justified. As the law requires that which *no man of himself can render, the human family are found guilty* before the great moral standard, and it is not in the province of law to pardon the transgressor of law. The standard of the law cannot be lowered to meet man in his fallen condition. No compromise can be made with the sinner to take less than the full requirement of the law. The law cannot acquit the guilty, it cannot cleanse the sinner, or give power to the transgressor to raise himself into a purer, holier atmosphere. Standing before a holy, good, and just law, and finding ourselves condemned because of transgression, we may well cry out, What shall we do to be saved? (*Signs of the Times*, May 30, 1895).

So when you are converted, even if you were to live a flawless life from then on, it would not be good enough. *You cannot manufacture a lifetime of absolutely perfect obedience*. Only Christ is able to provide that perfect grace for you! Thank God that He has, for He is the only human being to ever live an absolutely perfect and flawless life from birth to death! Our key text for this chapter is: "Therefore, as through one man's offense judgment came to all men, resulting in condemnation, even so through *one Man's righteous act the free gift came to all men*, resulting in justification of life. For as by one man's disobedience many were made sinners, so also *by one Man's obedience many will be made righteous*" (Rom. 5:18, 19). It is by one man's obedience that we are made righteous. This text cannot be expanded to include two people! There is only room for one. It is not Jesus *plus* my obedience or Jesus *plus* my sanctification or Jesus *plus* my character development. It is not Jesus *plus* anything else! It is by one man's obedience—and one man's obedience alone—that I am justified and that I receive the free gift of eternal life! His life, death, and resurrection alone—without any other contribution—have provided me with the free gift of eternal life.

Another text that makes the unique nature of Christ's gift totally clear is found in the tenth chapter of Hebrews. "By the which will we are sanctified through the offering of the body of Jesus Christ once for all" (Heb. 10:10). "For by one offering He has perfected forever those who are being sanctified" (Heb. 10:14, NKJV). Christ's absolutely perfect life and His death on Calvary provide my only perfection. Notice that the verse says that we are "perfected forever "by this one mighty offering. I can't add anything to it. It covers me, and God regards me to be as sinless as Jesus—even while I am *being* sanctified. This text shows how that it is God's perfect grace and the righteousness of Jesus alone that provide our perfection while we are still going through the process of sanctification—a process that will continue right up until the day that Jesus comes again.

> It was possible for Adam, before the fall, to form a righteous character by obedience to God's law. But he failed to do this, and because of his sin *our natures are fallen and we cannot make ourselves righteous. Since we are sinful, unholy, we cannot perfectly obey the holy law. We have no righteousness of our own with which to meet the claims of the law of God.* But Christ has made a way of escape for us. He lived on earth amid trials and temptations such as we have to meet. He lived a sinless life. He died for us, and now He offers to take our sins and give us His righteousness. If you give yourself to Him, and accept Him as your Saviour, then, sinful as your life may have been, for His sake you are accounted righteous. *Christ's character stands in place of your character, and you are accepted before God just as if you had not sinned.* (*Steps to Christ*, p. 62)

Only through Christ can you be perfect. He went before you and accomplished what you can never do. All you can do is accept the salvation

He has provided as a free gift. Perfectionists confuse sanctification with glorification. The perfectionist's theory is that all-comprehensive transformation should take place now. But notice what the book on the twenty-eight fundamental beliefs declares in the section entitled, "*Glorification and Perfection*":

> Some incorrectly believe that the ultimate perfection that glorification will bring is already available to humans. But of himself, Paul, that dedicated man of God, wrote near the end of his life, "*Not that I have already attained, or am already perfected*; but I press on, that I may lay hold of that for which Christ Jesus has also laid hold of me. Brethren, I do not count myself to have apprehended; but one thing I do, forgetting those things which are behind and reaching forward to those things which are ahead, I press toward the goal for the prize of the upward call of God in Christ Jesus" (Phil. 3:12–14). Sanctification is a lifelong process. Perfection now is ours only in Christ, but the ultimate, all-comprehensive transformation of our lives into the image of God will take place at the Second Advent. Paul cautions: "Let him who thinks he stands take heed lest he fall" (1 Cor. 10:12). (*Seventh-day Adventists Believe*, pp. 145, 146)

Take heed lest you fall. Glorification and absolute perfection will only come at the Second Advent. That is the teaching of the Seventh-day Adventist Church. The church's official position is very clear. It is backed by the following statement from the Spirit of Prophecy:

> "Be ye therefore perfect, even as your Father which is in heaven is perfect." Matt. 5:48. Christ presents before us the highest perfection of Christian character, which throughout our lifetime we should aim to reach.... Concerning this perfection, Paul wrote: "Not as though I had already attained, either

> were already perfect: but I follow after.... I press toward the mark for the prize of the high calling of God in Christ Jesus" (Phil. 3:12–15).
>
> How can we reach the perfection specified by our Lord and Saviour Jesus Christ—our Great Teacher? Can we meet His requirement and attain to so lofty a standard? We can, else Christ would not have enjoined us to do so. He is our righteousness. In His humanity He has gone before us and wrought out for us perfection of character. We are to have the faith in Him that works by love and purifies the soul. (Ms. 148, 1902, in *That I May Know Him*, p. 130)

She is encouraging you to receive it, not to achieve it! Yet, some believe that absolute perfection is something that we can achieve, earn, or accomplish. They emphasize the message of "Yes, we can." It is true that we can be perfect, but it is only by accepting what Christ has wrought out for us. He is our righteousness. By accepting, by faith, His perfect character as ours, as a free gift, His perfection is credited to our account, and God accepts us as if we had never sinned. Consider Ellen White's words again: "If you give yourself to Him, and accept Him as your Saviour, then, sinful as your life may have been, for His sake you are accounted righteous. *Christ's character stands in place of your character, and you are accepted before God just as if you had not sinned*" (*Steps to Christ*, p. 62). This is the message of 1 John 1:9—we are cleansed of "*all* unrighteousness." Paul declared that he had not attained perfection (Phil. 3:12), and no other person in the Bible ever attained it either. The Bible says, "All have sinned and come short." Remember, only a *lifetime* of unbroken perfection can meet the law's demands. Don't make the arm of flesh your trust.

Notice what Ellen White says about John and Peter: "We become changed into the image of that upon which we dwell ... John was not perfect; Peter denied his Lord; and yet it was of men like these that the early Christian church was organized. Jesus accepted them that they might learn of Him what constitutes a perfect Christian character. The business of every Christian is to study the character of Christ.... It is not an uncommon thing to see imperfection in those who carry on God's work ... Everything that causes us to see the weakness of humanity is in the Lord's purpose to help us to look to Him, and in no case put our trust in man, or make flesh our arm" (*Review and Herald*, Aug. 15, 1893, in *That I May Know Him*, p. 182). John was imperfect, and not just at the beginning of his relationship with Jesus. He regarded himself as imperfect at the end of his life, when the enemies of Christianity attempted to kill him by boiling him in oil. "John declared, '... I am only a weak, sinful man, but Christ was holy, harmless, undefiled, separate from sinners. He did no sin, neither was guile found in his mouth.' John's words, while suffering at the hands of his enemies, had an influence, and he was removed from the cauldron by the very ones who cast him in" (*Christ Triumphant*, p. 312).

Paul, Peter, and John were not perfect, so what makes us think that we are going to be? What kind of gall is that? The closer we get to Jesus, the more we see our own sinfulness and, conversely, the less perfect we will appear in our own eyes. We are on dangerous ground if we try to mix in our own character development and works into the salvation equation. The true everlasting gospel is *Jesus plus nothing!* Once we are converted, we obey out of love. The obedience of faith is the fruit of our relationship to Jesus. We don't teach Roman Catholicism, that salvation is faith plus works. There is no absolute perfection apart from Christ. We need to look to Jesus and let Him change us into His image. We need to dwell, reflect, and meditate on Him. We need to study His perfect character. We should not make our own flesh or that of anyone else something in which we put our trust. Christ is our only righteousness. He is the great pattern, and it is our privilege to copy and imitate that pattern. Nonetheless, we will never equal the pattern. Just because we don't deliberately sin does not mean that we are not "sinful." We *are* sinful as John said.

The following comments of Ellen White make it clear that Christ is our only hope.

> *Never can we equal the goodness and the love of Jesus*, but he calls upon every man and woman, youth and child, to behold him, and by beholding his perfection of character, to become changed into his image. Call every talent into exercise to *copy* the Pattern. (*Signs of the Times*, Nov. 28, 1892, emphasis added)
>
> Christ is our pattern, the perfect and holy example that has been given us to follow. We can never equal the pattern; but we may imitate and resemble it according to our ability. When we fall, all helpless, suffering in consequence of our realization of the sinfulness of sin; when we humble ourselves before God, afflicting our souls by true repentance and contrition; when we offer our fervent prayers to God in the name of Christ, we shall as surely be received by the Father, as we sincerely make a complete surrender of our all to God. We should realize in our inmost soul that all our efforts in and of ourselves will be utterly worthless; for it is only in the name and strength of the Conqueror that we shall be overcomers. (*Review and Herald*, Feb. 5, 1895)
>
> Higher than the highest human thought can reach is God's ideal for His children. He wants our minds to be clear, our tempers sweet, our love abounding. Then the peace that passeth knowledge will flow from us to bless all with whom we come in contact. The atmosphere surrounding our souls will be refreshing.... (*Sons and Daughters of God*, p. 348)

But there is no need for us to be alarmed. Ellen White makes it clear that Christ's perfection is on a far more exalted level than ours. Our relative perfection exists solely because of Him, and it is really only a faint attempt at imitation, a mere reflection of the absolute glory and majesty of Christ's holiness. She understood this fact. So, when you read her encouragements to strive for perfection, always remember to interpret her statements in context, remembering that our "perfection" is *always relative*, within the sphere of our abilities, faults, and limitations. God is so wonderfully fair. He only wants us to be the best that *we* can be. He accepts our best efforts, as empowered by the Holy Spirit, as loving obedience in Christ. Jesus' righteousness is so much greater and more glorious than even the noblest of human achievements that it is blasphemy to suggest that any human being could ever equal it. His righteousness is greater than that of Moses, of Paul, of Peter, of James and John, and of all the great men of the Bible combined! "The divine beauty of the character of Christ, of whom the noblest and most gentle among men *are but a faint reflection* ..." (*In Heavenly Places*, p. 63). "As God is holy in His sphere, so fallen man, through faith in Christ, is to be holy *in his sphere*...." (*The Acts of the Apostles*, p. 559). "*They will be in sympathy with Christ, and in their sphere, as they have ability and opportunity, will work to save perishing souls as Christ worked in His exalted sphere for the benefit of man*" (*Testimonies for the Church*, vol. 3, p. 483). In these two statements, we see that Ellen White distinguishes between our sphere and Christ's "exalted sphere." Moral and spiritual perfection is promised to everyone who will overcome by faith. We can indeed live holy, Christ-like lives by His grace. Yet, it would be blasphemous to suggest that our "relative perfection" could ever equal Christ's absolute perfection. That is why so many get confused and wander into perfectionism. Ellen White continues:

"As God is holy in His sphere, so *fallen* man, through *faith* in Christ, is to *be holy* in his sphere...."

> The truth of Jesus Christ does not tend to gloom and sadness.... We must look away from the disagreeable to Jesus. We must love Him more, obtain more of His attractive beauty and grace of character, and cease the contemplation of others' mistakes and errors. We should remember that our own ways are not faultless. We make mistakes again and again.... *No one is*

> *perfect but Jesus*. Think of Him and be charmed away from yourself, and from every disagreeable thing, for by beholding our defects faith is weakened. God and His promises are lost from sight. (Ms. 24, 1892, in *That I May Know Him*, p. 136, emphasis added)

We make mistakes again and again.... No one is perfect but Jesus.

Could she be any plainer? Could she speak any more clearly? "... our own ways are not faultless ... No one is perfect but Jesus.... by beholding our defects faith is weakened." When we stare at our own spiritual navals, beholding our own faults and imperfections, we are actually weakening our faith. We need to get our eyes off of our own faults and the faults of others and fixed upon Jesus. "Do not, because your thoughts are evil, cease to pray. If we could in our own wisdom and strength pray aright, we could also live aright, and would need no atoning sacrifice. But imperfection is upon all humanity ... Christ stands before His Father, saying, 'Lay their sins on me. I will bear their guilt. They are my property. I have graven them upon the palms of my hands" (*In Heavenly Places*, p. 78).

As we look at the first angel's message and realize that the law is part of the everlasting gospel, we should never diminish it in any way. The phrase, "by one man's obedience," means that Jesus paid it all. He lived the only perfect life, and He paid in full every sinner's debt to the law. Moreover, He magnified the law. We should do the same by pointing out that none of us has ever kept the law as Jesus did. Our obedience is unacceptable as a means of salvation. In the true everlasting gospel, there is room for only one man's obedience! Ellen White summed up my feelings on this subject when she wrote:

"We may commit the keeping of our souls to God as unto a faithful Creator, *not because we are sinless, but because Jesus died to save just such erring, faulty creatures as we are*, thus expressing His estimate of the value of the human soul" (*In Heavenly Places*, 80). "*The true penitent learns the uselessness of self-importance. Looking to Jesus, comparing his own defective character with the Saviour's perfect character, he says only—'In my hand no price I bring; simply to Thy cross I cling'*" (*In Heavenly Places*, p. 64). It is my prayer that we all come into the unity of the faith, standing only on the solid rock of Christ our righteousness.

Abiding in Him, claiming His perfect grace, we shall bear much fruit!

CHAPTER 3

THE GREAT GOSPEL PARADOX

For by one offering he hath perfected
for ever them that are sanctified.
—Hebrews 10:14

According to the dictionary, a "paradox" is a statement that seems contradictory, unbelievable, or absurd, but that may actually be true in fact. The everlasting gospel is itself paradoxical. How can God forgive lawbreakers who deserve death? How can sinners who are darkened with sin become clean through God's righteousness? There are many teachings in Christianity that are paradoxical. And if you don't understand the concept of a paradox, then you will not understand many of the great teachings of Christianity. Let's explore a few. How could a good God create an angel of light who became the devil, the epitome of evil? How can a sinful human being offer God perfect worship? When God will not accept anything but perfect, flawless worship, how can we worship Him at all? How can something totally light become something totally dark? I know what you're thinking! You're thinking that God made a beautiful angel and that that angel turned himself into a devil. Right? I'm with you. Yet, when God made Lucifer, wasn't Lucifer totally good? How could something so totally beautiful and good become something so absolutely evil? You do know that it's a mystery and that you can't explain it, right? If you could explain how evil came to be, you would justify its very existence. There is no reason for sin and evil. Neither is there an excuse. If you can explain it, you justify it. The Bible calls it the "mystery of iniquity" (2 Thess. 2:7). It is indeed paradoxical that a good angel could become an absolutely evil devil. It is counterintuitive. On the other hand, how can something totally evil become totally good? How can a sinner become perfect in Christ? How can human beings keep God's law perfectly? Seventh-day Adventists love to say, "We need to keep God's commandments!" Yet, who among us has ever perfectly kept even one Sabbath? (Of course, that doesn't mean there is no practical benefit in our imperfectly kept Sabbaths, for there is.) Would anyone claim flawless Sabbath keeping even for a single day? You know that sounds paradoxical to me. How can we keep God's law perfectly when we are so obviously imperfect? How can sinners be righteous by faith and keep God's commandments when we are obviously incapable of keeping even one Sabbath perfectly?[18]

The great paradox of the everlasting gospel is that God accounts us perfect while we are still being perfected. In other words, God credits us with holiness while we are being made holy. God treats us like joint heirs with Christ while we are putting our true selves to death! We are crucified with Christ; we are dead on the cross, and yet, we live! That's called the "mystery of godliness." Such a condition is a paradox. How can a person be both dead and alive? It seems absurd. It seems contradictory. But is it true? Hebrews 10:14 reads, "For by one offering He has perfected forever those who are being sanctified" (World English Bible). For me, that single verse explains Christian perfection in its paradoxical glory better than any other. "For by one offering He has perfected forever ..." By one offering on the cross, He perfected us forever ... that is, those who are being sanctified. Under the umbrella of Christ's sacrifice on Calvary, we have perfection ... *now*.

> ***"For by one offering He has perfected forever those who are being sanctified."***

God credits us with Christ's perfect character, and, when He looks at us, He sees a perfect person. While we are being sanctified, we are being changed, and we are being transformed. While we are being transformed, we are under the umbrella of God's perfect grace and love. By that one offering, we are perfected forever. Are you understanding this? Are you embracing it? Through the offering of Christ on the cross, we receive perfection that exceeds the righteousness of the scribes and Pharisees! Jesus said, "Unless your righteousness exceeds the righteousness of the scribes and Pharisees, you will by no means enter the kingdom of heaven" (Matt. 5:20, NKJV). Did Jesus exceed their righteousness? Accepting Him, we get credit for His life and, therefore, we too exceed the righteousness of the Pharisees! Jesus said that the least of His disciples would be greater than John the Baptist, who was the greatest prophet ever to live. Christ is the only one who has ever achieved perfection. His perfect life was absolutely true to God's law in every way. Thus, when the least of Christ's disciples accepts Him, he receives Christ's perfect righteousness, and even the least and the newest of baby Christians receives Christ's righteousness and is greater than John the Baptist! When we accept Christ, we receive His perfect life and are regarded by God as flawless, perfect, and holy. God looks at us as if we have never done anything wrong. He looks at us as if we have never sinned. Do you like *Steps to Christ?* I *love* that book! It is great. Ellen White wrote in it, "It was possible for Adam, before the fall, to form a righteous character by obedience to God's law. But he failed to do this, and because of his sin [Well, thanks, Adam!] our natures are fallen and we cannot make ourselves righteous. Since we are [present tense] sinful, unholy, we cannot perfectly obey the holy law. We have no righteousness of our own with which to meet the claims of the law of God. . . ." (Ellen G. White, *Steps to Christ*, p. 62).

Okay. News flash: We can't do it—we can't make ourselves righteous! So many of us have become discouraged because we realize that we can't do it. Congratulations! That realization is absolutely necessary before God can save you. The purpose of the law of God is to hold up the standard of moral behavior and to remind us that *we* can't do it. That is why Paul said that the law is our schoolmaster to lead us to Christ. The law comes to us and points out our every flaw and imperfection, and it has an easy time doing so because we have so many of them! "But …" the statement says, and I am so glad that it does not stop there.

> But Christ has made a way of escape for us. He lived on earth amid trials and temptations such as we have to meet. He lived a sinless life. He died for us, and now He offers to take our sins and give us His righteousness. If you give yourself to Him, and accept Him as your Saviour, then, sinful as your life may have been, for His sake you are *accounted righteous*. Christ's character stands in place of your character, and you are accepted before God just as if you had not sinned. (Ellen G. White, *Steps to Christ*, p. 62).

She said that we are accounted righteous. The word means even though we are not in fact righteous, we are *credited* with being righteous! That's the true gospel! And it means that Christ's character stands in place of our character. Do you want a perfect character? Accept Christ as your Savior, and then God will credit Jesus' character in place of your character.

People come to me and say, "Pastor Tom, don't you want to be perfect? Don't you want to have a perfect character?" I have attempted to live like that, and I don't want to do it again.

I respond, "Why do you work so hard for something that I already possess? Why are you so frustrated and angry, and upset *all the time?* Why do you have that miserable look on your face?"

"Because I'm very serious about God!"

"Why are you so serious?"

"Because if I don't perfect my character, I'll be lost and go to hell. And I'm really working hard at getting this right!"

Doesn't the Bible say that the fruit of the Spirit is love, joy, peace, long-suffering, goodness, gentleness, meekness, and temperance? The fruit of the Spirit is *love*—"and I love you," *joy*—"and I am happy!" and *peace*—"Ah! I don't have to worry about my salvation! Jesus took care of that. All I have to do is trust Him, stay in love with Him, and then everything will go well." However, if you're trying to work your way to heaven by being really, really good, then life becomes a very serious business, and every little mistake will potentially condemn you to hell. So, every time you mess up or have a little problem, you feel miserable. You actually believe that you always have to be right … to be perfect … to be saved. Well, do you think God wants us to live our lives like that? Doesn't the Bible say in Nehemiah that the *joy* of the Lord is our strength?

I'm happy, and I'm not wiping this grin off my face for anybody. It is no concern of mine whether you like it or not. I'm happy, and I'm joyful. I'm not going to walk around like I'm going to a funeral! I already had the funeral. I already died with Christ. I was already put on the cross. Then I was buried, and Christ rose in my place and ascended to heaven and sits at the right hand of God. I've already been there, done that. I've already died, when I was crucified with Christ. Yet, I am alive, and the life I now live, I live by the faith of the Son of God! (see Gal. 2:20). I'm excited. I'm happy. I am sorry if you are not. My sins have been washed away. I've been forgiven for everything wrong that I've ever done! I have God's forgiveness. And you can have it too. My friend, if that doesn't get you excited and joyful, nothing will! People say to me, "Pastor, why do you always talk about Christ and Calvary and righteousness by faith all the time?" Let me answer by quoting the following statement. Notice how it begins: "There is not a point that needs to be dwelt upon more earnestly, repeated more frequently …" That sounds pretty important, doesn't it? Let me start again: "There is not a point that needs to be dwelt upon more earnestly, repeated more frequently, or established more firmly in the minds of all than the impossibility of fallen man meriting anything by his own best good works. Salvation is through faith in

Jesus Christ alone" (Ellen G. White, Ms. 36, 1890, in *Faith and Works*, p. 18).

Ellen White also wrote: "Today iniquity prevails not only in the world polluting it as in Noah's day but it exists in the church …" (Ms. 31, 1890). Iniquity exists in the church? Uh oh! "As a counter influence the cross of Calvary must be lifted up." Did you catch that? Lifting up the cross of Calvary will counteract the evil influence of those who practice iniquity in the church. OK, iniquity in the church is awful to think about. Does that mean that there are sinners in the church? Does that mean that the wheat and the tares grow together until Jesus comes? Does that mean that I should preach to Seventh-day Adventists that they might be converted? Does that mean that three and a half years into Christ's ministry Peter would still be carrying a sword and whacking off a person's ear, leading Jesus to say, "Peter, you need to be converted! When you're converted, Peter, strengthen your brethren"? Are there unconverted sinners in the church who need conversion? Are there miniature spiritual Christians with great big carnal natures who yell at people and are mean and nasty? Have you ever seen people in the church sometimes saying and doing things that they shouldn't? Do you ever wonder why they do that? We're going to talk about that.

> ***"There is not a point that needs to be dwelt upon more earnestly, repeated more frequently, or established more firmly in the minds of all than the impossibility of fallen man meriting anything by his own best good works. Salvation is through faith in Jesus Christ alone."***

"… the cross of Calvary must be lifted up, the atoning sacrifice must be kept before the people, that men may behold sin in its true hateful character, and may lay hold upon the righteousness of Christ, which alone can subdue sin, and restore the moral image of God in man. … There is one great central truth to be kept ever before the mind in the searching of the Scriptures—Christ and Him crucified" (Ms. 31, 1890). "The point that has been urged upon my mind for years is the *imputed righteousness of Christ*. I have wondered that this matter was not made the subject of discourses in our churches throughout the land, when the matter has been kept so constantly urged upon me, and I have made it the subject of *nearly every discourse and talk that I have given to the people*" (Ms. 36, 1890, in *Faith and Works*, p. 18).

What did Ellen White say was the subject of nearly every discourse and talk she gave? It was the imputed righteousness of Christ! It was not sanctification and imparted righteousness (though she did talk about them). No, it was the imputed righteousness of Christ—the free gift of eternal life that Jesus gives us when we are willing to receive it! The imputed righteousness of Christ was the *focus* of her preaching and ministry—not what a person eats or wears, not prophecy or the end times, not the mark of the beast or the antichrist! These were not her *focus*. The great central truth that she talked about more than anything else, the subject of almost every discourse she ever gave, was the imputed righteousness of Christ, which is Jesus Christ and Him crucified! That was the great theme, the great "burden," as she would put it, of what Ellen White preached. Ellen White had a *Christ-centered message!* That may not be the Ellen White that you've heard about, but you are hearing about it now!

It is my great desire that Seventh-day Adventists be Christ-loving, fire-breathing, Spirit-filled, Jesus-uplifting people! I don't want people to say, "Oh, those Seventh-day Adventists—they're the people that keep the Sabbath and don't eat meat." No! I want them to say: "Seventh-day Adventists are the people that love Jesus, lift up Christ on the cross, and keep the Bible Sabbath as a symbol of resting in Christ's righteousness and not working their way to heaven." The merits of Christ on our behalf are our only hope for salvation and should be the focus of our conversation. We cannot duplicate or even come close to equaling the pattern of Christ's accomplishments. Christ our example, whom we are to imitate, is perfect and holy. "We cannot equal the pattern; but we shall not be approved of God if we do not copy it and, *according to the ability which God has given*, resemble it" (*Testimonies for the Church*, vol. 2, p. 549). Isn't it wonderful that our loving God only judges us based on our ability to understand His will and accomplish it? He judged our dear Savior by the letter of the law, and through His righteousness, He judges us according to the ability He has given us to offer the obedience of faith as a token of our love and willingness to obey Him. "We should remember"—you're going to love this—"that our own ways are not faultless. We make mistakes again and again ..." (*That I May Know Him*, p. 136). Then come the words you've been waiting for: "*No one is perfect but Jesus.*" For years, I've heard preachers proclaim: "You've gotta' be perfect." "You've gotta' do everything right." "If you're not perfect and you don't vindicate the character of Christ by achieving sinless perfection, then Jesus can't come! Christ can't come until the whole church is perfect." Well, if the whole church has to achieve absolute perfection before Christ can come, then—forget it!—He'll never come! We don't look for Christ to come because *the church* is perfect; we look for Christ to come because *He* is perfect! I don't want my children to be perfect little children; I want them to know the perfect Savior! The reason they need Jesus is because they're not perfect children, and they never will be! How could they be? They were raised by imperfect parents! What hypocrisy it is for Seventh-day Adventist parents to tell their children they have to be perfect! How laughable. Their kids look at their mom and dad, as if to say, *Are you kidding me? Have you ever looked in the mirror? Do you have a clue about your own life and your own "perfection"? And you're tellin' me that I have to be perfect?* How arrogant and egotistical it is to act as if we have all the answers!

This view came about because some overzealous preacher taught the people to think that way! I don't blame the parents. I blame the forty years of preaching a false gospel in which perfectionism has been urged upon people as a means of salvation, and it's all a lie. It's a heresy. Perfectionism needs to be repudiated as a teaching and rejected! "We should remember that our own ways are not faultless. We make mistakes again and again.... No one is perfect but Jesus!" (*That I May Know Him*, p. 136). Could Ellen White be any clearer or plainer? The true everlasting gospel of the first angel's message would never claim that anybody is faultless. Ellen White goes on: "Think of Him. Be charmed away from yourself and every disagreeable thing." Are you and I not disagreeable things? No wonder our kids often look at us and say, "You strive for perfection and expect me to do the same or I can't be a Seventh-day Adventist? Well, I'm not good enough, and I never will be. Good bye!" And the parents will say, "Why did my kids leave? Why don't they want to be like me and stay in the church?" I'll tell you why. They aren't fooled. They know that they can't do it. That is why they leave. When you start telling them, "*You* can't do it, and its okay. Christ has done it for you. Just come and accept Him, and He'll give you the righteousness you need." When they get *that* message—that you love them no matter what, that they don't have to be perfect, and that you accept them just the way they are, then they're going to look at you differently. Then they're going to look at the church differently. Then they're going to fall in love with a compassionate God who accepts people where they are, who doesn't judge and condemn them for not being something they could never be, no matter how hard they try! They're smart enough to realize that you have got to be crazy to teach them that, unless they do something they can never do, God will never accept them, and they can't go to heaven. It is as if we are saying to them, "Hey, kids! You have to be this perfect person, which you can never be, in order for God to accept you. So, go over to that brick wall and bang your head against it." And they'll be like, "Are you out of your mind? You aren't doing that. We've never seen anybody else do that, yet you're telling us that we have to do that? I don't think so."

"We should remember that our own ways are not faultless. We make mistakes again and again.... No one is perfect but Jesus!"

The reason we need Christ is because we can't do it ourselves! Let me read it again. "We should remember that our own ways are not faultless. We make mistakes again and again.... No one is perfect but Jesus. Think of Him. Be charmed away from yourself and every disagreeable thing. For by beholding our defects faith is weakened. I point you to Christ the Rock of Ages."

Ellen White is saying that, by focusing on your spiritual progress and saying, "Am I perfect yet? Am I growing?" you are looking at a big sinner, and, "by beholding you become changed." So the more you look at yourself, the bigger and badder a sinner you will become and the worse you will get. However, by beholding Christ, you will become changed into His image and start imitating Him, and you will start forgetting yourself and losing yourself in Jesus. Slowly and surely, you will become like Christ. That's what spiritual transformation is all about. Remember that we are not merely justified by faith, but we are also sanctified by faith. Jesus is our sanctification (see 1 Cor. 1:30; Heb. 8:10). By His one offering on the cross we are sanctified, and He becomes our sanctification BY FAITH. Don't forget that ALL our righteousnesses are as sinful rags. All our own good works ARE SIN. It's only when we are SANCTIFIED BY FAITH that we are truly set apart and made holy. That is a new concept for many Adventists. Many have the Catholic concept of sanctification. They believe they are justified for their past sins, but FROM NOW ON, they must live sinlessly. That is heresy. We can only be sanctified, moment by moment, BY FAITH. Sanctification by faith is as much a truthful necessity as justification by faith.

Being accounted holy in heaven and yet being sinful on earth is a paradox. The closer you get to Jesus, the more sinful you will appear in your own eyes. It seems contradictory. It seems absurd. It seems as if it cannot be true, but it is. It's a paradox. Yet, unless you start to think paradoxically, you'll never understand Christianity. The true everlasting gospel is paradoxical. "The divine beauty of the character of Christ, of whom the noblest and gentle among men are but a faint reflection." Jesus is "the express image of the Father's person." He "was a living representation of the character of the law of God" (*Thoughts from the Mount of Blessing*, p. 49). Notice that Ellen White says, "the noblest and most gentle among men are but a faint reflection" of "the character of Christ." Now, beloved, listen to me. For forty years, I've heard preachers telling folks, "Until you perfectly reflect the character of Christ," meaning, unless you're perfect like Jesus, "Christ won't be able to come, and you can't be saved."[19] Remember, while these false preachers are telling you that, unless you equal Christ's perfection, you can't be saved, Ellen White said that the greatest and noblest of men is but "a faint reflection" of Christ. Now if Daniel and Elijah and Moses are a faint reflection, how are you ever going to equal Christ's character except by faith as you accept Him as your Savior?

Do you see the insanity of this view? I admonish the preachers of harvest theology who have preached for so many decades. I admonish the magazine editors who have preached for decades that unless Seventh-day Adventists become flawlessly perfect, living absolutely sinless lives before Jesus comes, they cannot be saved. I admonish them all to repent of this heresy! This false gospel is totally untrue, though it was published for many years. Having sown the seeds of perfectionism, we will reap a harvest of legalism and righteousness by works. I encourage those who preached such messages to accept the true gospel and claim Jesus as their only perfection, by faith alone, and join us who lift Him up as our only hope of perfection and salvation! That having been said, we must wonder, how did this damnable heresy work its way into our church, discouraging the hearts of so many and turning some among us into legalistic, self-righteous people, who look at one another to see whether or not we're measuring up? And what happened to our children as they watched us go through this? Remember, our enemy is not those who have accepted false teachings and who had good intentions, but who were misled. Our real enemy is Satan, who is an evil surmiser, and so good at deception that he talked one third of the angels out of heaven! He is the true author of legalism and self-righteousness. He was the one whose first sin was pride. I say stop the insanity now! Let's get back to the Bible and the truths of God's Word! Let's quit putting words in Ellen White's mouth and making her say and teach things that she never said! Ellen White's writings are great! Yet, the purveyors of perfectionism have collected the stronger statements and reproofs from her writings and put them all into compilations with everything she ever said not to do. Be careful in using such compilations. It is better to read the original statements in context. I would recommend you get *The Desire of Ages*, *The Great Controversy*, *Steps to Christ*, *Ministry of Healing*, and *Thoughts from the Mount of Blessing* and read these. Marian Davis brought these together from Ellen White's writings, with Ellen White's input and approval.[20] They reflect more fully Ellen White's intent. If a book is a compilation produced after her death, be very careful. You are getting the compiler's viewpoint rather than Sister White's. People with the viewpoint that everyone needs to be perfect put together (and out of context) a book that told young people all the things that they should never do.[21] Isn't that great? And then, when young people get it and read it, they think, *I'm never going to make it because I can never be good enough*. Now, is it possible to use compilations in a good way? Sure. Pull out a quotation, look it up in the original source, and then read what Ellen White wrote in context. I guarantee you that, if you read the statement as a whole, it will be much more positive.

Now, in Romans 3:10, Paul wrote, "there is none righteous, no not one." In Mark 10:18, Jesus said, "No one is good but one, that is God" (Darby). In Revelation 15:4, John wrote, "Who shall not fear you, O Lord, and glorify your name? For you alone are holy" (NKJV). So God tells us over and over again that nobody is righteous. Nobody can keep God's law flawlessly—except Jesus. Nobody does good—"No not one" (Rom. 3:10). "They have all turned aside; they have together become unprofitable" (Rom. 3:12). Jesus said there's no one good but one, that is God. Revelation 15:4 says that only God is holy; no one else is holy. All that having been said, are you ready for the paradox?

Peter wrote, "You are a chosen generation, a royal priesthood, a holy nation, His own special people, that you may proclaim the praises of Him who called you out of darkness and into His marvelous light" (1 Peter 2:9). He also wrote: "Gird up the loins of your mind, be sober, and rest your hope fully upon the grace that is to be brought to you at the revelation of Jesus Christ; as obedient children, not conforming yourselves to the former lusts, as in your ignorance; but as He who called you is holy, you also be holy in all your conduct, because it is written, 'Be holy, for I am holy' " (1 Peter 1:13–16). There's the paradox: God tells us to be holy in all our conduct as He is holy! How is that possible? The Bible says that God alone is holy, that no man is holy, and that all our righteousnesses are as filthy rags, and then it turns right around and says that we are to be obedient children and that we should be holy in all our conduct because God is holy. Is it true that only God is holy? Yes, it is true. Is it true that God tells us to be holy? Yes, that is true, too. Are both statements, which seem to be contradictory, true? Yes, they are, and there is only one thing that can solve the great gospel paradox of how we who are sinful and unholy by nature can be as holy as Christ. There is only one answer: We are only holy through the righteousness of Jesus Christ. "We have no righteousness of our own"—none. Whatever we do that is right and good, we do because the Holy Spirit does it in us and through us, and we can claim no holiness of our own. Our imperfect attempts at being right and good, while being prompted by the Holy Spirit, have no merit towards salvation, but are accounted right and good, even though, in fact, we are not! Many Adventists need to understand that just because the Holy Spirit is transforming sinners by creating a new nature in them, the sin nature is still there, polluting even our best attempts at obedience. That's why we renounce our own works and claim Jesus as our only perfection. When we accept Jesus as our Savior, we are accounted perfect, we are accounted righteous through Him. It is His holiness and not ours that God demands be made manifest. The everlasting gospel is the greatest paradox—unholy sinners accounted holy saints! When God commands us to be holy, He is saying,

"Receive my Son and be accounted righteous through Him. Then let my Spirit reveal His holiness in your daily actions by His grace and power." Remember, according to God, our best works are inadequate and our strongest faith feebleness. It is Christ alone that can save us. We have two natures: one spiritual and one carnal; the two are warring against each other. In Ephesians 2:3, the Bible says that we are by nature "children of wrath." In Galatians 5:17, Paul says (and, wives, if you have ever wondered why your husband does the foolish things that he does, listen to this), "For the flesh lusts against the Spirit, and the Spirit against the flesh; and these are contrary to one another, so that you do not do the things that you wish." Sometimes, we men and you women do foolish things that deep down you don't want to do but, because your carnal nature rises up, you do them anyway. You get angry or you get lustful or you get impatient, and you ask yourself when you're done, "Why did I do that? I didn't want to do that! I didn't mean to do that." "I didn't mean to get mad, I didn't mean to yell." You know, the way you show whether you are really converted or not is how you treat the person that you can't stand in the church. Aren't we supposed to love one another even though we don't think alike and even though we may at times be irritating? "I, brethren, could not speak to you as to spiritual people but as to carnal, as to babes in Christ. I fed you with milk and not with solid food; for until now you were not able to receive it, and even now you are still not able; for you are still carnal. For where there are envy, strife, and divisions among you, are you not carnal and behaving like mere men?" (1 Cor. 3:1–3). The wheat and the tares grow together in the field, which includes the church. We have people who are converted in the church and people who aren't. We have Peter carving off someone's ear, when Peter was going to be a leader in the church! Jesus had to convert Peter and break him before he was willing to humble himself. None of the apostles were willing to wash Jesus' feet. Think about it—Jesus had to wash the disciples' feet because they were too arrogant and proud. And we're just like those guys. We sleep, like they did, when Jesus wants us to pray. We take our swords out, stab each other, fight with each other, and cause strife and divisions among ourselves when God wants us to love one another. We're just like the apostles, and we need to be converted. Paul says, "I am carnal, sold under sin. … It is no longer I who do it, but sin that dwells in me.… I delight in the law of God according to the inward man. But I see another law in my members, warring against the law in my mind, and bringing me into captivity to the law of sin which is in my members.… Who will deliver me from this body of death? I thank God—through Jesus Christ our Lord! So then, with the mind I myself serve the law of God, but with the flesh the law of sin" (Rom. 7:14, 20, 22–25, NKJV). From all these verses, we learn that human beings are carnal by nature, sold under sin. We have a carnal nature from birth, yet, when we are converted, our carnal nature—get this—*remains* until the second coming of Christ. Perfectionists often confuse sanctification with glorification, and think the all-encompassing perfection that glorification brings is available now—but it's not! They act as if the carnal nature is somehow miraculously removed before Jesus comes and as if we have to be glorified now. Yet, glorification doesn't take place until Jesus comes. But—thanks be to God—though the carnal nature *remains*, it does not *reign* in the life of the true Christian. The Holy Spirit is subduing and crucifying our carnal nature, and we are walking in the Spirit and not dwelling in the flesh. Paul explains in Romans 8 that we are all waiting for our new bodies so that we can be delivered from this body of death. He talks about our groaning for a new body so that we will no longer have this conflict within us. "We know that the whole creation groans and labors with birth pangs together until now. Not only that, but we also who have the firstfruits of the Spirit, even we ourselves groan within ourselves, eagerly waiting for the adoption, the redemption of our body" (Rom. 8:22, 23). Ellen White mentions the carnal nature many times in her writings, and she cautions against acting as if it were harmless or even nonexistent. She makes it clear that our natures are tainted, corrupted, and polluted with sin—utterly repulsive. She calls our nature "the corrupt channels of humanity" (Ms. 50, 1900). She says that our natures are perverse, that there is nothing good in them, and that all that we "have ever done is mingled with self and sin" (*Thoughts from the Mount of Blessing*, p. 7). As long as we live, we will have "self to subdue, besetting sins to overcome" (*The Acts of the Apostles*, p. 560). Paul made it clear. He declared that he and the other apostles and the great men of God were sinful by nature and that all believers need to understand and acknowledge that fact. Ellen White would agree with Paul that we are carnal. "The righteousness of Christ is presented as a free gift to the sinner if he will accept it. He has nothing of his own but what is tainted and corrupted, polluted by sin, utterly repulsive to a pure and holy God" (Ms. 50, 1900, in *Selected Messages*, vol. 1, p. 342). Only through the righteous character of Jesus can man come near to God. As the religious services of true believers and their prayers, praise, and confessions ascend as incense to the heavenly sanctuary, passing through the corrupt channels of humanity, they are so defiled that, unless purified by Christ's sacrifice and blood, they can never be of value to God. So, even our church services, our prayers, and our praise remain corrupt and foul unless Jesus mixes His righteousness with them. "We do not understand our perverse natures" (*Review and Herald*, June 3, 1884). "Those whose hearts have been moved by the convicting Spirit of God see that there is nothing good in themselves. They see that all they have ever done is mingled with self and sin" (*Thoughts from the Mount of Blessing*, pp. 7, 8). Do you see this gospel paradox at work in yourself? "So long as Satan reigns we shall have self to subdue, besetting sins to overcome; so long as life shall last, there will be no stopping place, no point which we can reach and say, I have fully attained. Sanctification is the result of lifelong obedience" (*The Acts of the Apostles*, pp. 560, 561). The apostles and prophets confessed the sinfulness of their nature. They put no confidence in the flesh, and proclaimed no righteousness of their own. "The nearer we come to Jesus and the more clearly we discern the purity of His character, the more clearly we shall discern the exceeding sinfulness of sin and the less we shall feel like exalting ourselves" (*Christ's Object Lessons*, p. 160).

Some people have misinterpreted Romans 7 and 8 as describing the Christian before and after conversion. This is a gross error. Paul is not dealing with the question of conversion. He is dealing with the question of *nature*. Romans 7 deals with the carnal nature, and Romans 8 deals with the spiritual nature. After conversion, the believer still has a carnal nature. It must be fought, and it still has to be subdued. Paul said that he was crucified with Christ (Gal. 2:20). He put his carnal nature to death daily and lived a supernatural life. It was a life centered in Christ. Paul walked in the Spirit and not in the flesh because his flesh was crucified daily. Do we ever totally achieve perfection in our obedience? No, only in a relative sense, being perfect in our "sphere" (*The Acts of the Apostles*, p. 559). According to our ability, we are to strive to imitate the pattern of Christ. He accepts us as His children as we do our best. Someone wrote the *Adventist Review* asking, "Where does it say in the Bible that when we do our best God accepts us? He only demands one thing: perfection." I answered the person's query (though my response was not published) with a selection from one of Ellen White's letters: "Christ looks at the spirit, and when He sees us carrying our burden with faith, His perfect holiness atones for our shortcomings. When we do our best, He becomes our righteousness. It takes every ray of light that God sends us to make us the light of the world" (Lt. 22, 1889, Jan. 18, to R. A. Underwood).

***Paul is not dealing with the question of conversion. He is dealing with the question of* nature.**

Thus, the great paradox of the Christian faith is that even sinners like us, who have a carnal nature, can be forgiven and redeemed if we will by faith accept Christ as our Savior and walk in the Spirit. The great paradox is that people so totally evil can become totally holy by accepting the holiness that comes only from God. It seems contradictory. It seems unbelievable. It seems absurd. Yet, it is undeniably true. "O God, I want to be saved. I want Your righteousness. I admit that I am not perfect. You are my only perfection, and I want to be obedient and live a life of obedience. I want to obey You, not to save myself, but because I love You and am grateful that You saved me."

If you feel as I do, then you accept the paradox of the true everlasting gospel, and God will write your name down in His book of life. Jesus will credit your account with His perfect righteousness and forgive every sin that you have ever committed.

God will wash away every sin and give you credit for Jesus' perfect life. Does that not sound like a great trade? Are you willing to trade your sinful life for Christ's perfect life? "Blessed assurance, Jesus is mine; O, what a foretaste of glory divine!" Will you join me in prayer?

Father, we thank You that we don't have to be absolutely perfect, as Christ is, but You accept our relative obedience in our limited sphere. We only need to accept the perfection that Christ offers us for free. Give it to us, Lord. Write our names down in the Lamb's book of life. Help us to not be obsessed with what we do for You. Help us to focus on what You have done for us. Help us to not emphasize what we have to do for You as much as we emphasize what You have already done for us. Thank you for giving us the free gift of eternal life. Now bless us, we pray, in Jesus' name, Amen.

CHAPTER 4

THE GREAT SABBATH PARADOX

Remember the Sabbath day, to keep it holy.
Six days you shall labor and do all your work, but the
seventh day is the Sabbath of the Lord your God.
In it you shall do no work: you, nor your son, nor your daughter,
nor your male servant, nor your female servant, nor your cattle,
nor your stranger who is within your gates.
—Exodus 20:8–10, NKJV

In the previous chapter we explored the paradoxical nature of righteousness by faith. Interestingly, when it comes to the Sabbath, there is also a great paradox that is rarely talked about or understood. What is the great Sabbath paradox, and how could we have missed it? Simply stated, the great Sabbath paradox is this: Even though Seventh-day Adventists exhort the entire world to keep the Sabbath holy, no Seventh-day Adventist has ever kept even one Sabbath perfectly holy. As I am writing these words, I can imagine minds whirring and thinking, "What are you talking about?" My response is: Aren't paradoxes grand? What does the Word of God teach concerning all our best efforts at righteousness apart from Christ? "All our righteousnesses are as filthy rags" (Isa. 64:6). Now notice the plural form of the word "righteousness." It points to not just one particular attempt at justification but all of them. Every attempt at self-justification is doomed to failure because "by the works of the law shall no flesh be justified" (Gal. 2:16). So, even our most earnest and sincere attempts at Sabbath worship fall far short of Jesus' perfect, flawless Sabbath worship. Our prophet puts it this way, "*... passing through the corrupt channels of humanity, they are so defiled that unless purified by blood, they can never be of value with God. They ascend not in spotless purity, and unless the Intercessor, who is at God's right hand, presents and purifies all by His righteousness, it is not acceptable to God. ... Oh, that all may see that everything in obedience, in penitence, in praise and thanksgiving, must be placed upon the glowing fire of the righteousness of Christ*" (Ms. 50, 1900, in *Selected Messages*, vol. 1, p. 344).

So this passage makes it clear that all our worship and even our prayers have to be placed upon the "glowing fire of the righteousness of Christ" or they are unacceptable to God. So isn't it paradoxical that Seventh-day Adventists are exhorting the entire world to keep the Sabbath holy, when they have never kept even a single Sabbath holy themselves? Of course, the same can be said for every other of the Ten Commandments, but the irony is especially observable when it comes to the Sabbath commandment. Nothing else demonstrates so well how we have somehow managed to miss the main point concerning the law and the first angel's message of the gospel, the sanctuary, and worship. Let's explore these themes in the light of our special message to the world concerning the Sabbath.

One cannot present the true gospel if one has a flawed view of the law of God. God's law is a reflection of His character, and the underlying principles that the Ten Commandments reflect also reveal the dilemma that God faced when Adam and Eve disobeyed that law in the Garden of Eden. It is precisely because God could not abandon, alter, or ignore His law that Adam and Eve were driven from the garden. The law is holy, "and the commandment is holy, and just, and good" (Rom. 7:12). So, the problem was not the law; the problem was man's breaking of the law. "The wages of sin is death" (Rom. 6:23). Consequently, Adam and Eve had to die.

Satan sat back and thought, *I've got God now. He can't save His precious humans without saving me. I broke the law, and now they have too*. The fatal flaw in Satan's thinking is his miscalculation of God's grace. He never expected God to take man's punishment upon Himself! Having become selfish and self-centered, Satan was incapable of comprehending the height and depth of God's love for fallen humankind. He was even incapable of comprehending God's love for him. God did everything He could to save Lucifer. Yet, it was to no avail, and now God would do everything He could to save the human race, including paying their penalty by the life of His only begotten Son. When humankind sinned, their fallen nature was corrupted, and they were rendered incapable of keeping God's law. The challenge to Adam had been for him to *maintain* righteousness, not to *attain* righteousness. That was also the challenge for the "last Adam" Jesus Christ (1 Cor. 15:45). Could Jesus succeed where Adam failed? Could Jesus "maintain" the righteousness that He was born with? Remember that Gabriel described Jesus to Mary as "that *holy thing*" (Luke 1:35). Jesus was born holy and had to *remain* that way. He didn't have to *achieve* holiness, and Jesus said, "The Father that dwelleth in me, he doeth the works" (John 14:10). So, all righteousness comes from God. Remember the plan of salvation in the Old Testament? The sanctuary system was an object lesson to teach the Israelites all about God's plan of salvation. The lamb that represented Jesus the Messiah had to be "without spot" (Num. 28:3, 9, 11), for only perfect holiness is acceptable to God.

The challenge to Adam had been for him to* maintain *righteousness, not to* attain *righteousness.

Now let's apply all this to the teachings and Sabbath keeping of Seventh-day Adventists. The first angel's message announces that we are to worship our Creator who made all things. The Sabbath message is an important part of the first angel's proclamation. But how has the Seventh-day Adventist Church typically presented it? I would suggest to you that we have presented it no differently than did the Jewish rabbis: *The Sabbath is a symbol of the Creation; God has commanded us to keep it; the seventh day is the only true day ever devoted to the Lord God in the Torah, therefore, we need to be obedient and not work on that day*. How has the Adventist message been significantly different than the Jewish teachers on the subject? The law is an important part of the gospel, the sanctuary, and worship because it is the foundation of God's government and no lawbreaker can truly worship God. Nonetheless, there are many religions that teach the importance of the moral law.

What are we missing in our Sabbath message that God is trying to get across to us? We are not emphasizing the most important part of the message! It's not about *our* Sabbath keeping, it's about *Jesus'* Sabbath keeping! We do not receive credit for even one Sabbath when it comes to keeping the law. *All* our righteousnesses are as filthy rags and unacceptable to God unless they are placed upon the glowing fire of Christ's righteousness. We are saved by *His* thirty-three years of perfect Sabbath keeping! Only His Sabbath keeping counts towards our salvation. We've never kept even one Sabbath perfectly. When Jesus went to the synagogue, He was focused on God alone. He read the Torah with absolute purity and devotion. He sang the songs with passion and enthusiasm. His mind never wondered or drifted away from the worship of the Creator. When Jesus left the worship service, He spent His Sabbaths serving the communities He went to. He never spent a single Sabbath overeating and sleeping away the day. His Sabbath days were totally dedicated to helping to lighten the load of humanity. When you compare His perfect Sabbath keeping with our feeble attempts at following His example, even the best, most dedicated Seventh-day Adventist would have to admit that he or she falls far short of Jesus' ideal Sabbath observance. Fortunately for all of us, by faith we can claim His righteousness, and His Sabbath keeping becomes ours! It is credited to our account, and God looks at us as He does His son, and He is pleased with our perfect observance of His holy day!

So, once we realize the ungodliness of our Sabbath keeping and we claim the perfection of Jesus' Sabbath observance, how should we proclaim the Sabbath to others? For purposes of this chapter, we will assume you've already settled the question of the law's immutability and agree that God's law should be honored by our best efforts to imitate Christ's character by the willing obedience of faith. What does God say the Sabbath is? He declares: "I gave them my sabbaths, to be a sign between me and them, that they might know that I am the LORD that sanctify them" (Ezek. 20:12). So, to God the Father the Sabbath is a sign, or a symbol, of righteousness by faith! He is the God who *makes us holy*. He sanctifies us. To sanctify means to make holy, to set us apart as righteous. So, the Sabbath is a sign, or a symbol, that we don't make ourselves holy. It is a sign, or a symbol, that God makes us holy through his Son Jesus Christ! The Sabbath tells us to rest from our own works, and to trust in the works of Jesus Christ. When Seventh-day Adventists begin to preach the Sabbath with true humility, instead of acting as if we are the only ones "keeping the right day," and we start admitting that we too are Sabbath breakers and that it's only through the righteousness of Christ that we can keep it, telling them that the Sabbath is a symbol of righteousness by faith, it is only then that we will get the world's attention on this important subject! The Bible clearly teaches that one of the most important things we receive when we come to Jesus is rest from our sins through Christ's merits. Jesus says, "Come unto me, all ye that labour and are heavy laden, and I will give you *rest*. Take my yoke upon you, and learn of me; for I am meek and lowly in heart: and ye shall find *rest unto your souls*" (Matt. 11:28, 29). The word for "rest" in this verse reminds us that, when you come to Jesus and learn of Him, receiving Him, you will find rest for your soul; you will find peace and rest in Christ![22] The writer of

The Sabbath tells us to rest from our own works, and to trust in the works of Jesus Christ.

Hebrews expressed similar thoughts when he wrote, "Let us therefore fear, lest, a promise being left us of *entering into his rest*, any of you should seem to come short of it.... For we which have believed *do enter into rest*.... God did rest the *seventh day from all his works* ... There *remaineth therefore a rest* to the people of God. For he that is entered into his rest, he also hath *ceased from his own works, as God did from his*. Let us labour therefore to *enter into that rest*, lest any man fall after the same *example of unbelief*" (Heb. 4:1, 4, 9–11). So, clearly, in Hebrews 4, the writer is using the Sabbath as an illustration of the experience of a person of faith—as opposed to a person of unbelief—for, "the one entering [God's] rest ceases from his own works as God did from His" (literal translation).[23] It is symbolic of his trusting in God for salvation! The Sabbath is used here as a symbol of the way we enter into a saving relationship with Jesus by entering His rest in claiming His good works as our own! The Sabbath should be preached as a wonderful symbol of perfect grace! We should be proclaiming that we are all Sabbath breakers, but when we accept Jesus, we become Sabbath keepers because the Sabbath symbolizes righteousness by faith, renouncing our own works, trusting only in the works of Jesus Christ on our behalf and accepting the perfect grace of God who does for us what we cannot do for ourselves! Like Paul, we choose to "be found in him, not having [our] own righteousness, which is of the law, but that which is through the faith of Christ, the righteousness which is of God by faith" (Phil. 3:9).

So the Sabbath is a great paradoxical symbol of righteousness by faith! It is a sign that we cannot make ourselves holy by our own works. It is a symbol that we are set apart by God and sanctified only by perfect grace and not by our own Sabbath keeping. It is a symbol that we have renounced our own Sabbath keeping and, like Paul, want to be found only in the righteousness of God, which is by faith. The great paradox is that those who claim to be the ultimate proclaimers of the Sabbath need to add a new concept to the Jewish idea of it being a sign of creation, and include it as a sign of God making us righteous. And they need to begin proclaiming the Sabbath as the symbol of God's perfect grace, accomplishing through God's Son what we ourselves could never humanly accomplish. The Sabbath is the great leveler at the foot of the cross, pointing out how an unholy person could never keep even a single Sabbath holy. In Exodus 20:8 we are told: "Remember the Sabbath day, to *keep it holy*." John wrote in Revelation, "for *thou only art holy*: for all nations shall come and worship before thee" (Rev. 15:4). Not only are we to keep one Sabbath holy, but we must continue keeping the Sabbath holy for a lifetime. From the moment of our birth, every minute of every Sabbath we were required to maintain its absolute holiness! We must present to God only perfect, flawless Sabbath worship every minute of every Sabbath, for only such worship is acceptable to Him! No wonder the heavenly intelligences proclaim, concerning the Lamb: "Thou only art holy"! Only Jesus Christ is holy! That's what the Bible teaches. The Sabbath keeping of Jesus, the perfect Lamb of God, is our *only true* Sabbath keeping! He alone is holy!

Is it absolutely true that no human being since the fall has kept even a single Sabbath holy apart from Christ? That is indeed true! Is it true that every Sabbath Christ kept is absolutely holy? Yes! Does God command us to keep his Sabbath day holy? Yes! Is His requirement paradoxical? Yes! Can we be as holy as Jesus? Can we keep the Sabbath? Can we obey his commandments? Can our righteousness exceed the righteousness of the scribes and Pharisees? Can we be greater than John the Baptist? Can we keep His commandments if we love Him? The answer to all these questions is "*yes*"! But how is that possible? There is only one way—through the righteousness of Christ by faith! He alone is holy, and, when you receive Him as your Savior, He stands in your place, and God looks at you as if you have never sinned! Hallelujah! The very Sabbath itself is a symbol of the rest we find by faith in the righteousness of Christ! When we begin to proclaim it as a symbol of perfect grace and meet our fellow Christians in humility at the foot of the cross, the Sabbath will be welcomed in a way that we have yet to experience. Let us make Christ and His righteousness the very center of our Sabbath message from henceforth! The Sabbath is a sign that we are resting in the accomplishments of Christ's righteousness alone and not in our own works.

We have Sabbath rest from being achievers when we rest as receivers of the white robe of Christ's righteousness!

The Sabbath is a sign that we are resting in the accomplishments of Christ's righteousness alone and not in our own works.

CHAPTER 5

KEPT FROM FALLING

Now unto him that is able to keep you from falling,
and to present you faultless before the presence
of his glory with exceeding joy.
—Jude 24

As I have endeavored to teach the gospel to Christians who already have very definite views about the gospel, I have been amazed at how many in the church have accepted a Roman Church gospel. They will often tell me that they are saved by faith *and* works. Of course, not their own works, they say, the works come from the Holy Spirit. Little do they realize that this view is right out of the Catholic catechism! Perfectionism is actually a stage in Christian growth. Many Christians have to pass through this misunderstanding in order to get to the place where they really comprehend the true gospel. Those holding this misunderstanding often quote Jude 24 to make the point that they won't fall. In their system of theology, not falling means to "keep them from sinning." This is not what the text is teaching. Christ will keep you from falling from grace, even if you inadvertently sin because of your carnal nature. We are sinful because we have a sinful nature that remains sinful even when we are sleeping! We are saved by perfect grace through faith alone, and works are not in the equation for salvation. They are the fruit that comes after we are born again, not the basis for our being born again. In order to understand this text fully, I searched the Bible and the Spirit of Prophecy to see how it is applied. Let's see how God uses these phrases and what context He puts them in. Here is some of what I found:

> The indulgence of spiritual pride, of unholy desires, of evil thoughts, of *anything that separates us from an intimate and sacred association with Jesus, imperils our souls*. We must have living faith in God. We must "fight the good *fight of faith*," if we would "lay hold on eternal life" [1 Tim. 6:12]. We are "kept by the power of God *through faith* unto salvation" [1 Peter 1:5]. If the thought of apostasy is grievous to you, … then "abhor that which is evil; cleave to that which is good" [Rom. 12:9]; and *believe in Him* who is "able to keep you from falling, and to present you faultless before the presence of his glory with exceeding joy." (*Review and Herald*, May 8, 1888)
>
> We have no reason to fear while looking to Jesus, no reason to doubt but that He is able to save to the uttermost all that come unto Him; but *we may constantly fear lest our old nature will again obtain the supremacy*, that the enemy shall devise some snare whereby we shall again become his captives. We are to work out our "own salvation with fear and trembling, for it is God that worketh in you to will and to do of His good pleasure" [Phil 2:13]. With *our limited powers* we are to be as holy in *our sphere* as God is holy in His sphere. To *the extent of our ability*,

The indulgence of spiritual pride, of unholy desires, of evil thoughts, of **anything that separates us from an intimate and sacred association with Jesus, imperils our souls.**

we are to make manifest the truth and love and excellence of the divine character. As wax takes the impression of the seal, so the soul is to take the impression of the Spirit of God and retain the image of Christ. (*Signs of the Times*, Jan. 2, 1907)

There must be a steadfast resistance of temptation to sin in *thought or act*. The soul must be *kept from every stain*, *through faith in Him* who is able to *keep you from falling*. We should *meditate* upon the Scriptures, thinking soberly and candidly upon the things that pertain to our eternal salvation. The *infinite mercy and love of Jesus*, the *sacrifice* made in our behalf, call for most serious and solemn *reflection*. We should *dwell upon the character* of our dear Redeemer and Intercessor. We should seek to comprehend the meaning of the *plan of salvation*. We should *meditate* upon the mission of Him who came to save His people from their sins. By constantly contemplating heavenly themes, *our faith and love will grow stronger*. Our prayers will be more and more acceptable to God, because they will be more and more mixed with *faith and love*. They will be more intelligent and fervent. When the mind is thus filled … the believer in Christ will be able to bring forth good things from the treasure of the heart. (*Sons and Daughters of God*, p. 109)

If they will keep Bible precepts ever as their textbook, they will have greater influence over the youth; for the teachers will be learners, having a living touch with God. All the time they are inculcating ideas and principles that will lead to a greater knowledge of God, and earnest, *growing faith in their behalf in the blood of Jesus*, and the power and efficiency of *the grace of our Lord Jesus Christ to keep them from falling*; because they are constantly seeking the strongholds of a healthful and well-balanced Christian experience, carrying with them qualifications for future usefulness, and intelligence, and piety. (*Fundamentals of Christian Education*, p. 388, written June 12, 1895)

Do not think you must indulge in this pleasure and in that. Determine that you will be on the Lord's side. If you will stand under *the blood-stained banner* of Prince Emmanuel, faithfully doing his service, you need *never yield to temptation*; for One stands by your side who is able to *keep you from falling*.... Christ is the greatest Teacher the world has ever known. *He must dwell in the heart by living faith. Then* his Spirit will be through you *a vitalizing power*. (*Youth's Instructor*, Aug. 3, 1899)

In the results of His work, Christ will behold its recompense. In that great multitude which no man could number, *presented "faultless* before the presence of His glory with exceeding joy," Jude 24, He whose *blood has redeemed and whose life has taught us* "shall see of the travail of His soul, and shall be satisfied." Isaiah 53:11. (*Education*, p. 309)

My brother, whom the Lord has honored by giving a message of truth for the world, in *God alone can you maintain your integrity*. "But ye, beloved, building up yourselves on your most *holy faith*, praying in the Holy Ghost, keep yourselves in the *love of God*, looking for *the mercy of our Lord Jesus Christ unto eternal life*. And of some have compassion, making a difference: and others save with fear, pulling them out of the fire, hating even the garment spotted of the flesh." While this hatred for the sin that spots and stains the soul is expressed, we are, with one hand, to lay hold of the sinner with the *firm grasp of faith*, while with the other we grasp the hand of Christ. "Now unto Him that is able to *keep you from falling*, and to *present you faultless* before the presence of His glory with exceeding joy, to the only wise God." (Lt. 38, 1894, to Brother A. T. Jones)

In the next statement, please note that it is not our works or performance that enables us to be presented faultless; it is Christ's works. Only through His life and perfect grace can we be considered faultless.

He alone is faultless, except by faith in His merits. Through faith alone, sinners cover every defect and receive His faultless character.

> If you give yourself to Him, and accept Him as your Saviour, then, sinful as your life may have been, for His sake you are accounted righteous. Christ's character stands in place of your character, and you are accepted before God just as if you had not sinned. More than this, Christ changes the heart. He abides in your heart by faith. You are to maintain this connection with Christ by faith and the continual surrender of your will to Him; and so long as you do this, He will work in you to will and to do according to His good pleasure. (*Steps to Christ*, pp. 62, 63)
>
> With what care, then, should we examine our hearts in the light of the divine law, and compare ourselves with the *one faultless Pattern*, that no defect may be found upon us in the day of God. We cannot afford to make a mistake in a matter in which eternal interests are involved. (*Signs of the Times*, March 9, 1882)

So as our ONE faultless Pattern, it would not be correct to interpret "keep you from falling" as suggesting that we can produce a faultless life through our own obedience. There is only one person who is faultless and can keep us from falling, and that's Jesus Christ.

> Make Christ your dependence. Thus you may every day be increasingly enriched by His love. But *without Him you are helpless, utterly unable to subdue one sin, or to overcome the smallest temptation*. May God help you to understand the words, "As the branch cannot

Make Christ your dependence. Thus you may every day be increasingly enriched by His love.

> bear fruit of itself, except it abide in the vine, no more can ye, except ye abide in Me." Connection with Christ is a positive necessity, if the fruit we bear is to be acceptable to God. *Connection* with Him *results in purity of heart, in a faultless life*. What is the fruit for which God calls? "Love, joy, peace, longsuffering, gentleness, goodness, *faith*, meekness, temperance." May God help us to *bear this fruit*, is my prayer. May He help us to put our capabilities and powers to a right use. Then we shall see things in their true bearing. (*Pacific Union Recorder*, Jan. 19, 1905)
>
> Now is fulfilled the Saviour's prayer for His disciples: "I will that they also, whom Thou hast given Me, be with Me where I am." [John 17:24.] "*Faultless* before the presence of His glory with exceeding joy" (Jude 24), Christ presents to the Father the *purchase of His blood… Oh, the wonders of redeeming love*! the rapture of that hour when the infinite Father, looking upon the ransomed, shall behold His image …! (*The Great Controversy*, p. 646).

In the next statement, please note that it is not our works or performance that enables us to be presented faultless, but, rather, Christ's redemption. Because we are redeemed, we are presented with a victory gained by Christ, gained in our behalf. By faith His victory is our victory. Yet the first angel's message is often missed, because we actually believe we can never sin again. There is only one person who can offer a lifetime of perfect obedience. The way Christ keeps us from falling is by exchanging His life for ours. How have we missed that fact? How can we even think for a moment that with our carnal nature we can be flawless? He alone is true.

> The Word of life is that by which the Christian is to live. From this Word we are to receive a continually increasing knowledge

> of truth. From it we are to gain light, purity, goodness, and *a faith* which *works by love and purifies the soul*. It is given us that we may be *redeemed, and presented faultless* before the throne of divine glory. *Wondrous victory, gained by Christ in man's behalf!* (Ellen G. White, Letter 60, 1900)

In the next statement, please note the question that Ellen White asks and the obvious answer, which is *No!* We are continually dependent on God's compassionate, loving grace. We are held accountable for every neglect, every failure to show the love of God to others. We have missed this in the first angel's message. We can't be blameless; we fall daily; we are not the holy one, only Jesus is.

> Can you stand before God and plead a faultless character, a blameless life? Often you have needed the forgiveness of Jesus. You are continually dependent on His compassion and love. Yet have you not failed of manifesting toward others the love Christ has manifested toward you? Have you felt a burden for the one you saw venturing into forbidden paths? Have you kindly admonished him? Have you wept for him and prayed with him and for him? Have you, by tender words and kindly acts, shown him that you love him? As you have associated with those who were faltering and staggering under the load of infirmities of disposition and faulty habits, have you left them to fight the battle alone? Have you passed these sorely tempted ones by on the other side, while the world has stood ready to give them sympathy and to allure them into Satan's snare? Have you said, like Cain, 'Am I my brother's keeper?' How must the great Head of the church regard the great work of your life? To Him every soul is precious. How, then, must He look upon your indifference with regard to those who stray from right paths? Be sure that He who is the true Watchman of

> the Lord's house marks every neglect. (*Pacific Union Recorder*, April 10, 1902)

In the next statement, please notice that it is not our works or performance that enables us to be presented faultless, but, rather, it is Christ's works that save us. The gospel is that He has never fallen, not us! Notice the way that God looks at those who stand with the devil and constantly point out the faults of God's workers and His people:

> Let no one be sharp and dictatorial in his dealing with God's workers. Let those who are inclined to censure remember that they have made mistakes as grievous as the mistakes which they condemn in others. Let them bow in contrition before God, asking his pardon for the sharp speeches that they have made, and the *unchristlike spirit they have revealed*. Let them remember that God hears every word they speak, and that as they judge, so they will be judged.
>
> Christ is pleading the case of every tempted soul, but while he is doing this, many of his people are grieving him by taking their stand with Satan to accuse their brethren, pointing to their polluted garments. (*Review and Herald*, March 17, 1903)

While some in the church are constantly pointing to the sinful clothing of their fellow members, continually trying to get them to take their eyes off of Jesus and focused on themselves and their sinfulness, Christ does not share their evil view. Don't let them get to you. Don't listen to them. They are doing Satan's work. She will ask pointedly, "Is your life faultless?" The obvious answer is *No!* She knew that "No one is perfect but Jesus" (*That I May Know Him*, p. 136).

It is troubling how the very ones always talking about perfectionism are often the most critical, unkind, and unloving in their attitude toward others. Perfectionism is a stage that many people go through, and it is a false religion, based on self-centered legalism. God has to open our eyes to the true gospel. No one is perfect but Jesus! Let's continue learning. Ellen White wrote under inspiration:

> None of the prophets or apostles made proud boasts of holiness. The nearer they came to perfection of character, the less worthy and righteous they viewed themselves. But those who have the least sense of the perfection of Jesus, those whose eyes are least directed to Him, are the ones who make the strongest claim to perfection. (*Review and Herald*, Dec. 1, 1885, in *Faith and Works*, p. 54)

It is the devil's way of turning your eyes from Jesus and tricking you into focusing on your own faults or the faults of others. Don't fall for it! Don't be misled! Keep your eyes on Jesus. He looks at you in an entirely different way than they do. In the next statement, you will see how Jesus looks at you while others are being so critical:

> Let not the criticized ones become discouraged; for while their brethren are condemning them, Christ is saying of them, I have graven thee upon the palms of my hands. By creation and by redemption thou art mine. God's word is, 'Honor all men. Love the brotherhood.' Show all men respect, even though they do not reach the standard you have set for them. They may have made mistakes, but *is your life faultless?* Have you censured your own errors as severely as you have censured the errors of others? (*Review and Herald*, March 17, 1903)
>
> The truth of Jesus Christ does not tend to gloom and sadness.... We must look away from the disagreeable to Jesus. We must love him more, obtain more of His attractive beauty and grace of character, and *cease the contemplation of others' mistakes and errors.* We should remember that *our own ways are not*

> *faultless*. We make mistakes again and again ... *No one is perfect but Jesus*. Think of Him and be charmed *away from yourself*, and every disagreeable thing, for *by beholding our defects faith is weakened ... I point you to Christ, the Rock of Ages*." (*That I May Know Him*, p. 136)

The Spirit of Prophecy declares: "our own ways are not faultless." It is only through Christ's merits that we can be presented faultless. As we have studied the application of this text, it should become obvious to even the casual reader that we are kept from falling from grace through the exercise of faith. It does not mean that we have no sin or that we don't have faults. We are to use our "limited powers" to be holy in our spheres "according to our ability." It is only by God's grace that we can overcome sin. It is only Jesus' victory that gives us our victory. Our works are not perfect, or faultless, except through Christ, through His life, and through His sacrifice. *We are presented faultless, not through our perfect performance, as some have suggested, but through His perfection by faith, and through His faultless merits*. The incense of the righteousness of Christ, when mingled with our best service, is what makes our service acceptable to God.

Our works are not perfect, or faultless, except through Christ, through His life, and through His sacrifice.

Can God give you victory by faith over sin? Absolutely! Is there any excuse for sin? *No*, there is not! Are we doomed to continue doing the things that displease God? Absolutely not! Will God accept deliberately imperfect service? No, He will not! We can overcome any hereditary or cultivated tendency to sin by God's grace. Do we merit any credit towards our salvation by our works? *No!* It is fruit, born of a relationship with Christ, which results from His Spirit changing our hearts and bringing us into a right relationship with God. "So let us labor for the master, from the dawn to setting sun, let us talk of all His love and wondrous care!" Do all you can do to give God glory, but never claim one bit of credit for it! Our works are filthy rags. Our best efforts are imperfect and fall short of the standard that Jesus set for us. However, mingled with His righteousness, when we do our best, God accepts us as if we had never sinned! (See *Steps to Christ*, p. 62.)

We are saved by perfect grace to work for God!

CHAPTER 6

THE TRUE GOSPEL'S OVERCOMERS

He that hath an ear, let him hear what the Spirit saith unto the churches; To him that overcometh will I give to eat of the tree of life, which is in the midst of the paradise of God.
—Revelation 2:7

The Apostle John used the word "overcome" more than any other biblical writer, more than all the others combined. In the book of Revelation, he used a form of the word "overcome" eleven times.

To the overcomers Jesus promises:

1. They will eat from the tree of life (Rev. 2:7).
2. They will not be hurt by the second death (Rev. 2:11).
3. They will eat hidden manna and receive a white stone with a new name written upon on (Rev. 2:17).
4. They will receive power over the nations and the "morning star" (Rev. 2:26–28).
5. They will be clothed in white garments and not have their names blotted from the book of life, and Jesus will confess their names before the Father and His angels (Rev. 3:5).

6. They will be made pillars in the temple of God and will have the name of God, the New Jerusalem, and Jesus' new name written upon them. Jesus will also have received a new name, and that glorious name will be written upon the overcomers (Rev. 3:12).
7. They will sit with Jesus on His throne (Rev. 3:21).
8. They will inherit all things and be the sons and daughters of God (Rev. 21:7).

What a precious list of promises and rewards! What wonderful benefits! Could it get any better than this? Could God give us more incentives to overcome?

There's only one problem. All these rewards sound great, but how do we get them? How do we overcome? Without the *how*, the rewards become irrelevant. We can rejoice in the fact that God also gives us the *how*.

Let's open our Bibles to John's first epistle where John explained how God expects us to overcome. Then we will read further explanations from other passages.

"Ye are of God, little children, and have overcome them: *because greater is he that is in you*, than he that is in the world" (1 John 4:4).

"For whatsoever is born of God overcometh the world: and *this is the victory that overcometh the world, even our faith*" (1 John 5:4).

"And *they overcame him by the blood of the Lamb*, and by the word of their testimony; and they loved not their lives unto the death" (Rev. 12:11).

"Knowing that a man is *not justified by the works of the law, but by the faith of Jesus Christ*, even we have believed in Jesus Christ, that we might be justified by the faith of Christ, and not by the works of the law: for by the works of the law shall no flesh be justified" (Gal. 2:16).

"But now the righteousness of God without the law is manifested, being witnessed by the law and the prophets; even the *righteousness of God which is by faith of Jesus Christ unto all and upon all them that believe*: for there is no difference: for all have sinned, and come short of the glory of God; being *justified freely by his grace* through the redemption that is in Christ Jesus" (Rom. 3:21–24).

"But Israel, which followed after the law of righteousness, hath not attained to the law of righteousness. Wherefore? Because *they sought it not by faith, but as it were by the works of the law*. For they stumbled at that stumblingstone; as it is written, Behold, I lay in Sion a stumblingstone and rock of offence: and whosoever *believeth on him* shall not be ashamed" (Rom. 9:31–33).

Righteousness by faith was a stumbling block to the Jews, and it is a stumbling block to many today. The Jews tried to attain righteousness by their own works of law keeping, by doing good and right things. There is a certain pride of achievement in right doing, even if we are doing right for the wrong reasons. They performed good works, but they did not perform them by faith. They did them because they wanted power and control. The carnal mind hates the gospel of submission, surrender, and helplessness. The evil within us always wants to have something to be proud of, something to feel just a little bit self-satisfied with. To admit that we are helpless to change ourselves and that any good works we do are inferior at best and downright wretched at worst is a horrible blow to the carnal ego. When Isaiah the prophet said, "But we are all as an unclean thing, and *all our righteousnesses are as filthy rags*; and we all do fade as a leaf; and our iniquities, like the wind, have taken us away" (Isa. 64:6), he meant it! The Hebrew word meant the rags a woman used when she was unclean. That's why we are told that, even when we are in church, our most pious prayers are an abomination unless they are sanctified by Christ's righteousness. The human heart wants to exalt itself, to be in control, to have power over itself and others. It is a terrible blow to the carnal mind for people to admit that they are powerless to change their life and take self off the throne and for them to allow Jesus to fully convert them and rule in their heart.

Do you remember Simon in the book of Acts? He wanted God's power so that he could use it for his own purposes: "And when Simon saw that through laying on of the apostles' hands the Holy Ghost was given, he offered them money, saying, *Give me also this power*, that on whomsoever I lay hands, he may receive the Holy Ghost" (Acts 8:18, 19).

But Peter reprimanded him, saying: "Thou hast neither part nor lot in this matter: for *thy heart is not right in the sight of God*" (Acts 8:21). The motives of his heart were more important than having the power of God. Simon simply wanted to use God's power. People who are truly converted want God to use them. Our motivation for obeying God is even more important than the fact of our obeying Him. The Jews sought to be righteous by doing works of right doing and had a form of godliness, a form of piety that was very impressive to the outside observer, but their hearts were far from Him. They had no love, joy, faith, or tolerance. They were quick to criticize and condemn others. They felt that they were God's special people, a cut above all those "nominal Jews" that didn't measure up to them in their piety.

Our motivation for obeying God is even more important than the fact of our obeying Him.

Do you remember the prayer of the Pharisee, "I thank you that I am not as other men"? In other words, *Thank you, God, that I am not like that pathetic loser over there!* The Pharisee had a very high opinion of himself and a very low opinion of everyone else in the temple that day. It was much the same for other Pharisees. Consequently, they rejected the message of love and forgiveness that Jesus preached because it contained no self-aggrandizement to lift them up. The righteousness of God's Son, Jesus Christ, so outshines our righteousness, even with the Holy Spirit in us, that it is like comparing the light of the sun and the moon. The moon but imperfectly reflects the light of the sun, but it cannot compare to the sun's *brightness and glory*.

Now, what we will consider next is the statement that is mistakenly used to teach "harvest theology":

> Christ is waiting with longing desire for the *manifestation of Himself* in His church. When *the character of Christ* shall be

> *perfectly reproduced in His people*, then He will come to claim them as His own. (*Christ's Object Lessons*, p. 69)

Notice that the statement refers to "His people." That's plural. Jesus longs to see His character manifested, to see Himself manifested, in His church. He longs to see His people become loving and lovable Christians. He longs for them to become involved in soul winning and in ministering to others as He did. It doesn't mean that each individual must equal the perfection of Jesus Christ. It means that the church will *reproduce His character collectively.* It means that the body of Christ will become a reproduction, or a reflection, of her Bridegroom. A reproduction may be perfect in a relative sense, but it is still never an exact duplicate of the original. "The more we behold Christ, talk of His merits, and tell of His power, the more fully we shall *reflect His image in our own characters*" (*In Heavenly Places*, p. 127). "He is to walk and work in *the Savior's companionship*. As he does this his faith will increase. *Constantly beholding Christ, he will be changed into the same image from character to character*" (*In Heavenly Places*, p. 183). Ellen G. White makes it very clear in her writings that Jesus is in one sphere of perfection and we are in another. He is the only one to whom she ever ascribed absolute perfection. All human beings other than Christ can only attain relative perfection based on a sliding scale of individual circumstance. God judges us based upon our abilities and opportunities, even taking into account where we were born and what advantages and disadvantages we have had in our lives.

"As God is holy in His sphere, so fallen man, through faith in Christ, is to be holy in his sphere…." (*Acts of the Apostles*, p. 559). "They will be in sympathy with Christ, and in their sphere, as they have ability and opportunity, will work to save perishing souls as Christ worked in His exalted sphere for the benefit of man" (*Testimonies for the Church*, p. 483).

Here we see that Ellen White made a clear distinction between our sphere and Christ's *"exalted sphere."* Moral and spiritual perfection is promised to everyone who will overcome by faith. We can live holy,

Christ-like lives, by His grace. But it would be blasphemous to suggest that this "relative perfection" can ever equal Christ's absolute perfection. That is why so many get confused and wander into perfectionism. If Ellen White were saying that, in order for us to be saved, we have to equal Christ's righteousness or His perfection, she would be a false prophet who should be rejected. There would be no way to reconcile her previous statements on perfectly reproducing a perfect character with ones like this: "The truth of Jesus Christ does not tend to *gloom and sadness.... We must look away* from the disagreeable to Jesus. We must *love Him more*, obtain more of His attractive beauty and grace of character, *and cease the contemplation of others' mistakes and errors*. We should remember that *our own ways are not faultless*. We make mistakes again and again.... *No one is perfect but Jesus.* Think of Him and be charmed away from yourself, and from every disagreeable thing, for *by beholding our defects faith is weakened.* God and His promises are lost from sight ..." (*That I May Know Him*, p. 136).

Could Ellen White have been any plainer or spoken any clearer? "Our own ways are not faultless ... No one is perfect but Jesus ... by beholding our defects faith is weakened"! When we stare at our own spiritual navels, beholding our own faults and imperfections, we are actually weakening our faith. We must get our eyes off of our own faults and the faults of others, and we must look to Jesus. "Do not, because your thoughts are evil, cease to pray. *If we could in our own wisdom and strength pray aright, we could also live aright, and would need no atoning sacrifice. But imperfection is upon all humanity....* Christ stands before His Father saying, 'Lay their sins on me. I will bear their guilt. They are my property. I have graven them upon the palms of my hands'" (*In Heavenly Places*, p. 78). "We become changed into the image of that upon which we dwell.... *John was not perfect; Peter denied his Lord; and yet it was of men like these that the early Christian church was organized.* Jesus accepted them that they might learn of Him what constitutes a perfect Christian character. The business of every Christian is to *study the character of Christ.... It is not an uncommon thing to see imperfection in those who carry on God's work....* Everything that causes us to see the weakness of humanity is in the Lord's purpose to help us *to look to Him*, and in no case put our trust in man, *or make flesh our arm*" (*That I May Know Him*, p. 182, emphasis added).[24] John was imperfect, and not just when he first met Christ. He regarded himself to be imperfect at the end of his life, when his persecutors attempted to kill him in boiling oil. "John declared, '... *I am only a weak, sinful man*, but Christ was holy, harmless, undefiled, and separate from sinners. He did no sin, neither was guile found in his mouth.' John's words, while suffering at the hands of his enemies, had an influence, and *he was removed from the cauldron* by the very ones who had cast him in" (*Christ Triumphant*, p. 312). There is no absolute perfection apart from Christ. We need to look to Jesus and let Him change us into His image. We need to dwell on Him and study His perfect character. We should not make our own flesh or that of others something in which we place our trust. Christ is our only righteousness. He is the great pattern we should copy and imitate. Following the pattern is our privilege, but we will never equal the pattern, and it is legalistic and self-righteous to suggest, as some do, that unless we equal it, we won't be saved.

"*Never can we equal* the goodness and the love of Jesus, but he calls upon every man and woman, youth and child, to behold him, and by beholding his perfection of character, to become changed into his image. Call every talent into exercise to copy the Pattern" (*Signs of the Times*, Nov. 28, 1892). "Christ is our pattern, the perfect and holy example that has been given us to follow. *We can never equal the pattern*; but we may imitate and resemble it according to our ability. When we fall, all helpless, suffering in consequence of our realization of the sinfulness of sin; when we humble ourselves before God, afflicting our souls by true repentance and contrition; when we offer our fervent prayers to God in the name of Christ, we shall as surely be received by the Father, as we sincerely make a complete surrender of our all to God. We should realize in our inmost soul that *all our efforts in and of ourselves will be utterly worthless*;

for it is only in the name and strength of the Conqueror that we shall be Overcomers (*Review and Herald*, Feb. 5, 1895). "Higher than the highest human thought can reach is God's ideal for His children. He wants our minds to be clear, our tempers sweet, our love abounding. Then the peace that passeth knowledge will flow from us to bless all with whom we come in contact. The atmosphere surrounding our souls will be refreshing...." (*Sons and Daughters of God*, p. 348).

Nonetheless, there is no need for us to be alarmed. Ellen White makes it clear that Christ's perfection is on a far more exalted level than ours. Our perfection exists solely because of Him, and it is really only a faint attempt at imitation, an indistinct reflection of the absolute glory and majesty of Christ's holiness. Ellen White understood this. So, when you read her writings that encourage you to strive for perfection, remember that, in context, she always portrays our "perfection" as *relative*, taking into account our abilities, our faults, and our limitations. God is so wonderfully fair. He only wants us to be the best that *we* can be. He accepts our best efforts as loving obedience in Christ. Jesus' righteousness is so much more glorious and so much greater than even the noblest of men's achievements that it's blasphemy to suggest that any human being could ever equal it. It is greater than the achievements of Moses, Paul, Peter, James, John, and all the great men of the Bible combined! "The divine beauty of the character of Christ, of whom the *noblest and most gentle among men are but a faint reflection* ..." (*In Heavenly Places*, p. 63). "In *His life* Jesus of Nazareth differed from *all* other men.... He is the *only true model* of goodness and perfection" (*In Heavenly Places*, p. 14).

On your best day, in your holiest hour, you will never equal the righteousness of God's Son.

- You never equaled the righteousness of God's Son before you were converted.
- You will never equal the righteousness of God's Son after you are converted.

- You will never equal the righteousness of God's Son on your best day of keeping the law.
- You will never equal the righteousness of God's Son on this earth, even when you're in church, on your knees, praying your best prayer.
- You will never equal the righteousness of God's Son when you get to heaven, in your new nature, sitting on your golden throne!
- You will never equal the righteousness of God's Son throughout all eternity.

Jesus will always be holier, more righteous, and more glorious than we are, and He will be the only human being in heaven who will be worthy to be praised! We will be there, not because of what *we did*, but because of what *He did!* We will be in heaven, receiving all the rewards promised us, because of *His* deeds we overcome by faith, by the blood of the Lamb, by God's perfect grace! We don't move to victory—we move FROM victory. We already have it! Christ's victory becomes our victory the moment we accept Him. It will be by our receiving His works by faith, which is itself the gift of God (Eph. 2:8). Eternal life is a free gift. Only Jesus is worthy! His victory will be ours! Because He overcame, we will overcome!

All the human family in heaven will be there for one reason and one reason only: It is all about *Jesus*—Jesus' life, Jesus' death, and Jesus' resurrection. Glory to God! We will have overcome by faith in the blood of the Lamb! "And I said unto him, Sir, thou knowest. And he said to me, These are they which came out of great tribulation, and have *washed their robes, and made them white in the blood of the Lamb*" (Rev. 7:14). "The four and twenty elders fall down before him that sat on the throne, and worship him that liveth for ever and ever, and *cast their crowns before the*

All the human family in heaven will be there for one reason and one reason only: It is all about Jesus—Jesus' life, Jesus' death, and Jesus' resurrection.

throne, saying, Thou art worthy, O Lord, to receive glory and honour and power: for thou hast created all things, and for thy pleasure they are and were created" (Rev. 4:10, 11). On that day, we won't be singing that song, "Oh that will be glory for me, glory for me, glory for me," as if we deserved any credit! The glory for us on that day will be "when by His grace" we "shall look on His face." *That* will be our glory. We will be casting our crown at Jesus' feet and singing, "Thou art worthy!" "He alone is worthy of praise, and glory!" "We may commit the keeping of our souls to God as unto a faithful Creator, not because we are sinless, but because Jesus died to save just such erring, faulty creatures as we are, thus expressing His estimate of the value of the human soul" (*In Heavenly Places*, p. 80).

The wonderful thing is that Jesus will share it all with us. He lets us have a part in His throne, His government, and His life. To those who, by faith, overcome the evil one without and the evil within, He promises a life filled with rewards and happiness beyond anything we could ever imagine. To all the overcomers, He grants the pleasure of His company, an eternal relationship with the One who loved us, redeemed us, rescued us, and who now wants to live with us joyfully for all eternity! Don't forget the *how!* It's very important.

How do you build faith? The same way that you first received it. You heard the word of God preached or you read the Bible or someone shared his or her testimony with you, and then, as the word of God was planted in your heart like a seed, it grew, bore fruit, and here you are today. "So then *faith cometh by hearing, and hearing by the word of God*" (Rom. 10:17). Do you want to be among the overcomers? Then gain the victory by faith. Read the Word. Go where the Word of God is preached. Every time the church doors are open, be at the prayer meeting, the Bible study, the Sabbath school, and the worship service. Whenever and wherever the Bible is preached, be there. *Hear the Word, and faith will come!* "Christian fellowship is one means by which character is formed" (*In Heavenly Places*, p. 281).

Read the Word at home every day. Carry a pocket Bible with you and spend time with Jesus reading it whenever you get a chance, in the morning and in the evening, throughout the day and while you are at work. Does this sound fanatical? Does it seem to be a bit much? How much time do you waste sitting at red lights, waiting in the doctor's office, watching television, surfing the Internet, or doing things that are of far lesser importance? If you want to overcome a fault or defect in your character, behold the lovely character of Jesus in His Word. Study the life and personality of Jesus. "The true penitent learns the *uselessness of self-importance. Looking to Jesus, comparing his own defective character with the Saviour's perfect character*, he says only—'In my hand *no price I bring*; Simply to Thy *cross I cling*'" (*In Heavenly Places*, p. 64).

As you behold Him, you will find yourself miraculously changing. Things that you used to love, you will start to hate. Things that you used to hate, you will start to love. Jesus will crowd out all of those ugly traits of character from your life by filling your mind and heart with so many good things that you won't be able to keep up with the life-changing power of the Holy Spirit. Things that have bothered you for years will suddenly be unimportant to you, and they will be left behind as Jesus fills your life with so many wonderful things that you won't have room in your life for those besetting sins. "Just as I am without one plea, but that thy blood was shed for me!" We are loved and accepted even as we are being changed into His glorious image! "There is therefore now *no condemnation to them which are in Christ Jesus*, who walk not after the flesh, but after the Spirit" (Rom. 8:1).

God accepts us because of Jesus. He gives us the free gift of His salvation. He says, "neither do I condemn you, now go and sin no more"! We are free to obey, free to live without guilt or fear, free to overcome because of His blood, His love, and His acceptance! It is within the atmosphere of His love and acceptance that we can grow and learn. Obedience is a privilege, a gift from God, the natural result of our communion with God and of our accepting the divine nature as a recreative power in our lives. God recreates us in His image. We are in need of not just reformation but transformation. We cooperate with the Spirit in this transformation project. We begin to resemble and reflect our heavenly Father's image. "If you remain in me and I in you," Jesus says, "you will bear much fruit" (John 15:5, NIV). Our job is to concentrate on remaining in Him, or "abiding in Him," as the King James Version puts it! When we abide, we obey! Obedience is the fruit of the gospel root! We are to obey in love. This is the victory, even our faith. Read the Word. Build your faith. "They overcame … by the blood of the lamb …" (Rev. 12:11). Study the life of the Lamb; study the giving of His blood! We love Him because He first loved us. Love Jesus; be passionate in your worship, in your praise, and in your adoration of your best friend!

Spend time with Jesus in prayer and in His Word. Satan fears our prayers more than anything else! Prayer is the secret of spiritual power! As you are praying, go out into the world and serve the lost, the needy, and the downtrodden. *Take the Word of God out into the world, and conquer the world for Jesus! And, remember, you overcome, not by developing a perfect character, but by faith in the blood of the lamb!* Walk by faith and you will have already *overcome!*

God's perfect grace is sufficient! Christ is our only perfection and our only victory. He also is our only hope!

CHAPTER 7

MATURE AND MERCIFUL GOSPEL

But love ye your enemies, and do good, and lend, hoping for nothing again; and your reward shall be great, and ye shall be the children of the Highest: for he is kind unto the unthankful and to the evil. Be ye therefore merciful, as your Father also is merciful.
—Luke 6:35

To begin any study of perfection and perfectionism, we must define the terms to be used. As we saw in the last chapter, Ellen White talked about the absolute perfection of Jesus Christ as being a divine sphere and about human perfection in terms of our limited sphere. Yet, before we consider her usage of the word, it would help us in our study to examine its most basic meanings. The term "perfect" is used in the Old Testament to describe the *moral completeness* of the following individuals: Noah (Gen. 6:8, 9), the nation of Israel (Num. 23:21), David (1 Kings 11:4, 6), Asa (1 Kings 15:14), Job (Job 1:1), Zacharias and Elizabeth (Luke 1:6), and Nathanael (John 1:47). Such is the usual way the term was used in the Old Testament and sometimes in the New Testament. It meant that a person was mature, faithful, and loyal to God. Though all of these individuals had flawed records, they are still described as being "perfect." It is also worth our looking at some of the most famous perfection verses used to define perfection in Matthew and Luke.

Perfection in the Book of Matthew

We find the most famous quotation on perfection—and also the most misunderstood—in Matthew 5. Let's read it in context.

> Ye have heard that it hath been said, Thou shalt love thy neighbour, and hate thine enemy. But I say unto you, Love your enemies, bless them that curse you, do good to them that hate you, and pray for them which despitefully use you, and persecute you; that ye may be the children of your Father which is in heaven: for he maketh his sun to rise on the evil and on the good, and sendeth rain on the just and on the unjust. For if ye love them which love you, what reward have ye? Do not even the publicans the same? And if ye salute your brethren only, what do ye more than others? Do not even the publicans so? *Be ye therefore perfect even as your Father which is in heaven is perfect.* (Matt. 5:43–48).

The word "perfect," in the Greek, is literally τελειος (*teleios*). According to Strong's *Exhaustive Concordance*, the root meaning of this word, as translated into English, is "complete" or "mature," as in *adulthood*.[25] According to the Merriam-Webster dictionary, the definition of "perfection" is:

1. The quality or state of being perfect: such as (a) freedom from fault or defect: flawlessness; (b) *maturity*; (c) the quality or state of being saintly;
2. (a) an exemplification of supreme excellence; (b) an unsurpassable degree of accuracy or excellence;
3. the act or process of perfecting.

Perfection, in the parallel passage to that of Matthew in the Gospel of Luke, reflects the same meaning. "But love ye your enemies, and do good, and lend, hoping for nothing again; and your reward shall be great, and ye shall be the children of the Highest: *for he is kind unto the unthankful and to the evil.* Be *ye therefore merciful, as your Father also is merciful*" (Luke 6:35). So we see that Matthew stresses maturity while Luke stresses being merciful. Thus, God wants us to be mature and merciful.

What is Jesus' teaching us in these passages? Is He saying, "Make sure that you are sinless and are doing everything right or you won't be good enough to be saved"? Is that what He is saying? Or could He be saying, "You have to be as perfect as I am, or you can't be saved"? Or maybe, "Be as perfect as I am because I've got my eye on you, and, if you're not perfect, you are not good enough for me to accept"? No, absolutely not, although people have interpreted it in these ways for years!

Many preachers and teachers of previous generations have taught false theories about perfection. It is understandable that people would be confused. Notice how *Harper's Bible Dictionary* defines the term: "Perfect, perfection, the English translation of words signifying, respectively, 'being complete, sound, upright, or blameless' and 'the attainment of maturity' " (*Harper's Bible Dictionary*, p. 771). No wonder people are confused about perfection. There is great benefit in studying every text in the Bible that relates to this subject. You should learn all you can about it and not get confused. Truth is one thing and error is another, and the two cannot mingle. Thus far in this book, we have talked about what God *isn't saying*. Now we need to talk about what God *is saying* in these passages. In the passages in Luke and Matthew, Jesus is pointing us to the wonderful example of His heavenly Father. He is telling us how wonderful, kind and merciful His Father is. He makes a point about how God does not just love those who love Him, that is, the perfect people who never sin (see Psalm 14). But, rather, He loves even those who are unlovable, undeserving, and unworthy of His love. He is mature and adult about it, and He loves those who do not love Him back! Jesus' statement is a testimony about how great His Father is, followed by an admonition: "Be like my Dad," a challenge to be "merciful and mature" by loving those who don't love us.

We know we cannot live a life as perfect as Jesus' was. That would require absolute, perfect obedience for our entire lifetime. That is not what Jesus meant. He was not saying that we have to manufacture a lifetime of perfection or God won't accept us. How sad it is that so many teachers and preachers have missed the point of this text and turned it into a burden of performance that makes God seem like an exacting judge, when Jesus' point was the exact opposite of "Measure up to God's perfect standard or you're not good enough." Jesus was teaching that God loves even those who are *not performing well, who are not loving or holy, who are not paying Him back with good works*. God loves them *anyway*. That was Jesus' point! He was saying: *Consider how God acts and be like Him! Love like He does! Accept people like He does! Love them in spite of how they act!* That was what Jesus meant in telling us to be perfect and to be merciful. Jesus' perfection equals *love!*

Ellen White captured a similar thought in the following statement:

"I have repeated this wonderful statement; for it contains the very evidence that we are to present to the world—*the perfection of unity in the followers of Christ*. The members of the church of God *must reach this perfection*. I cannot do more than urge upon them that *this perfection is found in unity in Christ*. The Savior has presented before us how much will be gained in working out the unity that will *join one believer to another in the perfection of Christian love...*" (Ms. 9, 1906).

Isn't that beautiful?

The perfection Jesus was speaking about in Matthew 5:48 is the perfection of Christian love, which draws on God's love and is demonstrated in the unity of the saints! Now, that's a perfection we rarely hear about, but it is a objective that we desperately need to consider more often! Rather than trying to be right all the time in some legalistic, self-exalting, elitist kind of way, Jesus was encouraging us to imitate Him and to imitate His Father by being loving, merciful, and kind in the unified body of His Church. He did not want His disciples to follow the sad example of the self-righteous, pompous, legalistic, and elitist Pharisees who strutted around, in His day, claiming to be perfect in every way. The Bible, the twenty-eight fundamentals of our faith, and the writings of Ellen G. White all teach us that our perfection cannot equal the pattern but that we will not be acceptable to God if we do not let Him work through us to make us as much like Jesus as we can be. Paul said that he continued to press toward the mark of the high calling in Christ Jesus. Perfectionism is a heresy that we can live without. Perfectionism is a false religion that teaches that we can be absolutely perfect and will not be accepted by God if we are not.

The perfection taught is not the imputed righteousness of Jesus but an acquired character development accomplished through the Holy Spirit in believers, which equals Christ's work. This is a heresy and a lie of the devil. We are not saved by the work of the Holy Spirit in us or through character development by any means. We are saved by perfect grace, through Christ's righteousness by faith alone!

CHAPTER 8

PERFECT GRACE! FOUND ONLY IN CHRIST

Preach the word; be instant in season, out of season; reprove, rebuke, exhort with all longsuffering and doctrine.
—2 Timothy 4:2

When God called me to preach, He sent me with a message. He told me, "Whether they listen to you or not, preach the message. Let them know that He has sent a prophet among them, and let them know that you are going to preach My word no matter what." How many people think that a pastor should preach the message that God gives him, even if it's unpopular? How many people think that a preacher should listen to God and not man, even if some people don't like it, don't attend the church, and don't want anything to do with it? If God tells you to preach something, no matter how unpopular it is, you should preach it. A number of years ago, God called me to preach the gospel and to lift up Jesus Christ. God sent me out with a Christ centered message that I am sharing with you in this book. This chapter is a study of Christian perfection and Christ our righteousness based on the Scriptures, the twenty eight Seventh-day Adventist fundamentals of faith, and the writings of Ellen White (Commonly called "the Spirit of Prophecy"). This is the centerpiece of the message that God commissioned me to preach. Without a doubt, it is the most important message that anyone can preach. And, if we do not understand the doctrine of the gospel and salvation, how can we even hope to be saved?

Father in heaven, Your Word says, "I am not ashamed of the gospel of Christ, for it is the power of God to salvation for everyone who believes" (Rom. 1:16, NKJV). Bless my words and my heart that I might communicate in a way that would be pleasing in Your sight the precious truths of salvation and righteousness by faith. I pray that You would bless us as we turn to Your Word and consider this subject. In Jesus' name, Amen.

Perfection versus Perfectionism

To understand perfection is to recognize the absolute perfection of Jesus Christ and the limited, relative perfection of humankind in being mature, merciful, and faithful.

From its very inception, a scourge has affected the Christian church. That scourge is "perfectionism." Perfectionism is earning one's salvation by one's own works, attributing those works to the Holy Spirit, and claiming that we are somehow sinless. This is wrong and causes harm within the body of Christ. Some Seventh-day Adventists have even fallen into this heresy. It has become very popular in some very conservative circles of the church. Emphasizing the fact that, when Jesus steps out of the most holy place in heaven, unless you're absolutely flawless and perfect—and by that they mean that you don't do anything wrong—you will be lost. This is Roman Catholic theology, it is heretical, and you need to understand the true gospel message so you don't fall prey to its deception.

The sum of the matter is this: You are a sinner, and so is every other person on earth who ever lived except for one—Jesus Christ. He is the only one who is righteous; He is the only one who ever was or ever will be perfect. He is "holy, harmless, undefiled, separate from sinners" (Heb. 7:26). Christ is the only wholly righteous human being to have ever lived. God's righteousness is the only righteousness that there is. None of us is righteous apart from Christ. He is our only righteousness. What's more, we are hopeless apart from Christ. However, through Christ, we can have mercy and receive the free gift of eternal life. Our only hope is Jesus. Now, if you believe that, then you and I are in agreement. Do you understand? Good! I want to back it up though. Often when I have preached this message, I have given out a printed copy of the quotations from the Scriptures and the Spirit of Prophecy that I have used. I have backed up what I have said with the Word of God, and I always will. I'm putting it all out there for you to study. If there is anything that I have ever taught that is not biblical, *please* let me know! Seventh-day Adventists are a people of the Book. We have one rule of faith and practice—the Bible and the Bible only!

Now, who is going to be the focus of our faith? It is Jesus! He is what our faith is all about. We're going to focus on Him—not on what we eat, not on what we wear, and not on things that are minor teachings of the Christian faith. We are going to *major* in Christ our righteousness. In the course of so doing, we will also address these minor subjects. Yet, our emphasis is going to be on Christ our righteousness! Jesus Christ is going to be the focus of our faith. And we're going to lift up Jesus so high that He will draw all men unto Him. The Apostle Paul, one of the strictest and most obedient adherents of Judaism, wrote in Philippians: "For we are the circumcision, who worship God in the Spirit, rejoice in Christ Jesus, and have no confidence in the flesh … Yet indeed I also count all things loss for the excellence of the knowledge of Christ Jesus my Lord, for whom I have suffered loss of all things, and *count them as rubbish, that I may gain Christ and be found in Him, not having my own righteousness, which is from the law, but that which is through faith in Christ, the righteousness which is from God by faith*" (Phil. 3:3, 8, 9).

Paul declared that he didn't want to have his "own righteousness, which is from the law, but that which is through faith in Christ, the righteousness which is from God by faith" (Phil. 3:9, NKJV). Where does this righteousness come from? It comes "*from God by faith.*" Solomon, a very wise man, wrote: "For there is not a just man on earth who does good and does not sin" (Eccles. 7:20, NKJV). That eliminates everyone but Jesus. Only He is holy. Do you believe that? Who has kept an absolutely, flawless Sabbath—from sundown Friday to sundown Saturday—keeping it as perfectly as Jesus would have kept it? I had a guy answer that question one time by saying, "I was unconscious in the hospital one Sabbath!" Now, let me ask you: When he was unconscious in the hospital, did he still have a carnal nature? So was he not still a sinner? Absolutely. We are not sinners just because of what we do. We are sinners because of who we are. We are sinners by nature and by deed. That's what the scripture means when it says that there's not a just man on earth who "doeth good" and does not sin. If we can't claim to have kept even one Sabbath perfectly, how can we go around telling people that we are perfect? When we begin sharing the Sabbath as a symbol of righteousness by faith and of resting in the finished accomplishments of Jesus, people will listen. However, if humility is lacking, we are no better than the Jews who wandered in the wilderness and never completed their mission of entering Canaan. Are we not also wandering—wandering in our own desert of works-oriented salvation, failing to enter the heavenly Canaan? (See Hebrews 4.)

David wrote: "The fool has said in his heart, 'There is no God.' They are corrupt, they have done abominable works, there is none who does good. The LORD looks down from heaven upon the children of men, to see if there are any who understand, who seek God. They have all turned aside, they have together become corrupt; there is none who does good, no, not one" (Ps. 14:1–3, NKJV).

So, the Bible says that we are all sinners and that not one of us has done good. Now that's hard for us to understand because, if we have been Seventh-day Adventists, trying to be obedient and do what is right, we may have begun patting ourselves on the back and telling ourselves, "We're not like some other churches. We know which day to go to church on, and we know more about the Bible. We know the truth about the state of the dead." We may have also started patting ourselves on the back and saying: "Boy, we've really got it," and "Look how much we know," and "Boy, we're really great!" All the while, we fail to remember that we are sinners with a carnal nature and that even our Sabbath observance is polluted and foul if we don't have Christ and His righteousness taking our place. That is the subject we are studying in this chapter. Christ's righteousness is our *only* perfection, our only hope. Paul makes this even clearer in the epistle to the Romans. He says that not even one person is holy. "… 'There is none righteous, no, *not one; there is none who understands; there is none who seeks after God. They have all turned aside; they have together become unprofitable … But now the righteousness of God apart from the law is revealed, being witnessed by the Law and the Prophets, even the righteousness of God, through faith in Jesus Christ, to all and on all who believe. For there is no difference; for all have sinned and fall short of the glory of God'* … for the wages of sin is death, but the gift of God is eternal life in Christ Jesus our Lord" (Rom. 3:10–12; 21–23; 6:23, NKJV).

We have all fallen short of God's glory. None of us measures up to God's character. No one is perfect enough, or holy enough, to equal God's glory. Now, if eternal life is truly a gift of God, then, is there any way that we could earn it? No, there is not. Can we add anything to the gift in any way? No, we cannot.

If I say to someone, "I've got a gift for you!" and I give it to you, but tell you that, after church, I need you to go out and wash my motorcycle, okay? You would get the point, wouldn't you? Would I really be giving you a gift? No. Why not? Because it comes with strings attached—a *quid quo pro!* Besides, if you're a Seventh-day Adventist, you wouldn't wash my motorcycle on Sabbath anyway! Nonetheless, if I give you a gift, it's yours. You can keep it. You don't need to do anything to earn it; I just give it to you without strings attached. Jesus gives us the gift of eternal life, and you just say, "Thank you." It's just that easy! You don't try to add to it. You don't keep the Sabbath so that you can be saved or so that you can claim to have earned your way into heaven! You keep the Sabbath because you *are* saved! There's a big difference! Is it good to do "good" works? *Yes!* Should we all submit to God that we may "obey" God's law? Absolutely! Should we "obey" God's commandments by walking after the Spirit? Yes! Amen! Yet we must walk in the obedience of faith, always acknowledging that our obedience is imperfect and flawed, yet God accepts it as an offering of love. As long as it is mixed with the incense of Christ's righteousness, it will be accepted as a sweet-smelling savor. Should we accept our free gift that is given us by God, or should we try to earn our way? You can't *earn* your way! When God gives you a free gift, what can you say but "Thank you! I accept it!" You are complete in Christ's righteousness alone!

Isaiah wrote: "But we are all like an unclean thing, and all our righteousnesses are like filthy rags; we all fade as a leaf, and our iniquities, like the wind, have taken us away" (Isa. 64:6). Now, that term, "filthy rags," means very foul rags. Notice that the phrase "all our righteousnesses are like filthy rags" doesn't say, "All our sins are filthy rags." It says "all our *righteousnesses*"! But the good news is that God says, "if we confess our sins," He will forgive us for all our sins! So, we go to God, admit that we have filthy rags and that we are sinners, and God forgives us. Even the prophet Daniel acknowledged the sinfulness of Israel. "… all Israel has transgressed Your law, and has departed … Now while I was speaking, praying, and confessing my sin and the sin of my people Israel, and presenting my supplication before the Lord my God for the holy mountain of my God …" (Dan. 9:11, 20, NKJV). So, Daniel said he was confessing his sin.

Daniel, that great man of God, was a sinner and admitted that he was a sinner. The Apostle John was also humble enough to admit his sinfulness. He wrote, "If we say that we *have no sin*, we deceive ourselves, and the truth is not in us. If we confess our sins, He is faithful and just to forgive us our sins and to cleanse us from *all unrighteousness*" (1 John 1:8, 9, NKJV). When we ask Him for forgiveness to wash away our sins and cleanse us, God is faithful and just to accomplish that for which we have prayed. Isn't that good news, that, even though we're sinners, even though we can't earn our way to heaven, even though we can't earn "Brownie points" with God, we can get all the "Brownie points" we need if we just admit that we are sinners and ask for the free gift of eternal life? Once you are converted, if you have the love of Jesus in your heart, are you going to surrender your life that you may, to the best of your ability, through the obedience of faith, obey God's commandments and fulfill His will? Yes! Are you still going to fall short sometimes? Sure! But you should not plan on it. You aren't going to be sinning deliberately—at least I hope you're not! Well, maybe sometimes you are, but when you do sin deliberately, hopefully you will come to your senses. Amen? I mean, we all deliberately do wrong things sometimes that we shouldn't do. We all sin and even rebel sometimes, so let's admit it! But, when we come to our senses, when we realize that it is wrong, or when we snap out of it, hopefully, we will repent and ask God to help us to not continue behaving that way. Amen? Our behavior is dependent upon the relationship we have with our Savior! If we emphasize behavior all the time and don't talk about our relationship with our Savior, we're not going to get proper behavior. Rules without relationship always lead to rebellion. And we won't have a relationship with our Savior if we deliberately and habitually disobey Him! However, if you lift up Jesus, and focus on your relationship with Him, then you will get a great relationship with your Savior—as well as better behavior!

Rules without relationship always lead to rebellion.

Now, let's examine Ephesians 2:8–10: "For by grace you have been saved through faith."

So, how is it that we are saved? "By grace … through faith." Faith is not your Savior; *Christ* is your Savior. We are saved by the perfect grace of God through faith. Faith and works are like oars on a boat. Perfect grace is the boat. Faith is one oar, and works are the other. Nonetheless, perfect grace is the boat! Now, if you only have one oar in the water, what is going to happen to you and your boat? You are going to go in circles and get *nowhere!* So, if you just talk about faith but have no works, you had better read the obituaries because your faith is dead (James 2:17, 20, 26)! And if you just talk about works without having faith, then you're a legalist. And no legalist will see eternal life unless they repent, as Paul did. Paul was once a legalist, but he got converted! It's great when Pharisees get converted! Paul was a fire-breathing Pharisee! But, boy, when he got converted, he was strong in the Lord! So there's nothing wrong with a good Pharisee who gets converted. Nicodemus was also a Pharisee who got converted and became a *powerful* Christian! So, if you have pharisaical tendencies, don't give up, there's hope for you. And if you're a liberal, there's hope for you, too! And for you moderates who never want to argue or fight with anybody, there's even hope for you! God loves us all, and He says, "Go down the king's highway. Don't go too far to the right; don't go too far to the left. Stay on the king's highway." And that's what I want to encourage you to do. Now, let's go back to Ephesians: "For by grace you have been saved through faith, and that not of yourselves; it is the gift of God, not of works, lest anyone should boast. For we are His workmanship, created in Christ Jesus for good works, which God prepared beforehand that we should walk in them" (Eph. 2:8–10, NKJV). Good works have already been prepared for us! Jesus has already lived a perfect life. His good works that we are to walk in have been prepared for us before the foundation of the world! And if you're saved and in Jesus, and if you have accepted Christ as your Savior and are filled with the Holy Spirit, you're going to walk in the Spirit and do what God wants you to do! You're not going to be deliberately going down the wrong road! Don't say that you're saved or converted or that you love the Lord and then deliberately do the things that you know are wrong! That's not grace, that's *dis*grace based on cheap grace. And let me tell you, perfect grace wasn't cheap! It cost Jesus everything! So please, please, don't preach that works are not important—for they are. Yet, works are the cart; they are not the horse. Let's put the cart behind the horse, not out in front!

What is the focus of our faith? Christ our righteousness! A man went to Jesus and called Him "good," and what did Jesus say? "Why do you call Me good? No one is good but ... God" (Mark 10:18). That's humility, isn't it? This is the message that God called me to preach. This is the centerpiece, the foundation, the Rock upon which we are to build God's house. Even Jesus claimed no righteousness but God's. "Do *not* enter into judgment with Your servant, for *in Your sight no one living is righteous*" (Ps. 143:2).

If anyone tells you that they are perfect, they are misguided. The Bible clearly teaches that no mere human is righteous. Only God is righteous, and all our righteousness comes from Jesus alone. "Who shall not fear You, O Lord, and glorify Your name? For *You alone* are holy" (Rev. 15:4, NKJV). Do you believe that? If you believe that, would you say, "Amen"? "*For You alone are holy.*" Christ is called the "Lord our righteousness." Who is the only holy One? Christ, "Emmanuel," "God with us." Now, Revelation is referring to the Lamb here when it says, "*You alone are holy.*" God the Father, the Son, and the Holy Spirit—God is holy, and only God is holy. When we accept Him, He is the Lord our righteousness. The Bible says, "... not by works of righteousness which we have done, but according to His mercy He saved us, through the washing of regeneration and renewing of the Holy Spirit" (Titus 3:5, NKJV). So we are not saved by the works that we have done, but by Christ's works alone. "But of Him you are in Christ Jesus, who became for us wisdom from God—and righteousness and sanctification and redemption" (1 Cor. 1:30, NKJV). Christ is our sanctification; Christ is our redemption.

"For by one offering He has *perfected forever* those who are *being sanctified*" (Heb. 10:14). And there it is, my friends, by the one offering of Jesus Christ, He has perfected us forever! When Jesus died on the cross two thousand years ago, He died to make you perfect in Him. And when He was sacrificed on the cross, He paid the price for your sins. That's why it always makes me sad when people get all worried that God won't love them because they fall into sin or that they are rejected because they made a mistake, causing them to avoid God for a while because they have been bad. And they try to live a good life for a week so that they can earn their way back into God's favor, thinking: *Boy, I really blew it, I guess I'd better try to be good for a while so I can pray again!* Don't do that. Go right to God—even when you fall. He will accept you, love you, and help you through it. Don't stay away from Him. Don't you know that two thousand years ago He died on the cross for that very sin? He knew that you were going to commit it two thousand years ago, and He already paid for it way back then! When you talk to him about it, you're not going to tell Him anything that He doesn't already know about you or your sins. He died for all your sins, all the sins that you are going to commit from now until the day you die or are translated! He's already paid for them! By that one offering, He has already made you perfect forever! And when you accept Him, your perfection is Christ's perfection! "For by one offering He has perfected forever those who *are being* sanctified" (Heb. 10:14, NKJV). Isn't that beautiful? Even though you are in the process of being sanctified and are not totally holy yet, you are still growing in grace. Yet, you are still perfect in God's eyes forever through Christ's offering. Isn't that beautiful? Isn't that exciting? I can grow in grace and improve and develop my character all the while under the umbrella of God's great love, His perfect grace, and His acceptance. Wow! What good news is that! No wonder they call God's plan for saving us the gospel, which means "good news"! Man! That's good news to me!

In *Jeremiah 23:6*, Jesus is called, "*THE LORD OUR RIGHTEOUSNESS.*" Jesus is our righteousness. Now, as I said, some have mistakenly preached perfectionism in the Seventh-day Adventist Church, and I want to share with you what the twenty-eight fundamentals of our faith say about that. This is the true Adventist doctrine; anything else that you have heard or been taught is not true. So, we need to understand what's in our baptismal certificates, and we need to support and teach it because that is what the Bible teaches and what we have voted as a people to believe.

In *Seventh-day Adventists Believe*, you can find the following statements in the chapter, "The Experience of Salvation":

> By faith, Christ's perfect character becomes ours. People can never claim that perfection independently, as if it were their innate possession or theirs by right. Perfection is a gift of God. Apart from Christ human beings cannot obtain righteousness.... No one can add to what He has done. ... Some incorrectly believe that the ultimate perfection that glorification will bring is already available to humans.... (*Seventh-day Adventists Believe*, 2nd ed., pp. 143, 145)

So, if anyone is going around teaching that you have to be absolutely perfect or God won't accept you, then they're mistaken, okay? I want you to know that because there are people who do teach such things, even though the official church doctrine is: "Sanctification is a lifelong process. Perfection now is ours only in Christ ..." (*Seventh-day Adventists Believe*, 2nd ed., p. 145). I am merely repeating what's in the twenty-eight fundamentals of Seventh-day Adventist beliefs. "... the ultimate, all-comprehensive transformation of our lives into the image of God will take place at the Second Advent ..." (*Seventh-day Adventists Believe*, p. 145). Until Jesus comes, you will have a carnal nature. What's more, the book says, "By faith, Christ's perfect character becomes ours. People can never claim that perfection independently, as if it were their innate possession or theirs by right. Perfection is a gift of God. Apart from Christ, human beings cannot obtain righteousness" (*Seventh-day Adventists Believe*, p. 143).

You can be as good as you can possibly be, and you're still not going to earn a thing with God because even the best of your good works are contaminated apart from Christ. Pretty dramatic, isn't it? Now, can you see how this theology lays the glory of man in the dust? And can you see why the devil hates this subject? If people understand the gospel, Satan's power over them is broken. That's why I want you to understand this. "Neither Christlike character traits nor faultless behavior is the ground of our acceptance with God. Saving righteousness comes from the one righteous Man, Jesus, and is conveyed to us by the Holy Spirit. We can contribute nothing to Christ's gift of righteousness—we can only receive it. No one other than Christ is righteous (Rom. 3:10); independent human righteousness is only filthy rags (Isa. 64:6; see also Dan. 9:7, 11, 20; 1 Cor. 1:30). Even what we do in response to Christ's saving love cannot form the basis of our acceptance with God" (*Seventh-day Adventists Believe*, p. 146). That's from the twenty-eight fundamentals of Adventist belief. We believe that Christ is our only perfection and that perfectionism is a heresy that needs to be avoided in our teaching. When I left Catholicism to become a Seventh-day Adventist, I left righteousness by works behind. We are saved by perfect grace through faith just as Martin Luther said, and our works contribute nothing to our salvation—they are the fruit of the tree, not the tree. Jesus is the root; our salvation yields the fruit.

Well, now you know what the Bible says. We are all sinners. We are all lost. None are righteous. Only Christ is righteous, and you know what the twenty-eight fundamentals of our faith say. Our faith teaches that perfection is found only in Christ and that perfectionism is a heresy.

Now I would like to share some Spirit of Prophecy quotations with you that make it clear that we find perfection only in Christ and that He is our only righteousness and our only hope. The full quotations are given in the endnotes.[26]

Here are some of the most powerful, encouraging, uplifting quotes from the pen of inspiration that you will ever read. Why is it that these concepts have not been emphasized? Where has this message been? Could it be if our youth would have heard about this message they would have gladly embraced it? Let's take the time to focus the spotlight on the heart of Ellen White's message as a devotee of Jesus Christ. For her it was all about Jesus—and His love for us:

"God declares, 'There is none righteous, no, not one' (Rom. 3:10). ***All* have the same sinful nature.** All are liable to make mistakes. ***No one is perfect.*** The Lord Jesus died for the erring that they might be forgiven. It is not our work to condemn. Christ did not come to condemn, but to save" (*In Heavenly Places*, p. 292).

Instead of demanding perfectionism, she warns that we are ***liable*** to make mistakes. No one is perfect, nor is anyone expected to be. Isn't that a liberating thought? When under God's umbrella of perfect grace, we are free from condemnation.

God knows our nature is sinful and that we cannot obey his law sufficiently to save us. God's law "could not justify man because ***in his sinful nature he could not keep the law***" (*Patriarchs and Prophets*, p. 373). She also says, "We do not understand *our perverse natures*; and often when we are gratifying self, following our own inclinations, we flatter ourselves that we are carrying out the mind of God" (*Testimonies to Ministers*, p. 503).

My first discovery of this text was when I heard it quoted by Morris Venden in a week of prayer at Columbia Union College. "The divine beauty of the *character of Christ, of whom the noblest and most gentle among men are but a faint reflection…* Jesus, the express image of the Father's person, the effulgence of His glory; the self-denying Redeemer, throughout His pilgrimage of love on earth, was a living representation of the character of the law of God" (*Thoughts from the Mount of Blessing*, p. 49). As a young ministerial student, it arrested my attention and put man's potential for achievement in perspective.

Ellen White knew full well the depths of man's depravity. For her, it was all about Jesus because man had nothing within himself that is good:

> Those who know that *they cannot possibly save themselves, or of themselves do any righteous action*, are the ones who appreciate

> the help that Christ can bestow. They are the poor in spirit, whom He declares to be blessed...Those whose hearts have been moved by the convicting Spirit of God see that *there is nothing good in themselves*. They see that *all they have ever done is mingled with self and sin*. Like the poor publican, they stand afar off, not daring to lift up so much as their eyes to heaven, and cry, 'God, be merciful to me the sinner.' Luke 18:13, R.V., margin. And they are blessed. (*Thoughts from the Mount of Blessing*, pp. 7, 8)

Next we see her struggling to express her deep conviction of the futility of salvation by works.

> I ask, How can I present this matter as it is? The Lord Jesus imparts all the powers, all the grace, all the penitence, all the inclination, all the pardon of sins, in presenting His righteousness for man to grasp by living faith—which is also the gift of God. *If you would gather together everything that is good and holy and noble and lovely in man and then present the subject to the angels of God as acting a part in the salvation of the human soul or in merit, the proposition would be rejected as treason.* (*Faith and Works*, p. 24)

To me, as a young preacher looking to find my voice, this quotation became one of the foundation stones of my ministerial career. I began to immediately put her counsel into practice, looking for ways in every sermon to make it all about Jesus:

> *There is not a point that needs to be dwelt upon more earnestly, repeated more frequently, or established more firmly in the minds of all than the impossibility of fallen man meriting anything by his own best good works. Salvation is through faith in Jesus Christ*

> *alone*... Let the subject be made distinct and plain that it is not possible to *effect anything* in our standing before God or in the gift of God to us *through creature merit*. ... If any man can merit salvation *by anything he may do, then he is in the same position as the Catholic* to do penance for his sins. Salvation, then, is partly of debt, that may be earned as wages. *If man cannot, by any of his good works, merit salvation, then it must be wholly of grace*, received by man as a sinner because he receives and believes in Jesus. It is wholly a free gift. *Justification by faith is placed beyond controversy*. And all this controversy is ended, as soon as *the matter is settled that the merits of fallen man in his good works can never procure eternal life for him*. (*Faith and Works*, pp. 18–20)

Don't despair that you are powerless to help yourself—you have a friend in Jesus. When we do our best, He covers us with His white robe. Even if we are overcome by the enemy, Jesus sticks by us, no matter what.

Steps to Christ is a short but great book, and I recommend that everyone read it. If you have read it before, I recommend that you read it again, though this time with a little different emphasis. Is that alright? On page 62 it says that, because of Adam's sin, "our natures are fallen and we cannot make ourselves righteous."

Do you remember the old commercial featuring the elderly lady calls out, "I've fallen and I can't get up"? Well, we can say the same thing in our sinfulness—"My carnal nature has fallen, and I can't get up!" "Since we *are sinful*, unholy, *we cannot perfectly obey the holy law. We have no righteousness of our own* with which to meet the claims of the law of God. But Christ has made a way of escape for us.... He offers to take our sins and *give us His righteousness*. If you give yourself to Him, and accept Him as your

Saviour, then, sinful as your life may have been, for His sake you are *accounted righteous. Christ's character stands in place of your character, and you are accepted before God just as if you had not sinned*" (*Steps to Christ*, p. 62). Isn't that beautiful? When we talk about developing a Christian character, some Christians get all hung up on their performance, and they fear that, if they don't develop a perfect enough character, God will reject them. But, guess what? You can't develop your character perfect enough to qualify for heaven. Yet, if Christ is your Savior, He will still love you and accept you even though you're imperfect. No one will ever be saved who *isn't* imperfect. We cannot be perfect apart from Christ. It's that simple. He is our only perfection, our only hope. Ellen White states that very simply. Here's how her statement begins: "The truth of Jesus Christ does not tend to gloom and sadness. . . ." I love that thought! "The religion of Christ does not tend to gloom and sadness. We must look away from the disagreeable to Jesus. We must love Him more, obtain more of His attractive beauty and *grace of character*, and *cease the contemplation of others' mistakes and errors*. We should *remember that our own ways are not faultless* . . ." (*That I May Know Him*, p. 136).

"The truth of Jesus Christ does not tend to gloom and sadness...."

When we correct our children, we need to remember that we ourselves are not perfect. Ellen White said that we "should remember that our own ways are not faultless. We make mistakes again and again . . ." Do you make mistakes again, and again? I sure do, and I'm a preacher! I am a sinner like you. I have to pray every day for God to help me, and, every day I fall short. Every day I have to fall at the feet of Jesus and ask His forgiveness. Sometimes I weep at His feet because I'm so far from what God wants me to be. But He loves me anyway, and He is going to help me every day to become what He wants me to be. Ellen White finished the statement in the following way—you must hear this. Are you ready? It's just six awesome words. "*No one is perfect but Jesus* . . ." How straight is that? Then she says: "Think of Him and be charmed *away from yourself* ..." Quit looking at yourself and worrying about whether you're good enough, saying, "I'm not holy enough! I'm not righteous enough!" Quit worrying about your looks, saying, "I'm too fat! I'm too thin! I'm too tall! I'm too short! I'm too ugly!" *Get your eyes off yourself, and get them on Christ!* Whether you're tall or short, skinny, large or in-between, whether you're a woman or a man, whether you're black or white, Filipino, Asian, or Native American—whatever you are, the Great Creator God, who made everything there is, made *you*, loves *you*, died on the cross for *you*, and accepts *you* just the way you are! And continuing with the statement, we read, "... be charmed *away from yourself*, and from every disagreeable thing, for *by beholding our defects faith is weakened* ..." Looking at our defects weakens our faith, so stop beating yourself up! Your only hope is in Christ anyway! If you understand this, then you already understand why the devil's power is broken. The devil can't come around and say, "Wipe that smile off your face! You're no good" when your only goodness is in Jesus.

At the end of the statement she added, "I point you to Christ, the Rock of Ages" (*That I May Know Him*, p. 136). I know, some people would prefer to talk about what we wear, what we eat, and all that stuff. And those are all important things, but they are a *minor* part of Christianity. The *major* part is Christ, the Rock of Ages! He must be our emphasis. If we emphasize other things more than Christ, then we will become legalistic and will do God a disservice. He wants Jesus lifted up. Jesus said that, if you lift Him up, He will draw all men to Himself. Let's make Christ the focus of our faith. "God always demanded good works, the law demands it, but because man placed himself in sin where his good works were valueless, Jesus' righteousness alone can avail...." (Ms. 50, 1900, in *Selected Messages*, vol. 1, p. 343).

Our good works are valueless when it comes to the earning of our salvation. However, they are not valueless as an offering to God in love, even though they must be kept in proper perspective. Martin Luther made that perspective clear when He said, "Even our good works are sinful apart from Christ." As humans, we have a hard time with this concept. I am going to read a statement from *Selected Messages* that will amaze you. Here it is: "The religious services, the prayers, the praise, the penitent confession of sin ascend from true believers ..." Mrs. White is talking about your prayers and mine when we are in church, in our best Sabbath clothes, on our holiest day. We have established now that she is talking about true believers. "The religious services, the prayers, the praise, the penitent confession of sin, ascend from true believers as incense to the heavenly sanctuary, but passing through the corrupt channels of humanity"—That's us. We cannot claim any righteousness of our own. We are corrupt. "... passing through the corrupt channels of humanity, they are so defiled ..." Notice that these are *our prayers!* This is describing us when we are sitting in church, on our best day, in our best Sabbath clothes! So, if even the Sabbath worship experience is polluted when it is apart from Christ, how can we ever think that our works will be somehow acceptable to God? Are you beginning to understand? *There's no hope apart from Christ!* When I look at myself, I don't see how I can be saved. When I look at Christ, I don't see how I can be lost. He is our only hope. "... passing through the corrupt channels of humanity, they are so defiled that unless purified by blood, they can never be of value with God. They ascend not in spotless purity, and unless the Intercessor, who is at God's right hand, presents and purifies all by His righteousness, it is not acceptable to God.... Oh, that all may see that everything in obedience, in penitence, in praise and thanksgiving must be placed upon the glowing fire of the righteousness of Christ" (Ms. 50, 1900, in *Selected Messages*, vol. 1, pp. 344). *"Perfection through our own good works we can never attain*. The soul who sees Jesus *by faith, repudiates his own righteousness*. He sees himself as incomplete, his *repentance insufficient, his strongest faith but feebleness*, his most costly sacrifice as meager, and he sinks in humility at the foot of the cross. But a voice speaks to him from the oracles of God's Word. In amazement he hears the message, '*Ye are complete in Him.*' Now all is at rest in his soul. *No longer must he strive to find some worthiness in himself, some meritorious deed by which to gain the favor of God*" (*Signs of the Times*, July 4, 1892, in *Faith and Works*, pp. 107, 108). Is that clear enough? The sinner is saved by perfect grace through faith in Christ and can be complete in Jesus! When we fall at the foot of the cross with no hope, Jesus comes to us by His Spirit and says, "Arise." And He takes away our filthy garments, places upon us His white robe of righteousness, covers us with His blood, and says, "Father, I present these dear ones to you!" Then, the Father says, "It is enough. I accept them as my children." When the Father looks at us, He sees Jesus standing in our place.

The heresy of perfectionism does a "bait and switch." You've seen a "bait in switch" in a department store, haven't you? The store advertises a super deal on a washer or dryer, and then, when you get to the store, the salesperson tells you, "Oh, they're all sold out, but we do have this one that costs just $200 more." That is a "bait and switch." Well, the advocates of perfectionism also do a "bait and switch." They say, "Yes, you came to Jesus just as you were, but, now that you are saved, the standard is raised. Now that you have accepted Christ, you must be perfect or God won't accept you." So they lure you in by the lovely truth of *Christ our righteousness*, and then, as soon as you accept that truth, they tell you, "From now on you have to work your way there. Oh, He forgives your sins of the past, but, boy, you'd better not do it any more!" They give you salvation by grace with one hand and then take it away with the other. I'll tell you what—I need the Savior past, present, and future! He is my only hope. If you teach that, unless you equal the character of Christ you cannot be saved, you are teaching a heresy first taught by M. L. Andreasen. Andreasen wrote that, through the last generation of humans living upon the earth, "God's final demonstration of what He can do with humanity will be given. He will take the weakest of the weak, those bearing the sins of their forefather, and in them show the power of God. They will be subject to every temptation, but they will not yield. They will demonstrate that it is possible to *live without sin*—the very demonstration of which the world has been looking for and for which God has been preparing. It will become evident to all that the gospel really can save to the uttermost. God is found true in His sayings" (Andreasen, *The Sanctuary Service*, p. 302).[27] Overly conscientious, Andreasen was one of Adventism's most prominent preachers in the 1930s and 1940s. He taught that we have to vindicate God's character and law by achieving sinless perfection as one of the 144,000 who lives a perfect life, and that, unless a person has lived an absolutely flawless and perfect life, he or she will be lost in the time of trouble. This heresy is repudiated in Adventist literature and in Ellen White's writings, but many people have accepted the heresy and spread it around until it is taught, in some extreme circles, as truth. Now, why am I telling you this? What they are saying is that, unless your perfect character equals Christ's perfect character, you can't be saved. And, if that is the case, how many people will be saved? None!

Now let me read you a statement that will debunk "Last Generation Theology." It is one little statement, and you are going to love it. "The divine beauty of the character of Christ, of whom the noblest and most gentle among men are but a faint reflection ..." Was Daniel one of the noblest? How about Peter, James, and John? All of them were but a faint reflection of Christ's divine beauty! How about Elijah and Enoch? They are all but a faint reflection of Christ's beauty! Now, if those godly men are but a faint reflection, what chance do you have to perfectly reflect Christ's character? And, if that's what a person has to do to be saved, then I'm giving up right now! That's like giving me money and then saying, "Go wash my car!" Oh, no! That isn't the way it works! That's not the gospel of Jesus Christ that I know. Christ is my only perfection!

But why should I have to do what's already been done when God will give it to me as a free gift? My Jesus says, *Come to me and accept me by faith, and I will forgive your sins past, present, and future. I will be your Savior. And, as long as you're in a relationship with me, I will save you. I will redeem you as long as you don't reject me and walk away. I will never leave you or forsake you.* Now if Enoch, Elijah, and Daniel are a faint reflection of the character of Christ, I think I'm a pretty dim bulb! And I am so glad that even the greatest and noblest of men is but a faint reflection because that helps me to understand that salvation is not about me; it's about Him! It's not about my working on my character and striving to be a holy person. It's about my accepting the holiness and perfection that Christ has already provided and letting Him work it out in my body and in my heart and in my soul! So, what I have to do is accept Jesus, and He gives me everything: *perfection, justification, and sanctification*. He gives me the whole package—all at once—and then He works it out in my life, day by day, as I continue living in Him. And the whole time that God is working it out in me, He is also saving me. I am perfected forever by the single offering of Christ's death on the cross for my sins.

In 1890 Ellen White wrote: "I ask, How can I present this matter as it is? The Lord Jesus imparts all the powers, all the grace, all the penitence, all the inclination, all the pardon of sins, in presenting His righteousness for man to grasp by living faith—which is also the gift of God. If you would gather together everything that is good and holy and noble and lovely in man and then present the subject to the angels of God as acting a part in the salvation of the human soul or in merit, the proposition would be rejected as treason" (Ms. 36, 1890, in *Faith and Works*, p. 24). She is saying that, if you took all the good works done by every good person on earth who ever did anything good and you added them all up and gave them to God to save one soul, the offer would be rejected as treason. "… the matter is settled that the merits of fallen man in his good works can never procure eternal life for him" (Ms. 36, 1890, in *Faith and Works*, p. 19). Justification by faith is beyond question! "Neither Joseph, Daniel, nor any of the apostles [ever] claimed to be without sin … [They] acknowledged themselves to be sinners, unworthy of His great favors. They have felt their weakness and, sorrowful for their sins, have tried to copy the pattern Jesus Christ" (*Review and Herald*, Aug. 25, 1885, in *Faith and Works*, pp. 43, 44). "… His perfect holiness atones for our shortcomings. When we do our best, He becomes our righteousness…." (Letter 22, 1889, in *Faith and Works*, p. 102). "Even if we are overcome by the enemy, we are not cast off, not forsaken and rejected of God. No; Christ is at the right hand of God, who also maketh intercession for us ..." (*Steps to Christ*, p. 64). "The closer you come to Jesus, the more faulty you will appear in your own eyes; for your vision will be clearer, and your *imperfections* will be seen in broad and distinct contrast to *His perfect nature*. This is evidence that Satan's delusions have lost their power; that the vivifying influence of the Spirit of God is arousing you" (*Steps to Christ*, pp. 64, 65).

For years, some among us have taught our children and others that, unless they have achieved character perfection, they cannot be saved, thereby imposing upon them an impossible standard of perfection. We have been so harsh and demanding of our children—always wanting them to do everything perfectly—that they have grown up thinking, because of our misrepresentation of God's character, that He is some kind of ogre who was standing over human beings, making sure that we do everything right or He would condemn us! And the fact of the matter is that it is just the opposite of that! Ellen White is saying here that the closer you get to Christ, the more imperfect you will look! Then, the teaching that the closer you get to Christ, the more perfect you have to become is actually a satanic deception! Woe unto us! She says that the closer we get to Jesus, the more we will see His perfection, His glory, His goodness, and the less we will see in ourselves that is unpolluted or worthwhile. The fact that you see yourself as less worthy is evidence that you are coming closer to God! She says that you were always that evil anyway, you just didn't realize it! God is just opening your eyes so that you can see who you really are. That may sound depressing, but it shouldn't be. It's the opposite of what people have been claiming. If you have been reading your Bible a lot and praying, you may find yourself saying, *Man, I'm getting worse instead of better!* Have you ever felt that way? You feel like you're worse off than when you started studying, and you wonder, *Am I a true Christian? Shouldn't I be getting holier?* Well, congratulations! You are getting closer to Jesus! However, this is the exact opposite of what perfectionists teach. Instead of seeing ourselves getting holier, we see our own sinfulness, unworthiness, and imperfections more clearly.

The closer we come to Jesus, the more sinful we appear in our own eyes. The closer we come to Jesus, the more unholy we will look! This is the exact opposite of what some have been teaching. But, praise God that He's opening our eyes! Praise Him that we are seeing who we really are because that knowledge leads us to repent and ask God to take those sins away and to help us draw closer to Christ and do what is right. "No deep-seated love for Jesus can dwell in the heart that does not realize its own sinfulness. The soul that is transformed by the grace of Christ will admire His divine character; but if we do not see our own moral deformity, it is unmistakable evidence that we have not had a view of the beauty and excellence of Christ …" (*Steps to Christ*, p. 65). If we don't see our own moral deformity, we aren't close to Jesus. If you are filled with pharisaical pride and self-aggrandizement and you pat yourself on the back, telling yourself that you're all right, pretty holy, and not as bad as those other churches down the street, then you are far away from Jesus, and you need to repent, see your own moral deformity, and say like the Publican, "Have mercy on me, a sinner!" "… The character is revealed, not by occasional good deeds and occasional misdeeds, but by the tendency of the habitual words and acts" (*Steps to Christ*, pp. 57, 58). "Their only hope is in the mercy of God; their only defense will be prayer" (*Prophets and Kings*, p. 588).

Many who teach this extreme perfectionism like to talk about how the 144,000 will be the perfect example of "harvest theology," popularized by Andreasen. Let's look at this group now. Notice the following statement from *Prophets and Kings:*

> While Satan has been urging his accusations, holy angels, unseen, have been passing to and fro, placing upon *the faithful ones the seal of the living God*. These are they that stand upon Mount Zion with the Lamb, having the Father's name

> written in their foreheads. They sing the new song before the throne, that song which no man can learn save *the hundred and forty and four thousand* which were redeemed from the earth. "These are they which follow the Lamb whithersoever He goeth. These were redeemed from among men, being the first fruits unto God and to the Lamb. And in their mouth was found no guile: for *they are without fault before the throne of God*." Revelation 14:4, 5. (*Prophets and Kings*, p. 591)

The legalists and perfectionists emphasize that the 144,000 are "without fault," and they attribute perfection to the accomplishments of this group of people. Why? The only way they could be without fault is through Christ's accomplishments. They have no righteousness of their own. The 144,000 acknowledge their sinfulness, and they recognize that they are only in heaven because of the imputed righteousness of Christ, which we see in the statement, "*For you alone are holy*" (Rev. 15:4, NKJV). We are told that our carnal nature is with us "as long as Satan reigns … so long as life shall last." Our sinful nature will be with us until the day Jesus comes. Right up until that time, we will only be righteous through Christ. Our sinful nature is not removed until the very end. Even so, as born-again believers, we live in the Spirit and not in the flesh and overcome the enemy by the blood of the Lamb through faith. Even though we would rather die than knowingly commit a wrong act, we will confess our sinfulness and never claim to be sinless:

> Sanctification is not the work of a moment, an hour, a day, but of *a lifetime*. It is not gained by a happy flight of feeling, but is the result of constantly dying to sin, and constantly living for Christ. Wrongs cannot be righted nor reformations wrought in the character *by feeble, intermittent efforts. It is only by long, persevering effort, sore discipline, and stern conflict, that we shall overcome*. We know not one day how strong will be our conflict

> the next. *So long as Satan reigns, we shall have self to subdue, besetting sins to overcome; so long as life shall last*, there will be no stopping place, no point which we can reach and say, *I have fully attained. Sanctification is the result of lifelong obedience.*
>
> *None of the apostles and prophets ever claimed to be without sin.* Men who have lived the nearest to God, men who would sacrifice life itself rather than *knowingly commit a wrong act*, men whom God has honored with divine light and power, have *confessed the sinfulness of their nature*. They have put no confidence in the flesh, have claimed *no righteousness of their own, but have trusted wholly in the righteousness of Christ. So will it be with all who behold Christ. The nearer we come to Jesus, and the more clearly we discern the purity of His character, the more clearly shall we see the exceeding sinfulness of sin, and the less shall we feel like exalting ourselves.* (*Acts of the Apostles*, pp. 560, 561)

Once again we can see that the truth is the opposite of what perfectionists have been teaching. The nearer we come to Christ the more clearly we see the purity of Christ and the sinfulness of self. Rather than self-exaltation, the normal Christian experience is to feel sinful and unworthy as one comes closer to Jesus.

> Ministers especially should know the character and works of Christ, that they may *imitate Him; for the character and works of a true Christian are like His*. He laid aside His glory, His dominion, His riches, and sought after those who were perishing in sin. He humbled Himself to our necessities, that He might exalt us to heaven. *Sacrifice, self-denial, and disinterested benevolence characterized His life*. He is our pattern. Have you, Brother A, imitated the Pattern? I answer: *No. He is a perfect and holy example, given for us to imitate. We cannot equal the*

> *pattern; but we shall not be approved of God if we do not copy it and, according to the ability which God has given, resemble it.* Love for souls for whom Christ died will lead to a denial of self and a willingness to make any sacrifice in order to be coworkers with Christ in the salvation of souls. (*Testimonies for the Church*, vol. 2, p. 549)

"We cannot equal the pattern." Who is the pattern? Jesus. Can we equal it? No. Then how dare we teach that, unless we equal it and are perfect, we can't be saved! That is heresy. "We cannot equal the pattern; but we shall not be approved of God if we do not copy it and, *according to the ability* which God has given, resemble it" (*Testimonies for the Church*, vol. 2, p. 549).

Even though God's ideal is higher than we can reach, and we cannot equal the absolute perfection of Christ, God wants us to strive, "according to our ability," with all our hearts to be the very best person we can be, living up to our maximum potential for Christlikeness. "If you love me, keep my commandments," Jesus says. Or, to put it another way, *Those who love Me will keep My commandments*. Relative perfection is a noble goal to strive toward. Pressing toward the mark is the Christian way. You've got to strive to be as much like Jesus as you possibly can. She is not saying that it is acceptable to sin, to do what is wrong, or to do whatever you want. What she is saying is that you should strive to copy and resemble Jesus' life, though you will never equal the pattern. We should do the best we can to be like Jesus. Is it not reasonable for God to ask us to do our best to follow Jesus' example? And she says, God will judge us according to our ability. If you are a brand-new Christian and you don't know the Bible, don't feel like you can't make it, for God takes your lack of knowledge and experience into account. He says, "Look, this person is new. He doesn't know that much yet. I'm going to take that into account. I'm going to give him perfect grace and mercy to cover him while he's growing and while he's learning." If you have been around a long time and studied the Bible a lot, and you are very familiar of what God requires of you, then you should be more mature in Christ. God *does* require more of you than He does of someone who doesn't know that much. Nonetheless, He will be fair with you. If you know more, you will also have more blessings, so why *shouldn't* you do more for God and be closer to Him?

Apart from Christ, we have no merit and no righteousness. Our sinfulness, our weakness, and our human imperfections make it impossible for us to appear before God unless we are clothed in Christ's spotless righteousness. Whatever our maturity level, Christ is our only hope. H. M. S. Richards, Sr., who has always been one of my favorite heroes of the faith, once told me: "Righteousness by faith is the *only kind there is*." I have been thinking about our conversation for forty years now, and I'm still mining deep meaning from it. In one of his books, he wrote: "*It is all of God* for 'their *righteousness is of me*, saith the Lord' (Isa. 54:17) 'Abraham believed God, and it was counted unto him for righteousness' (Rom. 4:3). And that's how we are righteous; it's accounted to us" (*The Promises of God*, p. 234). He affirmed that the only righteousness anyone could ever have is in the person "sitting at the right hand of God." Elder Richards went on to say: "*Righteousness by faith is the only righteousness a believer can have*. It comes from God and is 'by faith of Jesus Christ unto all and upon all them that believe' (Rom. 3:22)" (*The Promises of God*, p. 234). Elder Richards taught me that Jesus is our only source of righteousness and that no human being can duplicate or produce anything worthwhile for salvation. Even our noblest efforts at obedience are imperfect and corrupt. Of course, we are saved to obey and not to disobey, and, when our best efforts are mixed with the incense of Christ's righteousness, God accepts them as holy unto the Lord. Praise God! However, they are only accepted because of the accomplishments of Jesus Christ, our great high priest.

When you fall at the foot of the cross and you realize your sinfulness, don't give up. If you want to accept the free gift of Christ's righteousness, pray with me and accept it just now.

Father in heaven, there's nothing I can do to save myself. I claim the righteousness of Your Son as my only perfection! Please save me when He comes again, I pray, in Jesus' name, Amen.

God's perfect grace is sufficient! Jesus is our only perfection and our only righteousness. He is our only hope!

PERFECT GRACE!

PART II

THE JUDGMENT IN HEAVEN!

CHAPTER 9

THE INIQUITY OF HOLY THINGS: WORSHIP IN NEED OF HEAVENLY INCENSE!

So it shall be on Aaron's forehead, that Aaron may bear the iniquity of the holy things iniquity of the holy things which the children of Israel hallow in all their holy gifts; and it shall always be on his forehead, that they may be accepted before the Lord.
—Exodus 28:38, NKJV

"The iniquity of the holy things"—what an amazing paradoxical phrase is that! How paradoxical to think about holy things being iniquitous! The sanctuary is a place of sacrificial offerings and worship. Like the veil in the Holy Place that was lifted to enter the presence of the Almighty, a veil is lifted from our minds as we contemplate the sanctuary's meaning. What a disclosure of the corrupt human nature of man and the carnality of our nature! As we consider the subject of the heavenly sanctuary in the light of righteousness by faith, it is important to keep in mind that, at the core of our being, our motives are impure and imperfect and our judgment is impaired and our very nature is corrupt and vile. Therefore, any act of public worship by human beings—either believer or nonbeliever—is rife with sin and corruption. That is why Paul declares that, at Christ's second coming, "This corruptible must put on incorruption" (1 Cor. 15: 53). Ellen White was under no illusions of a different state of things when she described the carnal nature in the following passages.

- "When human beings receive holy flesh, they will not remain on the earth, but will be taken to heaven. While sin is forgiven in this life, its results [that is, the carnal nature] are *not now wholly removed. It is at His coming* that Christ is to 'change our vile body, that it may be fashioned like unto his glorious body' (Philippians 3:21)." (*General Conference Bulletin*, April 23, 1901, Art. A)
- "We cannot say, 'I am sinless,' *till this vile body is changed* and fashioned like unto His glorious body." (*Signs of the Times*, March 23, 1888)
- "When man sinned, all heaven was filled with sorrow; for through yielding to temptation, man became the enemy of God, a partaker of *the Satanic nature*. The image of God in which he had been created was marred and distorted. The character of man was out of harmony with the character of God; for *through sin man became carnal, and the carnal heart is enmity against God*, is not subject to the law of God, neither indeed can be." (*Signs of the Times*, Feb. 13, 1893)

It will humble and profit us to contemplate the sad situation that we find ourselves in. When properly understood, the righteousness of Christ truly puts the glory of man in the dust and reveals the truth of the fourteenth psalm, which says that there is none good, no not one. The iniquity of our public worship is seldom realized or dwelt upon, but it is iniquitous nonetheless. Charles Spurgeon described the "hypocrisy, formality, lukewarmness, irreverence, wandering of heart and forgetfulness of" the presence of God in our public worship as a cup of sins that is full and overflowing. He called attention to "our work for the Lord" with "its emulation, selfishness, carelessness, slackness, unbelief." What an accumulation of corruption we have there! Then he added: "Our private devotions, their laxity, coldness, neglect, sleepiness, and vanity, what a mountain of dead earth is there! If we looked more carefully we should find this iniquity to be far greater than appears at first sight" (Charles Spurgeon "The Iniquity of Holy Things").[28]

We are dumbfounded the first time it dawns upon us that, because we are so carnal through and through, we don't even realize how deeply corrupt our motives are. We are mortified then as it dawns on us how very callous, impudent and irreverent we are toward the holy and awesome God in presenting Him with such blemished offerings. And, finally, it hits us like a ton of bricks that the statement is not talking about our sins; it is talking about our "holy things," our best works, our most sacred offerings, our worship, our praise, our thanksgiving, and our supposed obedience. They are all corrupt, foul, filthy, and unworthy to be offered to a holy God. This startling revelation immediately brings to mind the biblical statement: "But we are all like an unclean thing. And *all our righteousnesses are like filthy rags*; we all fade as a leaf, and our iniquities, like the wind, have taken us away" (Isa. 64:6, NKJV).

Notice that the statement does *not* say, "All our *sins* are like filthy rags," but "all our *righteousnesses* are like filthy rags." (The Hebrew phrase is literally "menstrual rags.") The Bible makes it clear that our best works, our holiest prayers, our sincerest attempts at obedience and worship are filthy and unacceptable to God apart from Jesus Christ our righteousness! Ellen White elaborates on this thought, making it crystal clear that, even in church, on our knees, praying our most sincere prayer, our every act of worship is filthy apart from the incense of Christ's righteousness.

- "The righteousness of Christ is presented as a free gift to the sinner if he will accept it. He has nothing of his own but what is *tainted and corrupted, polluted with sin, utterly repulsive to a pure and holy God. Only through the righteous character of Jesus Christ can man come nigh to God*" (*Selected Messages*, vol. 1, p. 342).

- "*Let no one take the limited, narrow position that any of the works of man can help in the least possible way to liquidate the debt of his transgression. This is a fatal deception.* If you would understand it, you must cease *haggling over your pet ideas*, and with humble hearts *survey the atonement*. This matter is so dimly comprehended that thousands upon thousands *claiming to be sons of God are children of the wicked one*, because they will *depend on their own works*. God always demanded good works, the law demands it, but because *man placed himself in sin where his good works were valueless, Jesus' righteousness alone can avail.* Christ is able to save to the uttermost because He ever liveth to make intercession for us. All that man can possibly do toward his own salvation is to accept the invitation, 'Whosoever will, let him take the water of life freely' (Revelation 22:17). No sin can be committed by man for which satisfaction has not been met on Calvary. Thus the cross, in earnest appeals, continually proffers to the sinner a thorough expiation" (*Selected Messages*, vol. 1, p. 343).
- "The *religious services*, *the prayers*, *the praise*, the *penitent confession of sin* ascend from *true believers* as incense to the heavenly sanctuary, but passing through the *corrupt channels of humanity*, they are so defiled that unless purified by blood, they can never be of value with God. *They ascend not in spotless purity, and unless the Intercessor, who is at God's right hand, presents and purifies all by His righteousness, it is not acceptable to God.* All incense from earthly tabernacles must be moist with the cleansing drops of the blood of Christ. He holds before the Father the censer of His own merits, in which there is no taint of earthly corruption. He gathers into this censer the prayers, the praise, and the confessions of His people, and with these He puts *His own spotless righteousness*. Then, perfumed with the merits of Christ's propitiation, the incense comes up before God *wholly and entirely acceptable*. Then gracious answers are returned. Oh, that all may see that *everything in obedience*, in penitence, in praise and thanksgiving, must be placed upon the glowing fire of the *righteousness of Christ. ...*" (*Selected Messages*, vol. 1, p. 344).

The picture of human weakness, carnality and corruption painted before us is astoundingly horrible. What a tale of woe and hopelessness when even our best efforts and noblest attempts at worship and service are unacceptable! But, oh, how cheering and uplifting is the thought that, when Jesus our great high priest went into the most holy place to minister on our behalf, He wore on his forehead the words, "HOLINESS TO THE LORD," and that, while Jesus bears our sin, He presents before His Father's face, not our ungodliness or our attempts at Christian perfection, but *His own holiness* by His own perfect grace!

Jesus has gone into the very throne room of heaven and now stands before His Father in our behalf. He takes the golden censer and fills it with the incense of His own righteousness and purifies the prayers of the saints. The Holy Spirit interprets our prayers to God as Jesus presents us before His father, not in our own holiness, but in the precious holiness of the Lamb of God without spot and without blemish! God accepts Christ's character in place of our imperfect character, and He accepts us and looks at us as if we had never sinned! (See *Steps to Christ*, p. 62.)

The Holy Spirit interprets our prayers to God as Jesus presents us before His father, not in our own holiness, but in the precious holiness of the Lamb of God without spot and without blemish!

May God give us the perfect grace we need to keep our eyes on Jesus, our great high priest, the Author and Finisher of our faith (Heb. 12:2)! Let us observe Him with the eye of faith as He does for us what we can never do for ourselves! Jesus is the Mount Everest of righteousness, and the holiest prophet is a mere molehill! He alone is holy! (Rev. 15:4.) His perfect life, death and resurrection even covers the iniquity of our holy things! As our great High Priest, Christ is able to save to the uttermost those who come to God through Him, seeing He ever lives to make intercession for us (Heb. 7:25)! Christ *is* perfect grace personified! Amen and Amen!

CHAPTER 10

SANCTUARY PRIEST

Not with the blood of goats and calves, but with His own blood He entered the Most Holy Place once for all, having obtained eternal redemption.
—Hebrews 9:12

Let us read Hebrews 9, beginning with verse 16:

> For where there is a testament, there must also of necessity be the death of the testator. For a testament is in force after men are dead, since it has no power at all while the testator lives. Therefore not even the first covenant was dedicated without blood. For when Moses had spoken every precept to all the people according to the law, he took the blood of calves and goats, with water, scarlet wool, and hyssop, and sprinkled both the book itself and all the people, saying, "This is the blood of the covenant which God has commanded you." Then likewise he sprinkled with blood both the tabernacle and all the vessels of the ministry. And according to the law almost all things are purified with blood, and without shedding of blood there is no remission. Therefore it was necessary that the copies of

> the things in the heavens should be purified with these, but the heavenly things themselves with better sacrifices than these. For Christ has not entered the holy places made with hands, which are copies of the true, but into heaven itself, now to appear in the presence of God for us; not that He should offer Himself often, as the high priest enters the Most Holy Place every year with blood of another—He then would have had to suffer often since the foundation of the world; but now, once at the end of the ages, He has appeared to put away sin by the sacrifice of Himself. And as it is appointed for men to die once, but after this the judgment, so Christ was offered once to bear the sins of many. To those who eagerly wait for Him He will appear a second time, apart from sin, for salvation. (Heb. 9:16–18, NKJV)

The entire sanctuary service revolved around God's plan of perfect grace. It was filled with object lessons and word pictures of perfect saving grace. Over the next several chapters we will be looking into the Bible teaching of the sanctuary. The Seventh-day Adventist Church is one of the few churches that actually preaches this message. Very few churches deal with the concept of the sanctuary, even though the New Testament has sanctuary messages all through it. The entire books of Hebrews and Revelation are all written in sanctuary language. Sanctuary references abound in the modern praise songs that are sung in churches today. The song, "We Were Made for This," talks about "dwelling in Your courts" and "coming into Your courts, Lord, I come into the most holy place to behold your glory." All through these modern praise songs the sanctuary message is being proclaimed in song to the world. And so, I say, let the churches sing about God's sanctuary. Let them lift up God's sanctuary, for this is the very message the world needs to hear. All these praise songs are pointing them toward the sanctuary. When the many young kids and young adults who sing praise music start looking toward the sanctuary, they will begin to see the Shekinah glory. Then, when they hear our sanctuary message, they will already be prepared to receive it! I believe strongly that the Holy Spirit is going forth in mighty power and reaching out to people in every denomination. I also believe that someday soon He will bring everyone to the point that they will understand the underlying purpose of the Seventh-day Adventist Church.

We are moving into the last days, and things are happening very, very rapidly. You may have heard about the beautiful November 2005 article in *National Geographic* that features the Seventh-day Adventist health message and how Seventh-day Adventists live longer. As a result of their investigation, the staff of the *National Geographic* now have a great respect for Seventh-day Adventists. You will see more on this as God turns the attention of the world toward Seventh-day Adventists, and you better be ready because, when it comes, it's going to come hard and fast. People are going to be showing up in our worship services to tape and report on them. With the increased scrutiny, the controversy over Sabbath and Sunday and over the Ten Commandments will heat up. You better be prepared!

"Not with the blood of goats and calves, but with His own blood He entered the Most Holy Place once for all, having obtained eternal redemption" (Heb. 9:12, NKJV). (The Greek for this is *ta hagia*, which is properly translated "the holy places," as in Hebrews 9:24, or "the sanctuary," as in Hebrews 8:2.) "He then would have had to suffer often since the foundation of the world; but now, once at the end of the ages, He has appeared to put away sin by the sacrifice of Himself. And as it is appointed for men to die once, but after this the judgment, so Christ was offered once to bear the sins of many. To those who eagerly wait for Him He will appear a second time, apart from sin, for salvation" (Heb. 9:26–28, NKJV). Christ *is* the sanctuary priest who enters the presence of God in the heavenly sanctuary at the "end of the ages." Are we at the end of the ages? Most certainly. In keeping with the symbolism of the Old Testament sanctuary, Christ entered, in 1844, the most holy place to begin the work of putting away sin once and for all! And how does He put away sin? By the sacrifice of Himself. He has entered the most holy place. The first message of this passage in Hebrews is three words: "*Jesus is alive!*" and He is in heaven! Rising on the third day, He ascended into heaven. Jesus Christ is alive today! Right now, He is standing before the throne of God, wearing His priestly garments, listening to our prayers, and presenting them to His Father! Jesus is alive!

Hollywood likes to talk about spiritual things in this world as if they are not true. They talk about the most incredible spiritual realities as if they are fairy tales, and they portray the most incredible fairy tales as if they were real. I don't care about the "Lord of the Rings." I care about the "Lord of the *Kings*"! I don't look to the world for answers. I look to the Creator of the world for answers. Who is your authority? Hollywood or holy wood? Is it the world or the cross? For my part, I look to God's Word! I look to the heavenly most holy place. That's where I am looking for answers—not to politicians or to Hollywood. What the Bible says will happen *shall* happen. In 1844, the judgment began. You can read about it in Daniel 7:9, 10, and 13. "I watched till thrones were put in place, and the Ancient of Days was seated; His garment *was* white as snow, and the hair of His head was like pure wool. His throne was a fiery flame, its wheels a burning fire; a fiery stream issued and came forth from before Him. A thousand thousands ministered to Him; ten thousand times ten thousand stood before Him …" (Dan. 7:9, 10, NKJV). (We will go into greater detail in the next chapter.)

How many angels are there in heaven? Billions. I have heard it said that a million angels can dance on the head of a pin. If that be true, then, employing the atomic substructure of the universe, a billion angels can become so small that they can fly through the eye of a needle without touching it. God's reach is vast. He has created dimensions that you can't even imagine. In the heavenly holy place, there are billions of angels, and God has a huge throne room that is hundreds of miles across, hundreds of miles high, and God sits upon that throne "high and lifted up!" The Bible says that His throne has wheels within wheels with flames of fire coming out of them. Daniel says, "The court was seated, and the books were opened."

Sanctuary Books

People mock Seventh-day Adventists for saying that God is going to go over the books of heaven. "Oh, how silly!" they say. "He probably has video up there with high-tech celestial DVDs! Books are so outdated!" My Bible tells me that He has "books." Now I don't know how He uses them to make records, but when the Bible calls them "books," that's good enough for me. "The court was seated, and the books were opened. I watched then because of the sound of the pompous words which the horn was speaking; I watched till the beast was slain, and its body destroyed and given to the burning flame. As for the rest of the beasts, they had their dominion taken away, yet their lives were prolonged for a season and a time. I was watching in the night visions, And behold, One like the Son of Man, coming with the clouds of heaven! He came to the Ancient of Days, and they brought Him near before Him" (Dan. 7:10–13, NKJV).

Notice Daniel said "thrones"—and they are *moveable* thrones—one for the Father, one for the Son, and twenty-four thrones for the twenty-four elders of Revelation. In the heavenly court, thrones were set up and the judgment began. Daniel described Jesus as entering the most holy place to "put away sin." He is finishing His priestly work. On earth, the high priest entered the Most Holy Place on the Day of Atonement to put away sin, to remove it from the sanctuary. Jesus, our great High Priest, will finish His priestly ministry by winning His case in the trial of the ages. Every case that He has represented will be victorious, and you will get off scot-free from every sin that you have ever committed. You will be found not guilty because Jesus paid the penalty for your sins! He will win the trial and destroy all sin in the universe. We are living right now between verses 13 and 14 of Daniel 7! In verse 15, Jesus comes back to earth! "I was watching in the night visions, and behold, One like the Son of Man, coming with the clouds of heaven! He came to the Ancient of Days, and they brought Him near before Him. Then to Him was given dominion and glory and a kingdom, that all the peoples, nations, and languages should serve Him. His dominion is an everlasting dominion, which shall not pass away, and His kingdom the one which shall not be destroyed" (Daniel 7:13, 14, NKJV).

When Jesus returns, He will destroy Satan and his angels, sinners, and all sin based on the justice of the "sacrifice of Himself." You cannot make Jesus love you any more or less than He already does. We think that our sin makes Him love us less. We think that, because we are sinners who do foolish things, God doesn't love us as much or that our sins have somehow wounded Him and now He doesn't love us! You can't make God love you any more and you can't make God love you any less—His love never changes.

God even loves until the very end those who will be lost. Salvation is not a question of His love. If you have bought the old lie of the devil that you are just too bad to be saved or that you are just too sinful and evil for God to heal or that you are too broken for God to fix—I am telling you right now that God can heal you and every other person who allows Him to do so. God can save anybody. God's perfect grace is radical. And what I am describing is radical grace! "Son of Sam," David Berkowitz, walked up to seven cars and shot fourteen people dead. He did it because he said the devil spoke to him through his dog and told him to go kill them. While he was in prison, a person came and showed him the gospel and preached Christ to him, and David Berkowitz gave his heart to Jesus Christ. For the last ten years he has been teaching a Bible study group of over 100 people every week in prison. When you look at Berkowitz's face now, it beams with the love of Jesus. You can see Christ shining in his eyes. The demons have been banished, the love and peace of Jesus Christ have filled his soul, and he has found help in his time of need. That's radical grace! (See http://1ref.us/mz)

God's perfect grace is powerful enough that it could have even saved Adolph Hitler and Jeffrey Dahmer. God's perfect grace can save anyone—no matter how wretched, no matter how evil. That it can't is one of the devil's lies. The devil says, "You're just too bad to be saved. You could never be saved—you're too evil." That's a lie. Don't listen to the devil's lies. He frequently uses two big ones. The first big lie is: "You're too bad to be saved." The second big lie is: "You're too good to be lost." He tricks more people with that lie than with the first. The truth is: We need Jesus! There is only one way to be saved. The Bible says, "... without the shedding of blood there is no remission of sins." Only one person has the correct DNA to save you, and that's Jesus Christ. Only one person's life can save you, and that's the life of Jesus. There is only one person's blood that can save you, and that's the blood of Jesus! Romans says: "By one man's obedience many are made righteous."

Your obedience cannot make you righteous. Your blood cannot make you righteous. No matter how good you are, no matter how often you go to church, no matter how hard you work to become an absolutely flawless Christian, no matter what you do, you can't save yourself. Your sacrifices won't save you. Your lifestyle won't save you. Your goodness won't save you. Only the blood of Jesus can save you. Nothing else can! There is no other blood that can save you. He must take His blood into the most holy place and put it on the altar for you. If you don't have His blood, then you are not forgiven. If you don't have His forgiveness, then you are lost. Only through Jesus Christ can you be saved. "The obedience of one," mentioned in this text, doesn't have room for two. So, if you're a Christian or Seventh-day Adventist Christian elitist who thinks that somehow you are going to become such a perfect person that when you finally get to the door of the kingdom, God will say, "We're so lucky to have you here," then, forget it! It's not going to happen.

We are told that "The divine beauty of the character of Christ, of whom the noblest and most gentle among men are but a faint reflection" (*Thoughts from the Mount of Blessing*, p. 49). There is only one way that any of us will get into God's kingdom, and that is by the blood of Jesus. Without Christ's blood, you cannot be saved. Once you are saved, then, by all means, live a righteous Christian life and, through the power of the Holy Spirit, live as obediently as you can, but always remember that you are under the umbrella of perfect grace.

The sacrifice He made on the cross of Calvary gives Him the right. It was by His blood, and He is our heavenly high priest. He has perfect righteousness, and He cleanses the sanctuary records of sin. The sins of the saints are blotted out and remembered no more! Hallelujah! Praise Jesus! At the present time, Christ still has the censer in His hand. In Hebrews 4:16 it says, "Let us therefore come boldly to the throne of grace, that we may obtain mercy …" (NKJV). Do you need mercy? I surely do. "… and find grace to help in time of need." Come boldly to the throne of what? "Grace"—yes, perfect grace! God's throne is a throne of mercy and of perfect grace!

But here is something to think about. How graceful are we when we share the Adventist message with people? Do we tell them that God's throne is a throne of grace and that perfect grace is the most important thing that we can share with them? Are we satisfied with just a drop of grace when God wants to give us an abundance of it? How can we be satisfied with a drop in the bucket when God has a whole ocean of grace? We stand holding our little thimbleful of grace and think we have enough. Oh, come on! Leap into the ocean by faith! We often have a quick prayer in the morning and then out the door we run. We get a brief feeling of blessedness when we could dwell in the most holy place every minute of every day and pray without ceasing. The Bible teaches in Col. 2:6 "As ye have therefore received Christ Jesus the Lord, *so* walk ye in him." We need to be born again daily, and the same way we came to Jesus, we need to walk in Jesus. We can have mercy and perfect grace. We can have help whenever we need it. We can have Jesus in us and with us all day long. Let's get bold—bold, I say! Let's study the Word and pray boldly all day long. Let's take the kingdom of God by force![29] Let's praise God all day long in song and in our hearts, and let's make the devil flee as we go boldly studying, praying, and praising Jesus. Let's even do this in church, even during the sermon! If the preacher is preaching and you are not getting much out of it, then take the Bible in your hand, open it up, and start reading!

As you are sitting at a red light, keep a Bible on the seat of your car. So what if they have to honk at you. Open it up and read a psalm! If you're sitting at the laundromat or waiting in line, keep your Bible with you and open it and read it and pray without ceasing. Are you with me? You could be driving down the road and some guy cuts you off. You could just look at him and say, "Praise the Lord! I'm so glad, Lord, that You protect me in this ungodly world! Please help me, Lord, to be merciful!" You can pray without ceasing every minute of every day. You can lift up your heart to the Lord in prayer and praise. "Therefore let us draw near with confidence to the throne of grace, so that we may receive mercy and find grace to help in time of need" (Heb. 4:16, NASB). Receive Christ's righteousness by faith, and become perfect in Him. "By that will we *have been* sanctified through the offering of the body of Jesus Christ *once for all*" (Heb. 10:10, NKJV). Notice that we "have been [past perfect tense] sanctified once for all."[30] When Jesus died on the cross, He became our sanctification (1 Cor. 1:30). So the verse says that we have been sanctified through the offering of the body of Christ. That is past perfect tense. We have been sanctified though we are also being sanctified. "For by *one offering* He has *perfected forever* those who are *being* sanctified" (Heb. 10:14, NKJV). By Christ's offering on the cross, He perfected you and He perfected me forever because he wrote down "forgiven" by our name and gave us credit for His life. "For by *one offering* He has *perfected forever* those who are *being* sanctified." By this single offering, He has perfected us forever at the same time that we are being sanctified.

As I mentioned before, when I told H. M. S. Richards, Sr. that I had a question about "the righteousness of Christ," he responded, "Good, Tom, because that's the only kind there is!" He was right. There is no other kind. We "have been" (past tense) sanctified "once and for all" and made perfect "forever," even though we are still imperfect down here on earth and "being" sanctified. In the book, *I Used To Be Perfect*, George R. Knight says, "… we are perfect but not yet perfect; sinless but not yet sinless." Oh, yes, it is a paradox, but it is so beautiful and so true. Ellen White writes, "Entire justice was done in the atonement. In the place of the sinner, the spotless Son of God received the penalty, and the sinner goes free as long as he receives and holds Christ as his personal Saviour. *Though guilty, he is looked upon as innocent.* Christ fulfilled every requirement demanded by justice" (The Youth's Instructor, April 25, 1901).[31] Like Martin Luther, she believed we are sinful, yet holy. We are perfect in Christ and fully accepted in Him, even though we are not finished being sanctified. Sanctification is simply the process of becoming more loving. Once and for all, He made us holy with His life! There is only one way to heaven: the merits of Jesus. While we are changing into the image of the character of God, He covers our shortcomings and mistakes with His perfect grace.

Whenever I preach this subject and talk about our great high sanctuary priest, some will mistakenly say, "Pastor, it's too much grace! It's cheap grace! You're preaching cheap grace!" They may think that I am preaching once saved, always saved. But am I? No way! I don't believe in that. I might believe in once saved *almost* always saved. Let me explain what I mean by that. You cannot read Hebrews 10:29 and believe in once saved always saved. That's *not* grace, that's *disgrace!* "How much severer punishment do you think he will deserve who has trampled under foot the Son of God, and has regarded as unclean the blood of the covenant by which he was sanctified, and has insulted the Spirit of grace?" (Heb. 10:29, NASB). The next verse says that a fiery judgment awaits such a person. Let me ask you a question: Can a person be sanctified and not be saved? No, that is not possible. This is talking about a saved person who leaves Jesus and goes back into the world. Now people always say, "Oh, well, if he goes back and does that, then he was never saved in the first place." That's not true. That is a lie. You can be saved and then reject Jesus and go back into the world. You can accept Christ and then renounce Him. If you can be born again into God, you can be born again back into the world. But to do so you have to deliberately forsake Him and deliberately leave Him, and deliberately resist Him and deliberately fight Him. You see, I believe that God's perfect grace is so powerful that it is drawing everyone and, if you don't resist it, you will be drawn into it and God will save you. The condition is that you don't resist. You have to fight against God to be lost.

Paul gives us a strong warning in Hebrews 6, in the case of "those who were *once enlightened*, and have tasted of the heavenly gift, and have become partakers of the Holy Spirit, and have tasted the good word of God and the powers of the age to come, if they fall away, to renew them again to repentance, since they crucify again for themselves the Son of God, and put Him to open shame" (Heb. 6:4–6, NKJV). What Paul is saying is this: "There is no way—absolutely no way—if you crucify Christ afresh and reject His sacrifice, to be saved. And you will be lost even if you have been saved in the past by accepting Christ."

Let's try to clarify what Paul is saying. If I were in that state, my thought would be: *My rejection of Christ has caused me to be lost. If I stay in this state and persistently insist on disobeying Him, there is no way I can be saved. However, if I am willing to repent and turn away from sin by choosing to confess my sins and placing my trust in Christ, then He is faithful to forgive and cleanse me from my sin.*

Now, why do I say that I believe in once saved *almost* always saved? In order to be lost, you have to listen to the devil and one-third of the angels. In order to be saved all you have to do is not resist God. What is more, you have the Father, the Son, and the Holy Ghost all on your side, and they are much stronger than the devil or anybody else. Plus, the Father, the Son, and the Holy Ghost are backed by two-thirds of the angels. With them, you outnumber the devil and his angels two to one! It is true that the worldly people who are going to be lost outnumber the saved, but I think two-thirds of the angels and God Himself are more than a match for the people of the world. So, I'd say it's harder to be lost than it is to be saved. And I think that, if you just listen to the Holy Spirit and don't resist Him, God will save your soul. You have to reject the Holy Spirit and deliberately choose to sin in order to be lost. You have to fight against God to be lost! So, before the judgment ends, while Jesus still has the censer in His hand, you need to come to Him.

In order to understand Hebrews better, I'd suggest that you read Revelation. In chapter 8, John describes the angel with a golden censer in his hand. "Another angel came and stood at the altar, holding a golden censer; and much incense was given to him, so that he might add it to the prayers of all the saints on the golden altar which was before the throne. And the smoke of the incense, with the prayers of the saints, went up before God out of the angel's hand. Then the angel took the censer and filled it with the fire of the altar, and threw it to the earth; and there followed peals of thunder and sounds and flashes of lightning and an earthquake" (Rev. 8:3–5, NASB). While the heavenly high priest is making atonement for us in the most holy place, we should seek to become perfect in Christ through His righteousness. How do we become perfect in Christ through His righteousness? By accepting His free gift of salvation and letting Him write our name in His book of life as He covers us with His white robe of righteousness. There is still time.

The door of God's mercy is swung wide on the hinges of His perfect grace. Will you go through the door? Will you look into the throne room of God? "After these things I looked, and behold, a door standing open in heaven, and the first voice which I had heard, like the sound of a trumpet speaking with me, said, 'Come up here, and I will show you what must take place after these things' " (Rev. 4:1, NASB). "And no one in heaven or on the earth or under the earth was able to open the book or to look into it. Then I began to weep greatly because no one was found worthy to open the book or to look into it; and one of the elders said to me, 'Stop weeping; behold, the Lion that is from the tribe of Judah, the Root of David, has overcome so as to open the book and its seven seals.' And I saw between the throne (with the four living creatures) and the elders a Lamb standing, as if slain, having seven horns and seven eyes, which are the seven Spirits of God, sent out into all the earth" (Rev. 5:3–6, NKJV).

According to Revelation 4 and 5, of all those who are in heaven or on the earth or under the earth, only Jesus is worthy. He was the only one worthy to open the scroll and secure for us eternal life. Keep looking into that heavenly holy place, and you will see through the open door into the most holy place.

"And the temple of God which is in heaven was opened; and the ark of His covenant appeared in His temple, and there were flashes of lightning and sounds and peals of thunder and an earthquake and a great hailstorm" (Rev. 11:19, NKJV). Can you see the very throne of Jesus in the most holy place next to the Father's throne? Can you see our great sanctuary priest pleading each of our cases? Can you see Him there? Yes, it is an awe-inspiring place. Daniel saw the one like a "son of man" lifted up, and Isaiah saw the Lord "high and lifted up." When they did, they fell as dead men. The same will be true of us. But what does Jesus say to us? He says, *Come, boldly My child to my throne of grace. Come, see Me. Look into My sanctuary; look into My most holy place. Hear Me, abide with me, live with Me, bring your sinful, imperfect character to Me, and I will give you mercy. I will give you grace. I will help you in your time of need!* That's what Jesus says to each of us!

Once He finishes His work as sanctuary priest, He will cast that golden censer down and put on His kingly robes, and He will come back to earth apart from sin. Hebrews says that Jesus is coming "to those who eagerly wait for Him … for salvation" (Heb. 9:28, NKJV). When Jesus throws down that censer, the angels bring His kingly robes, and He puts on His kingly crown, and then He comes to earth to rescue His people. When He comes this time, it will be as the Lion and not the Lamb, and He will come apart from sin, to bring salvation! At last, we will be "once saved, always saved!" We will be delivered from this body of death, and this corruptible will put on incorruption. And those who are excited, eager, and panting for His presence, as a deer for water, will have their every hope and dream come true when Jesus appears in the sky. If you want your friends and family to hear this message about the sanctuary and all that it means, then you need to bring them to a Seventh-day Adventist church. If you want your children to hear this message, you need to educate them in a Seventh-day Adventist school. That's where they will hear this message. You won't hear it at any other church. Come boldly before the throne of grace, and you will find help in time of need. Can you see Jesus, the sanctuary priest, with the incense in His hand ministering before the most holy place as the smoke goes up? Do you want to have your prayers ascend with the incense of Jesus' righteousness and have Jesus forgive your sins, win your case in court, pronounce you "not guilty," and save you when He comes again, based on His perfect grace? If you do, would you join me in prayer?

Lord Jesus, save me when you come back; rescue me, Lord! Declare me innocent based on your pleadings in the most holy place! Mix my prayers in with Your incense and present them to the Father. Put the blood upon them, Lord, the only blood that can save me, the blood of the Lamb. Only your obedience can save me, only your life, dear Lord. Credit me with Your life and cover me with Your blood. Thank you, Lord, for leading me to this book in which your message is proclaimed!

Thank you, Lord Jesus. We come to you, our great sanctuary priest! We praise you, and thank you for pleading our case. You alone are worthy of our praise! Write our name in Your book of life. Cover us with Your white robe and help us to live in Your presence every day. Help us to be steadfast in our daily devotions, in our Bible study, and in our prayer time. Help us to be faithful, Lord, every day and save us as we eagerly await your return, we pray in Jesus' name, Amen.

CHAPTER 11

SANCTUARY LAWS FOR WORSHIP

So it was, when Moses had completed writing the words of this law in a book, when they were finished, that Moses commanded the Levites, who bore the ark of the covenant of the Lord, saying: "Take this Book of the Law, and put it beside the ark of the covenant of the Lord your God, that it may be there as a witness against you ..."
—Deuteronomy 31:24–26, NKJV

The entire earthly sanctuary system of the Jews was centered on God's character as reflected in the Ten Commandments. The sanctuary was also established to deal with the sins of God's people. Its purpose was to teach the people about God's law, the awfulness of sin, the forgiveness and removal of sins, and the coming of the Messiah who would be sacrificed for the sins of God's people. The entire ceremonial system was instituted to teach the people that God loved them and that He would make provision through Jesus Christ for their redemption. If we wish to study the sanctuary and the laws that were part of the sanctuary system, as Christians, we will inevitably turn to the apostle Paul. For Christians, he is the main architect of New Testament theology. Originally, Paul was a Pharisee and a member of the Sanhedrin, the ruling council in Jerusalem. He was also a Roman citizen and spoke several languages. As an elder and leader of the Jewish people, he understood the law and claimed to be a Pharisee of Pharisees (Acts 23:6). Paul wrote seventy percent of the New Testament, including the major epistles to the Romans, the Galatians, the Colossians, the Ephesians, the Corinthians, as well as other books including the general epistle to the Hebrews.

Paul's treatise on the relationship of the Ten Commandments to the gospel is found in the first eight chapters of Romans and throughout the rest of his epistles. The epistle to the Hebrews spells out the relationship of the old covenant system, with its two main laws, to the heavenly sanctuary and the ministry of Jesus the Great High Priest. We will look at the Pauline system of theology concerning the law and the gospel, the law under the old covenant, and the law in the new covenant. We will also examine the ceremonial law of Moses and the Ten Commandments, which are also called "the covenant" of the Lord (Joshua 3:11) and "his testament" (Rev. 11:19). One of the main lessons we can learn from this sacrificial system is how God revealed to the human race the evilness of sin and what sin's consequences are. From the creation of the human race, God's moral law has been known and understood. The measure of sin has always been the suffering and pain that it has caused. The Bible says that there is no sin where there is no law, "for by the law is the knowledge of sin" (Rom. 3:20).

If by the law we receive the knowledge of sin, then we can't do away with it or sin would not exist, for where there is no law, there is no sin. When Adam sinned, the Ten Commandments were obviously present and binding. Otherwise, Adam could not have sinned or been held accountable for sinning. Likewise, there had to be a law that said, "Do no murder," or Cain could not have been held accountable for his actions. "What shall we say then? is the law sin? God forbid. Nay, *I had not known sin, but by the law:* for I had not known lust, except the law had said, Thou shalt not covet" (Rom. 7:7). "... by the law is the knowledge of sin." Even without a law inscribed in stone, God says, in Romans 2, that He has written His law in the hearts of the heathen who know right and wrong "by nature."

"For when the Gentiles, which have not the law, do *by nature the things contained in the law*, these, having not the law, are a law unto themselves" (Rom. 2:14). Where there is no law, there is no reckoning of sin, and there is no need for a sacrifice. Human beings are as evil as human experience has shown them to be, but without a sacrifice, there is no salvation, and ultimately, there is no God.

Yet, Scripture declares that God's law is holy and that his commandments are holy, just, and good. God Himself is holy, just, and good. So any gospel that does away with God's law, does away with sin and does away with salvation, and it attacks the very nature of God. Anyone who tells you that the Ten Commandments have been abolished is preaching a false gospel. Keep in mind that the epistle to the Romans was written around 58 AD. That's over twenty-five years after Jesus died, rose, and ascended into heaven. Decades later, Paul declared that God's law, the Ten Commandments, is still in place and that he is keeping them. Nowhere in Paul's writings does he mention the keeping of any day but the Sabbath—the day that he observed throughout Acts (see chaps 13, 14, 16, 17, and 18)—nor is there any mention of the Ten Commandments being obsolete or unnecessary. At the end of Romans, he exhorted his disciples to continue in the "obedience of faith."

For Paul, the law of God is the foundation of God's sanctuary system, under both the old and the new covenants. The ark of the covenant is revealed to be part of both tabernacles, of the copy, or model, made according to the pattern in the old covenant, and of the ark of the covenant in heaven where God reigns. Let's listen to what Paul, the Apostle wrote: "Therefore the law *is* holy, and the commandment holy and just and good" (Rom. 7:12, NKJV). "For I *delight in the law of God* after the *inward man*" (Rom. 7:22, NKJV). "I thank God—through Jesus Christ our Lord! So then, with the mind *I myself serve the law of God*, but with the flesh the law of sin" (Rom. 7:25, NKJV). "*Do we then make void the law through faith? God forbid: yea, we establish the law*" [Greek: *nomon oun katargoumen dia tēs pisteōs mē genoito alla nomon istanomen*] (Rom. 3:31).

Notice that Paul used the words, *mē genoito*, translated "God forbid" in the King James Version and meaning "may it never be!"

Mē genoito is the strongest negative in the Greek language, and Paul used it on purpose because he wanted to answer the question, "Do we then make void the law?" in the most emphatic way possible—we *absolutely* do *not!* Today we might answer the question about the invalidation or doing away of the law through faith by saying, *"You've got to be kidding! Don't even go there! Don't even think about it!"* So, after Paul gives the strongest "no" possible, he adds, "Yea we establish the law." In other words, we not only do *not* invalidate the law by faith, but by faith we confirm the law's role and validity. Thus, Paul declared that the law of God is firmly established by faith—and his statement was written twenty-five years after Christ had ascended into heaven! What astounds me is how that people can read Colossians 2:14 and Ephesians 2:15 and say that Paul taught the Colossians and Ephesians the exact opposite of what he taught the Romans—that faith abolishes the law. But that is self-contradictory and absurd. As you can see in his writings, Paul taught that the Spirit uses the law to convict sinners of their sins and to lead them to repentance. God's law "kills" them by convincing them of their sinfulness and making them guilty before God. Then God's Spirit uses their conviction of sin to turn them to repentance. Once they have a knowledge of their sin through the law and have repented, then the Holy Spirit convicts them of "righteousness" (John 16:9, 10), which is "right doing," or law keeping. God's Spirit convicts the sinner of sin by putting "enmity" in the heart against sin and against Satan when He writes the principles of God's law in the heart.

The carnal mind is at enmity with the law of God and is not subject to it. We all have a carnal nature, but God's Spirit gives us a new nature that has spiritual power over the old nature. Paul wrote, "For we know that the law is spiritual: but I am carnal, sold under sin" (Rom. 7:14). It is the carnal mind, or worldly mindset, with its desire for sinful things that is at war with God's law and that does not honor it. "Because the *carnal mind is enmity against God*; for it is *not subject to the law of God, nor indeed can be*" (Rom. 8:7, NKJV). The only mind in the universe that is not subject to God's Ten Commandment law is a carnal mind. "Ye adulterers and adulteresses, know ye not that the *friendship of the world is enmity* with God? whosoever therefore will be a friend of the world is the enemy of God" (James 4:4).

Friendship with the world is enmity with God. The carnal mind is not subject to God's law. So, if someone is telling you that the Ten Commandments have been done away with, they reveal their carnal mind. They have a mind that is friendly with the world. What is more important to you? Holy-wood or Hollywood? Hollywood has a very worldly mindset, and the Bible says, "Therefore they are enmity against God." Hollywood is just like anybody else, it has good and bad, and you have to choose carefully what you will watch and participate in. If you are friends with the world—if everybody in the world loves you and thinks you're great—then you're not much of a Christian because the people of the world reject true Christians. They don't like true Christians. They persecute true Christians. Hollywood *hates* true Christians. They despise Christ and everything He stands for. So, if a person who hates Jesus has no problem at all with you and they're patting you on the back telling you that you're a great person, then you'd better check yourself out! They have a mind that is not subject to God, and they are telling you to do something that is against God. Remember, Paul said that the carnal mind *is enmity* against God and that it is not subject to God's law. So, if someone is telling you that you don't need to be subject to God's law, then they are at enmity with God, or carnal in their point of view. Are they safe to follow? Are

Friendship with the world is enmity with God. The carnal mind is not subject to God's law. So, if someone is telling you that the Ten Commandments have been done away with, they reveal their carnal mind.

they safe to listen to? Paul never taught that the Ten Commandments were done away with. He wrote that the Ten Commandment law *is—present tense*—holy, just, and good. He said, "I delight in God's law." He said that, with his mind, he "serves the law of God"; and he said that faith does not make the law void but that it establishes the law that says, "Thou shalt not covet."

We are not saved by the law, but neither is the law done away with under the new covenant. What Paul meant when he said that *the carnal enmity was abolished in his flesh and nailed to the cross* was that he died a carnal sinner's death. Jesus bore in His own body all the sins of mankind. Paul never taught that the Ten Commandments were done away with. He declared that the Ten Commandment law—in the present tense—is holy, just, and good. Paul said that he delighted in God's law. He said that he served God's law with his mind. He said that faith does not make void the law but, rather, establishes the law. We are not saved by the law but neither is it done away with in the new covenant. It is the everlasting covenant. What Paul said was that the carnal mind was enmity against God. And he said, in Ephesians 2:15, that Christ abolished the enmity in His flesh and nailed it to the cross, as He died a carnal sinner's death. Christ bore in His body the sins of all mankind. "Having abolished *in his flesh the enmity [the carnal mind, the carnal mindset]*, even the *law of commandments contained in ordinances*; for to make *in himself of twain* one new man, so making peace" (Eph. 2:15). The law that Jesus did away with on the cross was the carnal ordinances that had to do with the carnal mind.

Sanctuary Laws in the Old Covenant

In this next section, I want to talk to you about the carnality of the sanctuary service in the Old Testament. In the sanctuary in the wilderness, Christ's body was symbolized by all the sacrifices and ordinances that had to do with God's forgiveness and the removal of the sins of His people.

With regard to the law that had to do with carnality, which we have mentioned, there is a helpful but startling verse that Paul wrote in the epistle to the Hebrews: "… which stood only in meats and drinks, and divers washings, and *carnal ordinances*, imposed on them until the time of reformation [that is, until Jesus came]" (Heb. 9:10). So the sacrifices of the Old Testament sanctuary service are called "carnal ordinances." Did you know that? The reason they are called "carnal" is because the entire earthly sanctuary system was soaked in blood and covered in sin. It was foul from the top of its head to the bottom of its feet; the sanctuary was made filthy and polluted by its ministry of blood and sin. The holy and the most holy were the type of the great anti-typical place, in which is found the throne room of God. The holy and most holy types were covered with sin. Sin was everywhere. Blood was everywhere. Before the curtain hanging between the Holy Place and the Most Holy Place, blood splattered daily in the sanctuary and required cleansing once a year. The blood of animals was nearly everywhere. Why? Because of the sins of God's people. The blood was what symbolically transferred sin from the sinner to the sanctuary to bring atonement (see Leviticus 4). It was carnal. It was enmity. The carnal nature is symbolized by the carnal ordinances, the law of sacrifices—meat and drink offerings that were all shadows, or symbols, of Jesus Christ.

In Christ's body on the cross, He bore the sins of the carnal man. He was also the perfect human being. So, that is why it says that, in Christ's own body is the perfect Jesus who never sinned as well as the carnal man who is symbolic of all sinners and our sins. Both persons are in one body, in Jesus, and they both bring about peace (Eph. 2:15–17). That is why Paul said in Romans, "Knowing this, that our *old man is crucified with him*, that the *body of sin might be destroyed*, that henceforth we should not serve sin" (Rom. 6:6).

"The body of sin might be destroyed." "Our old man is crucified with Him." Did you know that your carnal nature, your carnal mind, which is enmity against God, was nailed to the cross when Jesus was crucified?

When Jesus died on the cross, He reconciled the carnal Adam and the spiritual Adam in one body. He killed our carnal nature—the enmity, the carnal mind, our friendship with the world, and sin—and He reconciled us to God by His death, as we read in Ephesians 2:16: "And that he might *reconcile both unto God in one body* by the cross, having *slain the enmity* thereby." When Jesus died on the cross, he reconciled the carnal man and the new man in one body. He killed our carnal nature, also described as the enmity, the carnal mind, and our friendship with the world, as well as our sin, and He reconciled us to God.

So when Paul wrote about the "carnal ordinances," or the ceremonial law, being done away with in Colossians 2:14, Hebrews 9:10, and Ephesians 2:15, he is not talking about God's doing away with the Ten Commandment law. Throughout the first eight chapters of Romans, Paul validates God's law in making sin known, in condemning sin, and in providing a foundation for the gospel that Paul preached. It is just this simple: God's law is right; sin is wrong. God is just to condemn sin. Christ's perfect obedience to the law is our ticket to forgiveness for breaking the law. We are saved by Christ's good works, by Christ's observance of the law. By His perfect obedience of God's law, He proved that Adam was wrong for sinning and soundly rebutted Satan's claim that obeying God's law was impossible. For Paul to argue so eloquently that God's law is holy, just, and good, for him to say that he delighted in God's law, served God's law, and that faith establishes God's law, he cannot also be saying that the law has been made void! Only the carnal mind is not subject to God's Ten Commandments. For Paul to support the law for eight chapters of Romans and then six short chapters later to totally contradict himself in Romans 14 that now we don't need to worry about the Sabbath, would be totally inconsistent. What people interject into Romans 14, Paul never says. Paul's theology on the law of God is clear: "Do we make void the law of God through faith? God forbid!" *No, absolutely not!* To this we might add: Do we make void the law through *grace*? God forbid! No, *absolutely not!* You cannot annul even one of the Ten Commandments or you will violate the entire system of theology, law, and salvation that Paul preached. The law is the foundation of the gospel. All the commandments must remain intact.

That's why our understanding of perfect grace is different from that of other Christians. Our view is different from that of the Calvinists. Our view is different from that of the Baptists. Our view is different from that of the Nazarenes. Our view is different from that of the Catholics. Our view is different from that of the Wesleyans. We fully preach the law as part of the New Covenant. We don't preach the "Nine Commandments" plus "one suggestion." We do not take the Ten Commandments that were chiseled in stone and chisel out the part of the fourth commandment where God says, "Remember." Chisel out that one word? No!—No, no, no! The Sabbath commandment is as valid today as it was in the Garden of Eden and as it will be ten million years from now! It has never been done away with, and it never will be done away with! That can be proven from the Scriptures. Isaiah 66:22, 23 says that we are going to keep the seventh-day Sabbath in the new heavens and the new earth.

The ceremonial law of Moses was a carnal law by nature. It was comprised of bloody sacrifices and offerings pointing to Christ's death on the cross. They were shadows, or representations of the heavenly. A shadow is always a semblance of the real thing that is casting it. These laws were shadows of Jesus Christ who would come and give His life as the Lamb of God. The ceremonial system stood squarely under the shadow of the cross. This is clearly revealed in Hebrews 10:1.

But let's look at Colossians 2:14: "Blotting out *the handwriting of ordinances* that was *against us*, which was contrary to us, and *took it out of the way, nailing it to his cross* …" There's a "handwriting of ordinances"—laws—"that was against us, which was contrary to us." That was what was taken out of the way and nailed to the cross. Therefore, "let no man judge you …" I need to pause to point out that this text does not say that we are to do away with the Sabbath. It simply says, *Do not let anyone judge you.* Don't be judgmental. "Let no man judge you in *meat, or in drink*, or in respect of an holyday, or of the new moon, or of the sabbath days [plural—in English and Greek, and the word "sabbath" has a small "s"]: *which are a shadow of things to come*; but the *body* is of Christ" (Col. 2:16, 17).

Whatever this is, Paul says that (a) it comes from a handwriting (a *cheirographon*, a handwritten document), (b) it was against them, and (c) it had meat and drink offerings, holydays, new moons, and sabbath days. Let me ask you a question: In the Ten Commandments, do you see anything that has to do with meat or drink offerings or new moons? Do you see anything that has to do with shadows? That would be a "no" for both questions. The shadow comes from the sacrifice of Christ on the cross. Notice verse 17, "Which are a shadow of things to come ..." The laws concerning sacrifice pointed forward to Christ. Christ's cross cast a shadow back into history and these shadows were cast by Jesus. These sabbaths, offerings, and new moons are all part of the ceremonial law. Connected with the festivals (Lev. 23:4ff) were seven yearly sabbaths: two with Unleavened Bread, one with the feast of Weeks (or Pentecost), one with trumpets, one with the Day of Atonement, and two with the feast of tabernacles. These special holy days and their sabbath days (plural, small "s") and new moons were are all a part of Moses' law that was not contained in the Ten Commandments.

Hebrews 8:5 also sheds some light on the shadows. "Who serve unto the example and *shadow of heavenly things*, as Moses was admonished of God when he was about to make the tabernacle ..." Referring to Exodus 25, Hebrews goes on to say that Moses made the sanctuary system "according to the pattern shewed to [Moses] in the mount." God showed Moses the tabernacle that He wanted him to build. He showed him everything in heaven, and Moses came back and made everything according to the pattern that God had showed him on Mt. Sinai. "For the *law having a shadow of good things to come*, and not *the very image of the things*, can never with those sacrifices which they offered year by year continually make the comers thereunto perfect" (Heb. 10:1). The verse says that the law Paul is talking about is a "shadow of good things to come" that had sacrifices in it. So, let me ask you a question: Do the Ten Commandments have anything to do with sacrifice? No, they do not. Do they have any sacrifices contained in them? Again, they do not. Are the Ten Commandments a shadow of things to come, that is, pointing forward to Christ? No. They are not. The fourth of the Ten Commandments point back to the Garden of Eden when God made the Sabbath. "Remember the Sabbath day … for in six days the LORD made heaven and earth …" The Ten Commandments point backward, not forward. That is why the Ten Commandments were never nailed to the cross, unless you are referring to Jesus' being the embodiment of the Ten Commandments because He lived out the Ten Commandments fully. Perhaps in that one sense you could say that the character of God was nailed to the cross in Christ. But that act only establishes His character and His law.

Jesus kept the Ten Commandments. Everything about Him demonstrated Him to be a commandment-keeping Savior. So it was *He* who was nailed to the cross, not the Ten Commandments. They were never taken out of the way or abolished. In the heavenly throne room, God showed Moses what he was to make, and everything constructed in the worldly sanctuary were according to the pattern. Moses made it very clear, as did the priests who administered the sanctuary services, that God's Covenant was composed of the Ten Commandments and that the law that Moses wrote with his own hand was a different law with a different purpose.

Let us compare Deuteronomy 31 with Colossians 2:14–17.

"And it came to pass, when Moses had made an end of *writing the words of this law in a book*, until they were finished" (Deut. 31:24). The book of the ceremonial laws was written by Moses with his own hand. Then it was rolled up in a scroll and placed in a leather pouch *in the side of the ark* of God. Notice that it was in *the side of the ark*. "That Moses commanded the Levites, which bare the ark of the covenant *of the LORD* …" (Deut. 31:25). Did you notice the designation of the ark of the covenant? It doesn't say that the Ten Commandments were the covenant *of the Jews*. It says that they were the covenant *"of the LORD."* What is the covenant? Moses had said: "And he declared unto you his covenant, which he commanded you to perform, even ten commandments; and he wrote them upon two tables of stone" (Deut. 4:13). Now, later, God says, "Take *this Book of the Law, and put it beside of the ark of the covenant of the Lord* your God, that it may be there as a *witness against you*" (Deut. 31:26, NKJV).

So the ark of the covenant contained the Ten Commandment covenant, which was God's law, and the law written by Moses was placed in the side of the ark on a scroll. So Moses' law on the side of the ark was different from the Ten Commandments that were in the ark. Notice the purpose of the law on the scroll: "that it may be there as a *witness against you.*" What was the witness against them? The law of Moses that was slid into the side of the ark. Notice in Colossians 2:14, "Blotting out the handwriting of ordinances that was against us." The law of Moses, the covenant that Moses wrote with his own hands, with its ordinances about the sacrificial system, was nailed to the cross because the great anti-typical Lamb of God fulfilled the sacrifices, making obsolete all the little symbolic lambs that represented Him, and the glory of that Old Testament earthly sanctuary faded as the New Testament glory of Christ reached its zenith.

Paul made a clear distinction between the ceremonial law of Moses and the Ten Commandments. For he delighted (present tense) in the law that said, "Thou shalt not covet"—that is, the Ten Commandments, which were still in existence and which he declared to be holy, just and good. The Ten Commandments were a law that he still served with his mind, while the ceremonial law was "carnal ordinances" (Heb. 9:10) that were a "shadow of heavenly things" (Heb. 8:5) and a "shadow of good things to come" that included imperfect sacrifices offered yearly (Heb. 10:1).

Paul said that *"it"* was "nailed to the cross." He also said that the "it" that was nailed to the cross is "the enmity" (Eph. 2:15). Now what is the enmity? We already established that the "enmity" is the carnal mind, that, in friendship with the world, hates the Ten Commandment law of God.

This carnal mind was symbolized by the ceremonial system. The "it" is the "handwriting of ordinances" that Moses wrote with his own hand and put in the side of the ark. The "it" was the law of Moses written as a "witness against you," and Paul called it "against us."

There is a lot of theology here. And you may say, "What does it matter to me?" In Christ's body, the entire earthly sanctuary system of sacrifices and the sins of the carnal man that the "it" represented were "crucified," "done away with" and "taken out of the way." The stone tablets of the worldly ark could only pass away in the sense that their glory was fading away because the earthly sanctuary system was reaching its culmination. Those small tablets, fashioned after the pattern in heaven, were only models of the heavenly. They only reflected dimly the glory of the original tablets in heaven. That is why some people get all upset when they are reminded that Paul said that the glory of the tables written in stone is fading away (2 Cor. 3:7). Paul was writing about the fact that, when Jesus died on the cross, as the priest was ready to offer the sacrifice, an unseen hand ripped the veil of the temple in two and the lamb was delivered. Under the new covenant, the Ten Commandments are in heaven in the very throne room of God. They are immense, glorious, and beyond any scale or grandeur that man can even imagine! The everlasting covenant is now being conducted in heaven, and that is why it is called everlasting! The principles of the Ten Commandments will endure for eternity! The former model on earth was grand, but it was nothing in comparison with the reality of the commandments found in the center of God's throne room in heaven.

The sacrifices of the lambs in the earthly tabernacle were mere symbols of Jesus' sacrifice on Calvary. He took our sins into His body. He became sin for us. He reconciled in His body the sinner and the perfect last Adam. He was Himself the sacrifice. He killed the enmity, or carnal, worldly mind upon the cross. The veil in the temple was ripped in two! God tore that thick curtain in half, and the earthly sanctuary system became history. The knife fell out of the priest's hand at the time of the evening sacrifice, at three o'clock, and the lamb ran away. The shadow met reality; the type of the earthly system met the anti-type of heaven!

That's why in Revelation 11:18 and 19 it says that, right before Jesus comes—while the world is raging and God's law is being exalted by His true people—right at that very time believers will look through an open door in heaven and see the ark of God's covenant. Inside that ark is God's testament, the Ten Commandments. And no man can reach up there and take those stone tablets out of the glory room and chisel "Remember the Sabbath day" out of them!

The veil in the temple was ripped in two! God tore that thick curtain in half, and the earthly sanctuary system became history. The knife fell out of the priest's hand at the time of the evening sacrifice, at three o'clock, and the lamb ran away.

Notice that Moses wrote the law and put it in the pocket in the side of the ark of the covenant *of the Lord*. The purpose of the ark was to house the sacred covenant that God gave to Moses on Mount Sinai. The Ten Commandments were written by God with His own finger. They weren't written by Moses and put in the side of the ark; they were written by God on stone and then God gave them to Moses. Remember, Moses said the God who wrote and gave him the Ten Commandments was named "I AM." "And God said unto Moses, I AM THAT I AM: and he said, Thus shalt thou say unto the children of Israel, I AM hath sent me unto you" (Exod. 3:14). Jesus said to the Jews, "Before Abraham was, I am" (John 8:58). Jesus wrote the Ten Commandments with His own finger. They are the commandments of Jesus Christ. The Bible makes this clear when it says: "There is one lawgiver, who is able to save and to destroy: who art thou that judgest another?" (James 4:12). There is one Lawgiver, one Author of the Ten Commandments; it is the I AM.

When Moses walked down the mountain, he saw the children of Israel cavorting below, and, in the glory that he had just beheld while communing with God, he was so affronted by the worldly carnal mindset of the dancing writhing apostates that he took the Ten Commandment law and threw it down from the mountain. As it hit the rocks and broke, it symbolized the broken covenant and how the children of Israel had lost their way because of their worldliness and carnality.

Afterward, Moses had to pick up the broken law and, according to Jewish tradition, put the broken set of Ten Commandments in the ark. Then, Moses made a new set of tablets and took them to God to inscribe. God was very gracious. He understood why Moses got so angry, and, with His own finger, He once again rewrote His law! He did so for Moses. Then Moses took the new set of Ten Commandments and put it in the ark with the broken ones.

The Ten Commandments had nothing to do with the sacrifices or the shadows. It had nothing to do with things to come. The Sabbath was not a yearly sacrifice. What Paul described as being abolished was the yearly system of sacrifices that was a shadow of "things to come." The Passover and the feast of tabernacles, with their yearly sabbaths, were part of this yearly system of sacrifices. They were abolished when Jesus died on the cross. But the Ten Commandments were not a shadow. They did not point forward to Jesus; they pointed back to principles established from the Creation. They are the foundation of the eternal government of God.

God's commandments are in force and binding upon Christians today.

Let me reiterate: God's commandments are in force and binding upon Christians today. Paul never taught that they were abolished. He made a clear distinction that was very specific about what he meant. His system of theology is clear for all to see. The Old Testament sanctuary service connected with the ceremonial law was nailed to the cross and taken out of the way. However, the Ten Commandments are holy, just, and good. They are established by saving faith. Also, Paul said, "I delight in the law of God." If people are preaching that you should no longer keep the Ten Commandments or honor them, or that you are no longer subject to the Ten Commandments, what kind of a mind do they possess? It demonstrates that they are of the carnal mind. Anybody telling you to do away with or to abolish one of God's commandments is using carnal reasoning. Pray for them! Hopefully they are just misguided and will someday see the light.

When God says, "*Remember*," I don't care who says to forget. I am not going to forget, rather, I am going to remember. And I don't care if it's some fancy television evangelist in an expensive suit living in a million-dollar mansion and driving a Rolls Royce. I don't care. If God says, "Remember the Sabbath day to keep it holy," and He says that the Sabbath is the seventh day, and Jesus says that He is Lord of the Sabbath and that we need to honor it, keep it, remember it, and obey it, then I have to say that I'm going to go with Jesus and I'm going to ignore the evangelist.

In fact, I'm going to ignore every church that teaches that you can violate one of God's commandments. If your church is not a Sabbath-keeping church, then I'm not going there. Sorry, that's just the way I feel. Now, I might visit and fellowship with you at your church once in a while, and I might go hear a good Christian singer sometime, but I am not going to keep the papal sabbath. I am going to keep God's Bible Sabbath, which He commanded to be kept. The other sabbath is not a sabbath at all.

The Bible says, "six days shalt thou labour" (Exod. 20:9). That makes Sunday just another workday to me. And I hope, if anyone is reading this for the first time, that you aren't offended to hear me say this. Don't be like I was. I was so offended that I was ready to hit the guy who told me. I apologize if the idea that Sunday is just another workday is new to you. Straightforward things need to be said, so I hope that you will put them in their proper context.

Since the law points out what sin is, do you feel that, if you do away with the law, you will do away with sin and, if you do away with sin, you will do away with the need of the Savior? Do you agree with me on that? Do you feel that you have broken God's Ten Commandment law and you need to repent of your lawbreaking? I hope so. Are you willing to admit that you are a sinner and a lawbreaker? Do you want Jesus to forgive you for your sins and help you, by his perfect grace, to no longer live in rebellion but, like Paul, to delight in God's law? Do you want to receive Jesus today, repent of your lawbreaking, and be filled with the Spirit of the living God? I pray that your answer is "yes."

The New Covenant Basis for Worship

We've been learning about the old covenant and the commandments in stone within the earthly tabernacle in the wilderness. We have recognized that Moses made everything according to the pattern that he saw in the heavenly sanctuary, shown him by God on Mt. Sinai. We saw that the first set of commandments that God gave Moses were carved out of stone by God and engraved by God's own finger, and we saw that Moses beheld a horrible spectacle when he came down from the mountain. The children of Israel were engaged in immoral dissipation at the base of the mountain, committing fornication and engaging in other sins as well. Having experienced the purity and holiness of God's presence on Mt. Sinai, Moses saw the great contrast of the people's behavior and, becoming angry, he threw down the Ten Commandments, breaking them into several pieces. God instructed him to carve out another set of tablets and bring them to Him. Then, once again, God carved the Ten Commandments into the stone, using His finger. Both sets of commandments were modeled after the commandments that Moses saw in heaven. Do you get the impression that God wanted them to be exact—that God wanted them to be correct? He made Moses bring the blank slates back to Him so that He could personally rewrite the commandments. It seems to me that God wanted His law to be unalterable. What do you think? Stone is a very durable medium. Would you not agree that stone makes it very hard to change?

Moses saw the ark of the covenant in heaven and made the model according to the pattern. That this is so tells us that the Ten Commandments are enshrined in the heavenly sanctuary in God's throne room beneath the mercy seat. God is seated upon His throne, and, as He looks down at the ark, He looks through the mercy seat, which represents the blood of Jesus that protects us from the judgment of the law. When God looks down at the law, He looks through the blood of the lamb, on the mercy seat, and He sees His Son's character in place of our character (*Steps to Christ*, p. 62). In Christ, the mercy and justice of God have kissed each other!

In the ark of the covenant, we see the Ten Commandments, God's moral law. Because there is a heavenly ark of the covenant, we recognize the law to be immutable, unchangeable. Above the law, we see the mercy seat and God enthroned above it. And as He looks at His law, He looks through the mercy that called for the blood of Jesus. And as we come to Christ, He gives us Christ's righteousness and then He sees us as if we had not sinned. What a beautiful picture of the love of God! What a beautiful picture of God's perfect grace! Because the law was broken, the blood had to be applied on the mercy seat. We also know that the Ten Commandments are in heaven because of what the Apostle John described seeing. In Revelation, chapter 11, verses 18 and 19, John says that, while the nations are angry and God is getting ready to come and destroy them for their sins, the nations will be judged and the temple of God will be opened in heaven, where is seen in God's temple the ark of His testament. "And the *nations were angry*, and thy wrath is come, and the time of the dead, that *they should be judged*, and that thou shouldest give reward unto thy servants the prophets, and to the saints, and them that fear thy name, small and great; and shouldest *destroy them which destroy the earth*. And the *temple of God was opened in heaven*, and there was seen *in his temple the ark of his testament:* and there were lightnings, and voices, and thunderings, and an earthquake, and great hail" (Rev. 11:18, 19). There in heaven is the ark of the covenant with the Ten Commandment law. If people tell you that it isn't important to keep the Sabbath day of the fourth commandment, tell them, "If it isn't important, then why does God keep a copy of His law in His most precious place?"

Some say that it isn't important which day you worship on. If that were true, then why are the Ten Commandments at the very foundation of God's throne, and why did God write them in stone, and why does He have them in heaven? So, is God commanding us to remember something that is unimportant, to keep an unimportant day? God forbid! Paul wrote: "Circumcision is nothing, and uncircumcision is nothing, but the keeping of the commandments of God" (1 Cor. 7:19). Paul said that the important thing is the keeping of God's commandments! "Remember"—don't forget—"to keep it holy" (Exod. 20:8)!

Notice that, at the end of the world, the judgment takes place in heaven. Just before Jesus comes, in the Temple of God, right there under the mercy seat, right there under the Shekinah glory, right there in the Father's presence are the *Ten Commandments in the very center of God's throne room!* I love it! There they are untouched by human hands. No human can corrupt them. No human can do away with them. Does that sound like the Ten Commandments have been abolished? I think not! They are right where God wants them! Up in heaven, written in stone, woven into the foundation of His throne, His government, and His kingdom. Right where men cannot touch them, change them, or abbreviate them. No preacher can preach them out of the throne room of heaven! No false church can strip God's law from the ark in heaven! Pictured in Revelation 11, they are where all can see where God put them—the law that was written by God's own finger! The judgment is going on today, and God's law is the standard that He uses in the judgment.

It's important that you understand God's law, that you understand the Ten Commandments. And I want you to find the path right up through outer space into the very throne room of God, right into the ark of the covenant. I want you to find that path right to the throne of Jesus and the mercy seat because that is what you need most of all! The most important thing is to know Jesus, the only one with a perfect character, and He will credit His perfect character to your account!

It is for this reason that the Apostle James wrote: "For whosoever shall keep the whole law, and yet offend *in one point*, he is guilty of all. For he that said, Do not commit adultery, said also, Do not kill. Now if thou commit no adultery, yet if thou kill, thou art become a transgressor of the law. So speak ye, and so do, as they that *shall be judged by the law of liberty*" (James 2:10–12). The Ten Commandments aren't done away with. James said that, if you break one, you break them all. It's obvious from the specific mention of "Thou shalt not kill" and "Thou shalt not commit adultery" in James 2:11 that, by the "royal law," he is referring to the Ten Commandments, which is the "law of liberty." Paul refers to this same concept in Romans 8 when he urges us not to use our freedom in the spirit for sinful purposes, to commit sin, but, rather, to fulfill the law by walking in the Spirit.

"That the righteousness of the *law might be fulfilled in us, who walk* not after the flesh, but *after the Spirit*" (Rom. 8:4). Notice that this verse makes it clear that fulfilling the law means to walk in the law. It means to walk in the Spirit. It means to keep the law by doing what's right. It does not mean to get rid of it. It does not mean to make it void or do away with it. The obedience of faith is the duty of every Christian; not as a means of salvation, but as a way to show love and devotion to our Savior who loves us. Jesus said, "I did not come to destroy [the law] but to fulfill [it]" (Matt. 5:17, NKJV).

It always amazes me to read the verse in the Sermon on the Mount in which Jesus said, "I came not to destroy the law, but to fulfill it," and then have people say that He meant that we don't have to worry about it anymore. "Fulfill" does not mean to do away with it! Jesus told John, at Jesus' baptism, to baptize Him to "fulfill all righteousness." So, did He do away with righteousness? *No!* If I obey the speed limit, and fulfill the law's demands, do I do away with the speed limit? Of course not! If I have *fulfilled* a contract, I didn't do away with it. No, I actually honored it by keeping its provisions. How do you honor the Ten Commandments? By keeping their provisions and by obeying God's law! Jesus said, "If you love Me, keep My commandments" (John 14:15). Love fulfills the law. No one will be turned away from the heavenly gates for being too loving. Can you imagine— … "I'm sorry; you're just too Christ-like, you can't come in." "You're just too kind and loving with those who disagree with you, you can't come in." I don't think there's any fear of that ever happening! Just before Jesus comes, we are told, God's judgment is taking place and the ark of the testimony is seen in the heavenly sanctuary. It is called the ark of the testimony *because* the ten commandments *are* the "testimony," which tells us the commandments are in heaven. There they are in the throne. How old is God's throne? Psalm 93:2 tells us: "Thy *throne is established of old:* thou art from everlasting" (Ps. 93:2). I don't know if God's throne is eternal. As I said, I don't know. I don't know if back in the eons of time, before He made any matter, that He made the throne. I don't know if the point is that the actual throne He sits on is from everlasting because sometimes Hebrew uses parallel structure and figures of speech, and the verse really only means that God's throne is very old while He Himself is from everlasting or if it simply means that *His dominion* is from eternity. So, I am assuming that the first thing that He made was His throne. I mean, if I were God, and nothing else existed, I might make a chair to sit on first. But, I don't know. His throne is very, very old. Can we all agree on that? So, the New Covenant is not only the Ten Commandments written in stone in the Old Testament tabernacle, but it is also God's throne, "established of old," when the Ancient of Days made His first piece of furniture and the ark of the covenant. When He made the ark, way back in the eons of time, He put His Ten Commandment law in it. Right there in His throne was His everlasting covenant, His law. God put His law in His throne to reflect His character. That's why God's covenant is everlasting. "The earth also is defiled under the inhabitants thereof; because they have *transgressed the laws, changed the ordinance*, broken the *everlasting covenant*" (Isa. 24:5).

What kind of covenant is it? It is the *everlasting covenant!* There is a difference between *eternal* and *everlasting*. You understand that, right? God's character is eternal; God's covenant is everlasting. There was a time when God made a covenant. To make a covenant requires making a covenant with someone. Therefore, God needed to make the covenant with the universe in some way. The covenant is everlasting in the sense that God made it at some point in time, and, from the day that He made it, it will never be done away with. It will be everlasting. And He identifies the Ten Commandments to be a part of that everlasting covenant. I want you to notice something here. The writers of Hebrew poetry use a lot of parallelism. Isaiah uses it as well. In Isaiah 24 he wrote that God is coming to "shake the earth like a leaf" and that He is coming to punish the inhabitants of the earth for defiling the earth. In Hebrew poetry, the writer expresses the same thought by "rhyming" the thought, that is, by expressing the thought in two parallel forms.

Isaiah wrote that they defiled the earth in three ways:

1. By *transgressing* God's law
2. By *changing* God's law and
3. By *breaking* the everlasting covenant.

The parallelism says that they transgressed, changed, and broke God's law. Let me ask you a question: Do Christians today have any problem with any other commandment besides the fourth? No, they do not. They are obviously not worried about the other nine. It is just the Sabbath commandment that bothers people today. They claim that it has been changed and that Christians should keep another day, don't they? Yet, God says that He is coming to punish the people on the earth who have transgressed His law, tried to change His law, and who are breaking His law.

Moses symbolically illustrated their breaking of God's law and violation of the covenant when he threw the tablets of the Ten Commandments down and broke them before Israel. Today people are breaking the law of God when they are lying, raping, committing adultery, and when murder seems rampant! There are people everywhere breaking God's law. Worse still, there are churches that are teaching people that it's okay to break God's law, and many churches—most churches, in fact—are breaking God's law.

There are false religious systems in the world, and the beast power has sought to "change times and laws." Daniel predicted that the "little horn" that comes out of Rome would transgress, and change, and break God's Ten Commandment law—the everlasting covenant. And John predicted that all the world will wonder after "the beast," that is identified with Rome, in the end times. Before NAFTA and before other changes in the world economic system, we wondered how there could be a worldwide economy. We also had a hard time visualizing a worldwide deception. Do you have a hard time still? Everything is now interconnected. We now have a worldwide economy. Can you see now how it will be possible, as the Bible says, that all the world will wonder after the beast and receive the mark of the beast? Do you see how a worldwide deception can come to be? Ostensibly teaching the commandments of God, this Roman church has placed its authority above the Bible, making itself a law unto itself. The one who is "lawless," who sits in the temple of God, exalting himself above all that is called God, has instituted a "new time, and a new law" in opposition to God's law. He defiled God's sanctuary. He taught the inhabitants of earth to defile God's law and God's planet. Don't forsake the everlasting covenant for this imposter's "new law."

Don't believe the Roman church that takes great pride in the fact that she instituted the first day of the week as the new day to worship God. It is a counterfeit, and it must be rejected. It is a deception and a lie of the worst kind, and, in following it, people are making a mistake at the very least. Be kind to your relatives and friends and people who don't understand. They're making a mistake. Someday they will learn the truth about it, and then they will have to make a decision. But be kind to them and help them to see their mistake and do what God says to do in his Word. The principles of God's character and His gospel are all reflected in His law and enshrined in His throne. God's law and His plan of salvation have been in God's mind and heart for all eternity, and that makes them everlasting. Hasn't God always been balanced? Hasn't God always worked and rested? I am certain that the divine Sabbath fellowship Jesus had with His Father and the Holy Ghost in the early days of eternity was just as sweet as it is today. I am certain that Jesus and his Father and the Holy Spirit kept the Sabbath and enjoyed Sabbath rest. I am certain that They fellowshipped and spent time in communion with each other. And I am certain that the Godhead has the sweetest fellowship of all in their relationship and interaction with each other—eternal oneness. Can you imagine it? Eternal oneness, eternal fellowship, eternal Sabbath rest. That's why I believe the Sabbath is eternal. According to Jesus, God made the Sabbath for all mankind (Mark 2:27). He said that He created the earth and then rested on the seventh day and then blessed the Sabbath because all that He had made was very good (Gen. 1:31). According to Scripture, God made the Sabbath before sin. He blessed it and made it a special day for this planet. I am certain that He shared a blessing with us that He Himself had long enjoyed. The new covenant does not do away with the Ten Commandments. The Bible says that, in the new covenant, God takes the law contained in stone and He writes it in our hearts (Jer. 31:33; Heb. 8:10; 10:16; 2 Cor. 3:3).

Are you familiar with the Scofield Bible and its Dispensationalist interpretation? Scofield wrote into the notes of his Bible that the Old Testament was the dispensation of law and that the New Testament is the dispensation of grace? In other words, those in the Old Testament had the law, but now, under the New Testament era of grace, the law is done away with. The problem with dividing the history of the world into dispensations is that the New Testament frequently repeats that God's law is still in force. However, according to Dispensationalism, the law no longer exists—it's been done away with. But what does God say in Hebrews, chapter 8? "For this is the covenant that I will make with the house of Israel after those days, saith the Lord; *I will put my laws into their mind*, and *write them in their hearts:* and I will be to them a God, and they shall be to me a people" (Heb. 8:10). "In that he saith, *A new covenant, he hath made the first old*. Now that which decayeth and waxeth old is ready to vanish away" (Heb. 8:13).

God repeats the same truth in Hebrews 10. "This is the covenant that I will make with them *after those days, saith the Lord, I will put my laws into their hearts, and in their minds will I write them*; and their sins and iniquities will I remember no more" (Heb. 10:16–17).

Isn't that beautiful! God wants to put His law in our hearts and minds. His new covenant takes what was written in stone, and, through the Holy Spirit, writes it in our hearts and minds! In addition, God forgives us of our sins, and He remembers them no more. Get that—He writes His law in our hearts and in our minds! God's law becomes part of our very nature. The sinner is transformed miraculously by the Spirit of God into a new creature in Christ as he or she is born again! The caterpillar crawling about in the grass is transformed into a beautiful butterfly with iridescent wings that enable it to fly! Not only is God's law in the sanctuary in heaven, but it is written in the hearts and minds of His people, and a beautiful butterfly has been formed in the chrysalis of God's law! "The carnal mind … is not subject to the law of God, neither indeed can it be" (Rom. 8:7). That's the way it is! However, the born-again Christian has the mind of Christ! Jesus' mind was always obedient to His Father's commandments, as we find in the following verses. "Let *this mind be in you*, which was also in Christ Jesus" (Phil. 2:5). "If ye keep my commandments,

The caterpillar crawling about in the grass is transformed into a beautiful butterfly with iridescent wings that enable it to fly!

ye shall abide in my love; even as *I have kept my Father's commandments*, and abide in his love" (John 15:10). The obedience of faith always claims Jesus' righteousness alone, as *He* obeys God.

The earthly sanctuary was purified with animal sacrifices, but the heavenly sanctuary will be cleansed and purified with a better sacrifice that replaces the symbolic sacrifices. "It was therefore necessary that the patterns of things in the heavens should be purified with these; but *the heavenly things themselves with better sacrifices than these*. For Christ is not entered into the holy places made with hands, which are the figures of the true; but into *heaven itself, now to appear in the presence of God for us:* Nor yet that he should offer himself often, as the high priest entereth into the holy place every year with blood of others; for then must he often have suffered since the foundation of the world: but *now once in the end of the world* hath he *appeared to put away sin by the sacrifice of himself.* And as it is appointed unto men once to die, but *after this the judgment:* So Christ was once offered to bear the sins of many; and unto them that look for him shall he *appear the second time* without sin unto salvation" (Heb. 9:23–28).

After a man dies, he will someday have to face Christ in the judgment. The judgment is the cleansing of the heavenly sanctuary from sin. At the close of the great anti-typical day of atonement now taking place, sin will be put away from the sinner forever. Christians will be separated from their sins forever. Their sins are blotted out in the times of refreshing, and Christians are pronounced "not guilty" in the heavenly courtroom. It's so wonderful to know that the whole purpose of the judgment is to now, once, at the "end of the world," have Jesus appear in the presence of God to put away our sins for all eternity. The beauty of the judgment is that we are pronounced "not guilty" and we are set free for all eternity from our sins. While the nations are angry, the judgment is taking place in heaven before the ark of God's testament. Paul taught that, after men die, they will be judged. Jesus pleads on our behalf, presenting His own sacrifice to put away our sins forever!

When Christ appears the second time, He will be sinless, and He will bring salvation to His church.

Would you like the Great High Priest in heaven to plead your case today? Would you like Jesus to lift His hands marked by the print of the nails and to raise them up before the ark of the covenant and say to the God of the universe, "Father, forgive them for breaking your law contained in the ark. Wash away their sins in My blood." Would you like the Great High Priest to mediate in your behalf right now? Would you like to receive eternal life based on His sinless life and His sacrifice for you on the cross? Won't you join me as I pray:

Yes, Lord, I would like You to represent me in the judgment and be my Great High Priest, to mediate my case, and to plead Your blood in my behalf.

God's law has been upheld and declared "holy, just and good." As Jesus is returning, He will declare: "whoever is righteous let them be righteous still." When He returns a second time to rescue His people, they will be the people who, according to Revelation 14:12, "keep the commandments of God and have the faith of Jesus." Of them it is said: "Here is the patience of the saints: here are they that keep the commandments of God, and the faith of Jesus" (Rev. 14:12).

God's faithful and true church on earth when Jesus returns will be preaching righteousness by faith and teaching Paul's view of the law. They will be keeping the commandments of God by faith, walking in them through the Holy Spirit. The law of God will be written in their hearts and minds, as Paul said, "That the righteousness of the *law might be fulfilled in us, who walk* not after the flesh, but *after the Spirit*" (Rom. 8:4). Summing up the ceremonial law and its decreasing importance with the moral law's continuing relevance, the Apostle Paul gets in the last word, when he says: "*Circumcision is nothing*, and uncircumcision is nothing, *but the keeping of the commandments of God*" (1 Cor. 7:19).

When the high priest was making the sacrifice the day that Jesus died and God ripped the veil of the Most Holy Place in two, the ceremonial law came to an end. Consequently, Paul wrote: "*Circumcision is nothing*, and uncircumcision is nothing, *but the keeping of the commandments of God*" (1 Cor. 7:19). Paul said that keeping God's commandments is what is important! When we say that we are to keep them, please, dear friend, understand that God wants you to be His obedient child. The obedience of faith is very important. He wants you to come to Jesus just as you are, but then, dear brother or sister, He will not leave you just the way you were! He forgives you for every lie that you have ever told, but that does not mean that He gives you permission to tell another! He forgives you for every single sin of the flesh. He forgives you and He washes you and He accepts you just as you are, as you come to Jesus, in the words of the hymn, "... without one plea but that His blood was shed for me!"

I've seen alcoholics come to the altar. I've seen illegal drug users come to the altar. I've seen the sexually immoral come to the altar. I've seen prideful church elders and even pastors come to the altar. I've seen Seventh-day Adventists who have been members of the church for fifty years come to the altar and place their pride upon it. And they come just as they are. I've seen them come and ask forgiveness for their judgmental attitude, for their sinful, carnal way of life, and I've seen Jesus come into their heart and transform and change them. And I will tell you this, when they walk away from that altar, they are changed! There is a difference! Faith without works is dead, dear brothers and sisters. The purpose of the law is to teach you your sinfulness, to show you how lost you are, how worldly your lifestyle is and how evil are the things you are doing. Its purpose is to convince you that you are incapable of changing yourself. Its purpose is to convince you that you cannot keep God's law apart from Christ and that the only way that you will ever be perfect is by coming to the altar and accepting Jesus as your personal Savior! Once you are saved by God's perfect grace through faith, God will come in and change you, and you will quit wallowing in your sins. Failure is

Failure is not falling down in the mud, brothers and sisters. It is lying in the mud and wallowing in it!

not falling down in the mud, brothers and sisters. It is lying in the mud and wallowing in it! Get up; go to Jesus. Repent, and He will wash you off. He will clean you up; He will put a new robe on you and turn you around and get you going in the right direction. If you fall eight times, get up and rise again eight times, and if you fall at all, fall *toward* the Lord, not away from Him! Every Christian has bad days. Every Christian sometimes does dumb, stupid stuff. Creating such a problem for yourself does not mean that you are not converted. Just come to Jesus. You need to be cleansed; you need to be changed.

If you are willing to come, you can tell Him today:

Lord, I need to be converted! I want you to convert me from the top of my head to the bottom of my feet. I want you to come in and take control of my soul and wash away my impure thoughts, wash away my carnal desires, and crucify my carnal nature on the cross. I want you to nail me to the cross, Lord. I want you to forgive me of my sins, and I want you to change me and transform me from the inside out so I don't have to do the evil things that Satan keeps trying to make me do. I want victory by faith today!

He is waiting to hear from you.

CHAPTER 12

THE PROPHECY THAT FAILED AND THE JUDGMENT IN HEAVEN

And I saw another mighty angel come down from heaven, clothed with a cloud: and a rainbow was upon his head, and his face was as it were the sun, and his feet as pillars of fire: and he had in his hand a little book open: and he set his right foot upon the sea, and his left foot on the earth, and cried with a loud voice, as when a lion roareth: and when he had cried, seven thunders uttered their voices. And when the seven thunders had uttered their voices, I was about to write: and I heard a voice from heaven saying unto me, Seal up those things which the seven thunders uttered, and write them not. And the angel which I saw stand upon the sea and upon the earth lifted up his hand to heaven, and sware by him that liveth for ever and ever, who created heaven, and the things that therein are, and the earth, and the things that therein are, and the sea, and the things which are therein, that there should be time no longer: but in the days of the voice of the ***seventh angel****, when he shall* ***begin*** *to sound, the mystery [secret plan] of God would be finished, as he hath declared to his servants the prophets. And the voice which I heard from heaven spoke unto me again, and said, Go and take the little book [scroll] which is* ***open*** *in*

> *the hand of the angel which standeth upon the sea and upon the earth. And I went unto the angel, and said unto him, Give me the little book. And he said unto me, Take it, and eat it up; and it shall make thy belly bitter, but it shall be in thy mouth sweet as honey. And I took the little book out of the angel's hand, and ate it up; and it was in my mouth sweet as honey: and as soon as I had eaten it, my belly was bitter. And he said unto me, Thou must prophesy [preach] again before many peoples, and nations, and tongues, and kings.*
> *—Revelation 10:1–11*

Verse 1 of Revelation 10 pictures a mighty angel with a rainbow on his head. Can you imagine that? "And he had a face like the sun, and his feet were like pillars of fire. And he had a little book, and the book was open in his hand. And he set his right foot on the sea and his left foot on the land."

John is portraying an angel coming down to earth to open a book and then standing on the land and the sea, a symbol of the whole world. This is a representation of a worldwide message that the angel was to bring. The angel has a rainbow around his head. In chapter 4, a rainbow is pictured as encircling God's throne. As a matter of fact, when you look in God's throne room, He not only has a rainbow over His head, but He has a rainbow *under* His feet that shines through a translucent floor, making it appear that God is sitting in the middle of a circular rainbow. This is a message that comes directly from God, which tells you that you should pay attention. Now notice that the angel had the little book *open* in his hand. That is significant. Then, in verse three, it says that he "cried with a loud voice, as when a lion roars: and when he cried out, the seven thunders uttered their voices." Amazing! What a picture!

One time when I was at the zoo, I was standing next to the lion cage, though I didn't know it. I was standing right next to the wall, and right on the other side of the wall, maybe two feet away from me around the corner through the bars, was a huge male lion. As I leaned against the wall, waiting for my family, that huge male lion let out a tremendous "*Roar!*" And I jumped almost high enough to go over the wall! I mean, I have never heard *anything* like that! Talk about loud! If I were in Africa and a lion came after me in the wild, it would really test my courage. Some tribes actually make it a test of manhood to kill a lion. I have a very close friend from Zimbabwe who told me that, as a teenager, he had to go out and find a lion and kill it. If I were in Africa, and a lion let out a roar in the wild like the one I heard at the zoo, I'm telling you, I'd be sprinting back to America. I would be out of there! Those animals are huge, maybe half the length of a church pew. Then John tells what happened after the seven thunders uttered their voice. "*And when the seven thunders uttered their voices, I was about to write but I heard a voice from heaven saying, 'Seal the things which the seven thunders uttered and do not write them.'*"

As I leaned against the wall, waiting for my family, that huge male lion let out a tremendous "Roar!"

I wonder if maybe that was God's chariot with the fiery wheels within a wheel sounding like a Harley. You know, those seven thunders sounded like thunder! I'd like to think that God's chariot has a thunder sound. I don't know if it does. John said that nobody knows what the seven thunders uttered, so let's not spend a lot of time there. Let's move on. Now, "*I heard a voice from heaven saying unto me, 'Seal up the things which the seven thunders uttered, and do not write them.*" Well, whatever they said, we're not going to know it.

"*And the angel whom I saw standing on the sea and on the land lifted his hand …*" In the Greek, it says that he raised his *right* hand "*up to heaven, and swore by him who lives for ever and ever …*" What did the angel swear? The New King James Version says, "*that there should be a delay no longer,*" and then adds, "*But in the days of the sounding of the seventh angel, when he is about to sound*"—not "*when he sounds,*" as in the King James

Version—"*the mystery of God*"—which is the plan of salvation—"would be finished, as he declared to his servants the prophets. Then the voice which I heard from heaven spoke unto me again, and said, 'Go and take the little book which is *open* in the hand of the angel who stands on the sea and on the earth.' And I went unto the angel, and said to him, 'Give me the little book.' And he said to me, 'Take and eat …' " And then John ate the little book, and what happened was just as he had been told: "… *and it shall make thy belly bitter, but it shall be in thy mouth sweet as honey.' And he said unto me, 'You must prophesy [preach] again before many peoples, and nations, and tongues, and kings.*' "

Immediately, John describes in the next chapter, "Then I was given a reed like a measuring rod. And the angel stood, saying, 'Rise and measure the temple of God, the altar, and those who worship there. But leave out the court which is outside the temple, and do not measure it, for it has been given to the Gentiles. And they will tread the holy city underfoot for forty-two months' " (Rev. 11:1, NKJV). This description mirrors what Jesus said when He foretold that Jerusalem was to be trodden underfoot by the Gentiles. The Roman Church controlled Jerusalem for 1260 years during the Dark Ages. Some estimate that millions of Jews were killed by the Papacy during this period. Thus, the Gentile Church persecuted the Jews, and they were trodden underfoot. Once again, in 1976, the city of Jerusalem came under Jewish control. However, from the time of Nebuchadnezzar in 586 BC until 1976, there was no Jewish nation in Israel. The nation of Israel was established with the 1967 war, however, Jerusalem was not under Jewish control until 1976. The title of this chapter, "The Prophecy That Failed," I got from J. Reynolds Hoffman, and I use it with a little bit of tongue in cheek because the prophecy *didn't* really fail; the people just thought it did. But, still, it's a handy way to make you think about this subject. There are questions people ask. Even if they don't ask them aloud, they at least think them. The questions go something like this: "When did the Adventist movement begin?" "What caused the Adventist Church to start? Is it a breakaway from some other church?" "Who were the early leaders of the Seventh-day Adventist Church?"

When we read Revelation 10 and study the prophecy that Supposedly "failed," we can begin to dig out the facts, and come to understand what this chapter is talking about. The prophecy is symbolic like the prophecy of the beast with the seven heads and ten horns. The word *angel* in Greek means "messenger." The angel with the rainbow comes from heaven bringing a message that is so important that it is preached in a loud voice like the roaring of a lion. It is heard in both land and sea—that is, all around the world. It roars like a lion, which shows that it is a powerful message! The angel has a little book, in fact, the entire scene depicted in Revelation 10 revolves around that little book. *Four times* John says that the book is *little*. *Two times* he says that the book is *open*. Only *once* does John tell us that it is a book of prophecy. This is in verse 11. The implication of the word "open" is that it was once closed. To interpret the prophecy, we need to understand what book this is. Right? When we go through the Bible, from Genesis to Revelation, there is only one book of prophecy that is small in size (it has 12 chapters) and that was described as having been closed—and even sealed. "But thou, O Daniel, shut up the words, and seal the book, even to the time of the end: many shall run to and fro, and knowledge shall be increased" (Dan. 12:4). "*Seal up* the book"—which book? The book of Daniel. Until when? Until *the time of the end*. Very interesting.

The only book in the Bible that was ever sealed is the book of Daniel, and the book of Daniel was to be sealed until the time of the end when many were to run to and fro. Notice what the heavenly messenger told the prophet. "And he said, 'Go thy way, Daniel: for the words *are closed up* and sealed [kept secret] till the time of the end'" (Dan. 12:9). Can we agree that many today are running to and fro and that, of all times on earth, this is the time of the end? This provides us solid evidence from which to conclude that Daniel is the little book described in Revelation 10.

The Time When the Opening Takes Place

Twice we are given clues regarding when it is that the prophecy was to be fulfilled. First, the text mentions the beginning of the seventh angel when it is about to sound. The seventh angel is the last angel. There are none after it. When the seventh angel sounds, what happens? It is the time of the end. What does the seventh angel point to? The return of Christ. So, when the seventh angel is about to sound, just before Jesus comes, the event described in Chapter 10 takes place.[32] The text also says, "*The mystery of God would be finished ...*" The "mystery of God," in Revelation 10:7, is the final proclamation of the gospel. The experience with the little book clearly must take place near the end of the world, as it helps to get the gospel out to the entire world. To better understand this prophecy, we will need to look at the mirror image of prophecy, which is history.

Daniel was rediscovered sometime after 1798. At this time, a worldwide movement was sweeping America called "The Great Awakening." Christians were studying the prophecy of the antichrist power of Daniel 7. Verse 24 of that chapter indicates that the antichrist power would pluck up three kings, or kingdoms. The three kings were the three Arian provinces that believed that Jesus was a created being and not eternal God. This was a heresy that the Catholic Church was willing to go to war over. In AD 493, the Ostrogoths, with the permission of Catholic Emperor Zeno, wiped out the Heruli, a Germanic barbarian tribe, plucking up the first of the three horns. After Justinian became emperor in AD 527, he issued the *Justinian Decree* in AD 533, elevating the Bishop of Rome to be "The Head of all the Holy Churches." But this decree could not go into *practical* effect until the Arian enemies were vanquished. In AD 534, Justinian sent his general Belisarius to destroy the Vandals. This he accomplished in one campaign season, thereby plucking up the second of the three horns. Finally, the Ostrogoths were defeated and driven out of Rome in March of AD 538. Some twelve hundred sixty years later, in 1798, Napoleon sent his general Berthier to capture Pope Pius VI and to bring him back to France. (The popes had humiliated European monarchs in many ways.[33] Napoleon was not about to be humiliated by any pontiff.)

The French Revolution proclaimed: "*God is dead! Reason is King!*" and dragged the Roman Church into the dirt and crushed its power. After

Berthier captured the Pope and brought him back to France, the pope died in captivity—fulfilling Revelation 13.[34] 1798 is a significant year because that was when the papacy was dealt its deadly wound and there was no pope for three and a half years. After that, there were two popes, and each excommunicated the other! Beginning sometime after 1798, in the early nineteenth century, there was an international, interdenominational, independent revival of the study of the book of Daniel. The revival of prophecy was sparked by William Miller's study of Daniel 8:14, which says, "Unto two thousand and three hundred [2300] days; then shall the sanctuary be cleansed [delivered]." Bible scholars everywhere began to teach that the sanctuary was the earth and that the second coming of Christ to the earth should be expected on or about 1844. On October 22, 1844, the prophecy was fulfilled.

The best-known preachers of the Advent in the United States were William Miller, who was a Baptist; Josiah Litch, who was a Methodist; and Charles Fitch, who was a Congregationalist. In general, half of these people were Methodists and a quarter were Baptists. Clergy who preached the Second Advent were Christian, Presbyterian, Lutheran, Quaker, and Episcopalian. They believed that the 2,300-day prophecy was to be fulfilled, a day for a year, according to Ezekiel 4:6 and that the starting point for the prophecy was the order to rebuild Jerusalem (Dan. 9:25). This order was given in 457 BC. Taking the prophecy 2,300 years from 457 BC takes you down to 1844. However, at first they miscalculated and came down to 1843. When Christ did not come in that year, they went back to the prophecy, recalculated the figures and realized that there was no year "0" between the last year of BC and the first year of AD, so they needed to add a year to 1843. And then they arrived correctly at 1844, and during the summer of that year, they calculated when the seventh month would be, and that brought them to October 22, 1844. How interesting! More than 700 preachers in England were telling this story about Daniel 8:14. Did you know they had a camp meeting in New England in 1842, 1843, and 1844, and did you know that more than a half million people attended[35] that camp meeting? We had a half million people go to Sturgis for "bike week" and half a million people go to Daytona Beach for another "bike week." That is a lot of people, but can you imagine how big a crowd that was in 1842–1844? Imagine—half-a-million people going to camp meetings to hear the preaching of the advent message. The reader should keep in mind that when the word "adventist" is used referring to this 1843–1844 Advent Movement, it is not referring to the Seventh-day Adventists denomination that was not founded until 1863.

Another influential person in the advent movement was named Manuel Lacunza. He was a Roman Catholic priest who went to South America and preached the advent message. Another very important Advent preacher was Joseph Wolfe, who was a converted Jew. He took the advent message to the Middle East, all of Europe, and South America. The message of the book of Daniel stirred the people of these regions.

The Advent awakening of 1798 to 1844 alone fulfills the prophecies of Revelation 10. The ministers named above and hundreds more preached the message that Jesus was coming and that the people needed to get ready for the event so they would be taken to heaven. They reasoned around Jesus' statement, "*No man knows the day or the hour,*" by thinking that certainly God had revealed the general time of Jesus' return. There were other things they missed. Why did God allow that to happen? Why did God allow them to misinterpret the prophecy? Why did the prophecy have to fail before they could understand what God was teaching through the prophecy? Wherever this message was preached it caused a tremendous division in the churches. These congregations were in turmoil. One Methodist would ask another, "*Are you an Adventist?*" And if he said that he was, they would vote him out of the church. They were inquiring as to the belief of the person regarding the soon return of Jesus. The Adventist question, "*Do you believe Jesus will return* in 1844?" divided many congregations regardless of denomination. People who believed that Jesus was coming sold their homes and businesses and put the money into the cause. People sold their plows, their wagons, and their horses. People sold their farms and gave away their clothes, leaving nothing but the clothes on their back. They put it all on the line. They *believed* the advent message. And remember that, at this time, there was no Seventh-day Adventist Church. The preaching of Daniel's prophecy was an international, inter-denominational worldwide phenomenon.

The "eating of the book," according to the angel, would be *sweet* in the mouth. There is nothing sweeter to a Christian's heart than the thought of seeing the dear Savior coming again, and these early Adventists believed that soon the heavens would open and they would see Jesus' face. But the Bible says that, after the sweetness, it would be bitter in their belly. And it was oh so bitter when these people did not see their Lord appear.

And it was doubly bitter because of the jeering of their friends, neighbors, and relatives. "*I see that you didn't leave. Funny thing, I thought you were supposed to fly up yesterday! I see you're still here. I knew you were wrong!*" "*Hey, Adventist, where are your wings? I just happened to notice that you haven't flown away yet!*" Can you imagine how those people felt? Can you imagine how bitter it must have been to be mocked and made fun of and to have lost everything and preached about something that absolutely did not happen? To preach a prophecy just to have it fail and be humiliated in front of everyone—the experience was very bitter![36]

In the midst of this darkness, the truth of 1844 began to be revealed with even clearer light. God called upon these people once again to do a work for Him, to "prophesy again" (Rev. 10:11). He had allowed them to misinterpret the prophecy because, like the disciples who had been disappointed by Jesus' death, they were looking in the wrong direction. Comparing the first verse of Revelation 11 with the last verse of Revelation 10, we find where their eyes should have been fixed. "*And there was given me a reed like unto a rod [10½ feet]: and the angel stood, saying*" (Rev. 11:1). This is the same angel, remember. "*… and the angel stood, saying, Rise, and measure the temple of God, and the altar, and them that worship therein.*" In the last verse of

In the midst of this darkness, the truth of 1844 began to be revealed with even clearer light.

Revelation 10, the angel had said, "Thou must prophesy *again*." So, God showed them that the temple of God, His sanctuary, was the key to what they were looking for! This call to study the sanctuary did not come from man; it came from God Himself. The answer to the great disappointment in chapter 10 is the sanctuary in chapter 11.[37]

What is the location of God's sanctuary? "Then the temple of God was opened in heaven, and *the ark of His covenant was seen in His temple*. And there were lightnings, noises, thunderings, an earthquake, and great hail" (Rev. 11:19, NKJV). Did you see that? Some people say that the Ten Commandments were done away with. Some people say that there is no *ark of the covenant*. But the *Bible* says that, when the temple of God *in heaven* was opened, right there *in heaven* was seen the ark of the covenant. Here was the flaw, the fatal flaw of the 1844 movement: The sanctuary of Daniel 8:14 was not the earth! The earth corresponds with the outer court, where the altar of sacrifice was. It was on the earth that Jesus laid down His life. But where is the temple? It is in heaven.

If you look in Hebrews 9:1–7, you will find that there were two rooms, or apartments, in the sanctuary. Each room had its furniture and sacred articles. The first room was called "the holy place," and it had the table of showbread, the altar of incense, and the lampstand. The second room was called "the most holy place," or the "holy of holies." It had only one piece of furniture: the ark of the covenant. The ark contained the Ten Commandments. In the Earthly Tabernacle the priest went daily into the first room, but only the high priest entered the Most Holy Place, and he did so only once a year. The physical arrangements of the temple are basic to an understanding of the tenth and eleventh chapters of Revelation and, for that matter, the whole of the Revelation.

> Then indeed, even the first covenant had ordinances of divine service and the earthly sanctuary. For a tabernacle was prepared: the first part, in which was the lampstand, the table, and the showbread, which is called the sanctuary; and behind the second veil, the part of the tabernacle which is called the

> Holiest of All, which had the golden censer and the ark of the covenant overlaid on all sides with gold, in which were the golden pot that had the manna, Aaron's rod that budded, and the tablets of the covenant; and above it were the cherubim of glory overshadowing the mercy seat. Of these things we cannot now speak in detail. Now when these things had been thus prepared, the priests always went into the first part of the tabernacle, performing the services. But into the second part the high priest went alone once a year, not without blood, which he offered for himself and for the people's sins committed in ignorance. (Heb. 9:1–7, NKJV)

Notice that Revelation 11:19 says: "... the temple of God was opened in heaven, and there was seen the ark of His testimony ..." The text does not say that the temple *was open* but that it was *opened*. The result of this opening was that the ark could be seen. If I were to open a door in my house and you were to see a refrigerator, what door would that be? The kitchen door. If God opened the door of the temple and the prophet saw an ark, what door has been opened? The "door" to the Most Holy Place. Obviously, Revelation 11:19 is depicting the Most Holy Place. The 1844 event was not the coming of the Lord to the earth, as people had expected, but it was the entrance of Jesus described in Daniel 7: "I watched till thrones were put in place, and the Ancient of Days was seated; ... the Ancient of Days came, and a judgment was made in favor of the saints of the Most High" (Dan. 7:9, 22, NKJV). Our Great High Priest, Jesus, went into the Holy of Holies and began His ministry to judge the world in righteousness at the end of the world to complete His priestly work and finish what Revelation calls "the mystery of God."

Comparing Revelation 14:7 with Revelation 10:6, we see that both texts refer to the same thing: the Creator declaring that the final *hour of judgment has come*.

"Saying with a loud voice, 'Fear God and give glory to Him, for the hour of His judgment has come; and worship Him who made heaven and earth, the sea and springs of water'" (Rev. 14:7, NKJV). "And swore by Him who lives forever and ever, who created heaven and the things that are in it, the earth and the things that are in it, and the sea and the things that are in it, that there should be delay no longer" (Rev. 10:6, NKJV).

The rediscovery of the Sanctuary Truth resulted in a revival and transformation of the early Advent believers. God's gracious invitation in Hebrews 10:19 to follow Jesus by faith into the holy of holies introduced the work of our Lord as the Great High Priest. His priestly ministry on behalf of God's children took on a new glory in the daily life of those who chose to obey and follow their Lord into the most holy place of heaven.

Some people refused to follow Jesus into the most holy place and gave up their faith in the message of Daniel 8:14. The command of God was to measure the temple and, in this discovery of the sanctuary message, they also discovered in the heavenly sanctuary the ark of the covenant (Rev. 11:19). In the ark was discovered the Ten Commandments, and the believers began to see their true relationship to redemption. Recognition of the Ten Commandments in heaven and in the three angel's message of Revelation 14 led to the discovery of the Sabbath by more and more believers, and the people were led to keep it holy and the Seventh-day Adventist movement was born. First and foremost, these were people who believed in the second advent of Christ, and, secondly, they honored God's seventh-day Sabbath. Isn't it curious that some would say that there is no commandment to keep holy the Sabbath day because the commandments have all been done away with! Somebody ought to tell the heavenly Father so He can remove the Ten Commandments from His throne room because He is obviously unaware of the fact that they have been done away with. They are called "*His* testament"! When you look into the most holy place in heaven above the ark of the covenant, Lucifer's place as one of the covering angels has been filled by another angel beside Gabriel. I'm not sure who the other angel is, but there they minister before the Shekinah glory of the awesomely powerful God who dwells in light that no man can approach. Seated between the angels, God looks down from His throne, and what does He see in the ark of the covenant? The Ten Commandments. And what is above the Ten Commandments? The mercy seat.

What is above the mercy seat? The Shekinah glory! What else is on the mercy seat? The blood of Christ!

Once a year, on the Day of Atonement, the priest would go into the Most Holy Place. On that day, he would take the blood of the Lord's goat and sprinkle it on the mercy seat. As God sits on His throne, He can look down between Him and the Ten Commandments and see the mercy seat. He doesn't see His law directly or all our imperfections; He sees the law of God *through the blood of Jesus* and has to look through the mercy seat to see the law. When you start talking about perfection and that we have to be perfect, there are no human beings who ever have been perfect or ever will be except for one, and that's Jesus.[38] He perfectly fulfilled the law of God by walking in it, *not* by destroying it! (Rom. 8:4–7) We receive His perfection by faith. That's why, in *The Great Controversy*, page 623, it says that now, while the door of mercy is swung wide on the hinges of perfect grace, now, while Christ is making atonement for us, we need to seek to become perfect in Christ through His righteousness.[39] We need to ask Jesus to credit us with His perfection, not to help us to somehow get rid of all our sins so that we can become a perfect little person. If it depends on me, then—forget it—I'll never reach the goal. But it depends on what God has done for me and not on what I do for God. I have no righteousness. My only righteousness is Christ and Him crucified. My only hope is that the blood is on the mercy seat, my sins are blotted out, and my name is written in the Lamb's book of life! That's my only hope, and in Him I trust. In Him I believe. Now the Sabbath truth has been restored, and truths that have been accumulating bit by bit since the beginning of the Reformation in the 16th century have been picked up off the ground, dusted off, and restored to their glorious beauty. (See Daniel 8:13, 14.)

People may say, "Aren't you Seventh-day Adventist the ones who said that Christ was coming back in 1844?" The answer is—no, we are not. The Seventh-day Adventist Church did not exist in 1844. It was only in the 1863 that the Seventh-day Adventist Church became a denomination. Therefore, the Seventh-day Adventist Church has never set a date for the second coming and never will. Seventh-day Adventists never made ascension robes. That is a myth. The early Adventists went up the mountain and other secluded places to wait for Jesus, but none of them had ascension robes.

Why didn't Martin Luther see the Sabbath? Why didn't Wesley and all the reformers see the Sabbath?

There is a very simple explanation for that question. *The door was shut!* Daniel wasn't open; and the door was not opened until 1844. Believers could not yet see the law of God in the most holy place of the sanctuary because the door was shut. But it's open now. You can see it today.[40] Just open the book of Revelation.

Aren't Seventh-day Adventists the product of a terrible mistake, the mistake of 1844? How could they possibly have the truth?

In Revelation 10, God has given ample evidence that He let this mistake happen—He allowed it. He covered that prophecy up and allowed them to fail to interpret it correctly for His own divine reason. How do we know that? He said, "Thou must prophesy again." On this, I can only venture a human opinion. The second coming of Christ had been lost sight of, and people always work harder under a sense of urgency. The glorious truth of our Lord's return was scattered further and faster this way than it would have been otherwise. The popular churches were offended by this. They stopped mentioning the second coming. For many years the churches had been agitated over this doctrine. They wanted to hear no more of it. This accounts for the silence in the average pulpit today—a backlash against the 1844 movement. However, now it's coming back; it's being preached, but it's being preached as a secret rapture. There is a "rapture," but *there's nothing secret about it!* Revelation 1:7 says, "Every eye shall see him," and I believe that what it says is true. Another backlash against 1844 was the development of Modernism, which says: *You must not take the Bible too seriously. Remember those nuts that were running around saying, "The world's ending! The world's ending!"*

Fanaticism rose up about this time, with a move into crisis religion and emotionalism. By 1844 the Mormons had come into existence. (Joseph Smith was killed on June 27, 1844.) You get the impression that old "claw foot" knew when that prophecy was to be fulfilled, and he figured that he would throw in a counterfeit just to confuse you! *Vestiges of the Natural History of Creation* was published in 1844, which paved the way for the acceptance of Darwin's *On the Origin of Species*.[41] So the Adventist movement continued on after the great disappointment. The majority of the half a million advent adherents quit discussing the return of Jesus. However, there were individuals and small groups here and there in New England that would not abandon the hope of our Lord's return. Slowly, the lines of communication began to form. Periodicals were printed, meetings were called, and a church organization was effected in 1863. Now, twenty percent of all the missionaries in the world are Seventh-day Adventists. Now, the church has publishing enterprises printing in over 300 languages. Now, Seventh-day Adventists have over 500,000 students in our church schools. As you look at the story of our Lord's return, it is being told in over 700 languages. The Seventh-day Adventist Church was not a church born of discontent, but a church born of a common hope in Jesus' soon return.

As the signs are fulfilling all around you—one storm after another—earthquakes, tsunamis, and odd weather—as God is ringing the bell, warning you that Jesus is soon to come, there is a church that is preaching the second coming of Christ! What is the message of God's church today? The answer is found in Revelation 10:11: "*Thou must prophesy [preach] again before many peoples, nations, tongues, and kings.*" So, once again, God is going to use that movement—the extension of the Millerite movement—to preach in all the world. Seventh-day Adventists now have more churches in more countries than any other church on the face of the earth. They are now a worldwide church, preaching, prophesying again, and teaching about the open book of Daniel seen in the angel's hand in Revelation 10. When something is done again, it implies that it was done once before. "Prophesy *again*" means that the same message must be repeated, and that message is that Jesus is coming again. The only difference is that we also need to preach the sanctuary and the judgment message of Jesus Christ. The judgment is going on even as we speak, according to Revelation 11:18 and 14:6. While the nations are angry, the judgment is going on in heaven. Many people think they can wait until Jesus comes and then, when they see Him, they can repent. But the Bible says that the censer is thrown down and Jesus declares: "... he who is unjust, let him be unjust still; he who is filthy, let him be filthy still" (Rev. 22:11, NKJV).

Jesus says, *When I come "my reward is with me* to give every man according to his works" (Rev. 22:12). It will be too late to decide then. When Christ comes, you get your reward. You will either saved or lost. That's it. You won't be able to repent then. It will be like it was in the days of Noah. Do you remember the story about when God sent His angels to close the ark's door, and the ark sat there for seven days while the people made fun of Noah and mocked him? They didn't realize that they were as good as dead—they were already judged; they were already eternally lost. For seven days everything seemed normal, and then the end came. When Jesus throws down the censer (Rev. 8) and the judgment is over in heaven, everything will seem normal. People will be "marrying and giving in marriage" (Matt. 24:38). People will be going to the movies, watching TV, and doing all the things they normally do, and they won't even realize that their fate has already been decided for all eternity. That's why now, while the door of mercy is swung wide on the hinges of perfect grace, you need to bring your life into harmony with God's call and surrender yourself to Jesus today! Today is the day of salvation! Jesus said in Matthew 24:14 that this message will be preached in the entire world and then the end will come. The Bible says that the church that is preaching in the end times will preach about the sanctuary, the ark of the covenant, and the seventh-day Sabbath that is in the heart of God's law. There is only one worldwide church that is preaching the seventh-day Sabbath and the sanctuary message, and that is the Seventh-day Adventist Church.

The whole purpose of your reading this book is to hear the message of God so you can be ready when Jesus comes and not be lost. What a day that will be when Jesus comes! Do you want to be ready? Do you want to be welcomed and given eternal life? Is there anything in your life more important than this? Don't let anything or anyone keep you out of the kingdom. The things the Bible predicts are real, and they are going to happen shortly! I believe we need to stay ready by living one day at a time trusting in Him. We need to read our Bibles, pray, put God first in our life, and not let anything keep us out of the kingdom. Won't you say "yes" to Jesus right now? Won't you let Him write your name in His book of life so He can save you when He comes? May this song be your experience with Jesus!

"In a Little While We're Going Home"
(Early Advent Hymn)

1. Let us sing a song that will cheer us by the way,
   In a little while we're going home;
   For the night will end in the everlasting day,
   In a little while we're going home
2. We will do the work that our hands may find to do,
   In a little while we're going home;
   And the grace of God will our daily strength renew,
   In a little while we're going home
3. We will smooth the path for some weary, way-worn feet,
   In a little while we're going home;
   And may loving hearts spread around an influence sweet!
   In a little while we're going home
4. There's a rest beyond, there's relief from every care,
   In a little while we're going home;
   And *no tears shall fall* in that city bright and fair,
   In a little while we're going home.[42]

Refrain

In a little while, in a little while,
We shall cross the billow's foam;
We shall meet at last,
When the stormy winds are past,
In a little while we're going home.

CHAPTER 13

THE INVESTIGATIVE JUDGMENT IS THE FOUNDATION OF WORSHIP

Saying with a loud voice, Fear God, and give glory to him; for the hour of his judgment is come: and worship him that made heaven, and earth, and the sea, and the fountains of waters.
—Revelation 14:7

In our last study we examined Revelation, chapter 10, and we discovered, while preachers of the Great Advent Awakening of the 19th Century had arrested the attention of the entire world, they had misinterpreted Daniel 8:14 and incorrectly concluded that the sanctuary was the earth, and that it would be cleansed by fire. The message was sweet in their mouths, as they looked for Jesus to come and receive them into glory. Yet, when Jesus did not come, they were bitterly disappointed. This chapter will examine the message of Revelation, chapter 11, which was the result of a closer look at the prophecies of God's Word. We will use chapter 11 as a springboard to open up the wonderful themes of prophecy that God wanted proclaimed to the world through the Great Advent Awakening experience. Out of this great disappointment, within twenty years, the Seventh-day Adventist movement developed. Notice, in the last verse of Revelation 10, how God told His people that they must repeat their prophetic message: "And he said unto me, Thou must *prophesy again* before many peoples, and nations, and tongues, and kings" (Rev. 10:11).

God made it clear that another movement, a Movement of Destiny, would arise like the Phoenix from the ashes of disappointment and would proclaim the same prophetic message, with one difference: The sanctuary in heaven would be the focus and not the earth. The cleansing of the sanctuary in Daniel 8:14 was to take place in heaven and not on the earth. They were instructed to leave out "the outer court" of the heavenly sanctuary. The outer court in the ancient sanctuary was where sacrifices were made. That outer court of the heavenly sanctuary is the earth, outside the city where Jesus was crucified, and the altar of sacrifice is Mount Calvary. "And there was given me a reed like unto a rod: and the angel stood, saying, Rise, and *measure the temple of God*, and *the altar*, and *them that worship therein*. *But the court which is without the temple leave out*, and *measure it not*; for it is *given unto the Gentiles*: and *the holy city* shall they tread under *foot forty and two months*" (Rev. 11:1, 2).

God made it clear that another movement, a Movement of Destiny, would arise like the Phoenix from the ashes of disappointment and would proclaim the same prophetic message, with one difference: The sanctuary in heaven would be the focus and not the earth.

The earthly outer court, God's beloved city, Jerusalem, would be trodden under foot by the Gentiles for a period of forty and two months. A Jewish month is 30 days. This means that the Gentiles would trod Jerusalem under foot for 1260 days. The Bible teaches, in Ezekiel 4:6, that a prophetic day equals a year in literal time. So, the outer court of Jerusalem would be trodden under foot for 1260 literal years. Daniel called this "the abomination of desolation." Jesus referred to this time as "the days of vengeance" that must be fulfilled as He is quoted in the book of Luke: "And when ye shall see Jerusalem compassed with armies, then know that the *desolation* thereof is nigh.... For these be the *days of vengeance*, that *all things* which are written may be *fulfilled*....And they shall fall by the edge of the sword, and shall be *led away captive into all nations*: and *Jerusalem shall be trodden down of the Gentiles, until the times of the Gentiles be fulfilled*" (Luke 21:20, 22, 24).

Jesus predicted that Jerusalem would fall, this prophecy was fulfilled in AD 70 when the Roman General Titus conquered Jerusalem. He laid siege to the city, starved and slaughtered men, women, and children, and the temple was leveled to the ground. When staring at the temple, the apostles thought the temple would stand forever. "And Jesus said unto them, See ye not all these things? verily I say unto you, There shall not be left here one stone upon another, that shall not be *thrown down*" (Matt 24:2, KJV). When Titus leveled the city, he did not destroy the temple. But the Prophet's words were true. "Angels of God were sent to do the work of destruction, so that one stone was not left one upon another that was not thrown down" (*Seventh-day Adventist Bible Commentary*, vol. 5, p. 1099). The Jews' probation as a nation came to a sudden and violent close, and they were scattered throughout the world.[43] This scattering of Israel is called "the Diaspora" and was predicted by many of the Old Testament prophets. Jerusalem remained under Gentile control until 1976, when the Jews would once again rule over Jerusalem. Now, for the first time since the days of King Nebuchadnezzar, there is a Jewish government in place in Israel, and Jerusalem is once again in Jewish hands. The Bible makes it clear that the next event to take place after Jerusalem is restored to Jewish control is the coming of Jesus (Luke 21:27).

"And then shall they see the Son of man coming in a cloud with power and great glory."

We are living in the last days, my friend. The message of the last church before Jesus comes again is a message centered in the prophecies concerning the sanctuary in heaven. The outer court, which is the earth, was to be ravaged by a power that would walk all over the Jewish people and would make war against the saints of the Most High.

This 1260-year period comes from a prophecy originally mentioned in Daniel 7.

"And he shall speak great words against the most High, and shall wear out the saints of the Most High, and *think* to *change times and laws:* and they shall be given into his hand until *a time and times and the dividing of time*" (Dan. 7:25). The period is also mentioned in Revelation 13: "And there was given unto him a mouth speaking great things and blasphemies; and power was given unto him to continue *forty and two months*" (Rev. 13:5). It is also mentioned in Revelation 11: "And I will give power unto my *two witnesses*, and they shall prophesy a *thousand two hundred and threescore days*, clothed in sackcloth" (Rev. 11:3). In all these places, the same prophetic period is specified. Who is this power, when does this period of time start and end, and how does it relate to the message of Revelation 11 concerning the sanctuary in heaven? God has called a movement to proclaim His last message to a dying world. God has never approved of the false religious-political power that, not only walked all over the Jewish people, but would slaughter the saints of the Most High. The time came and now is when God has directed that the truth about the sanctuary in heaven and the true priestly ministry of Jesus be proclaimed. A counterfeit religion was established by the dragon to deceive the world and to prevent God's true message from reaching the people. This false religious-political system has a blaspheming leader who will trample God's Word, set up a false temple, a false priesthood, and a false system of doctrine and worship. He will also murder God's people (2 Thess. 2).

The "little horn" of Daniel 7 is the political power that plucked up and defeated three kingdoms and began his rule of 1260 years. The three kingdoms were the three Arian provinces that believed that Jesus was a created being and not eternal God. This was a heresy that the Catholic Church was willing to go to war over. In AD 493, the Ostrogoths, with the permission of Catholic Emperor Zeno, wiped out the Germanic barbarian tribe of the Heruli, thus plucking up one of the horns. After Justinian became the emperor in AD 527, he issued the decree in AD 533 that elevated the bishop of Rome to the "Head of *All* the Holy Churches." But this decree could not go into *practical* effect until the rest of the Arian enemies were removed. In AD 534, Justinian sent his general Belisarius to destroy the Vandals. Belisarius was successful in one campaign season, thus plucking up the second horn. Finally, the last of the three Arian kingdoms, the Ostrogoths, were defeated and driven out of Rome in March of AD 538 (*Encyclopedia Britannica*). The "little horn" power that plucked them up is still in power today. It is the Roman Catholic Church. It is the only religious power on earth that was in power in AD 538 when Justinian's armies defeated the last of the three Arian tribes. Open your Bible to Daniel 7, and we will move quickly through the prophecy.

The characteristics of the "little horn" have been grouped below to show the characteristics of the judgment that takes place about the time the "little horn" stops warring against God's people:

The Titles of the Little Horn

1. The Little Horn
2. The Man of Sin, the Lawless One
3. Son of Perdition
4. That Wicked
5. The Antichrist
6. The Beast
7. Mother of Harlots
8. Babylon
9. The Great City

Scriptural References: Daniel 7:1–26; 2 Thessalonians 2:1–8; 1 John 2:18, 22; 4:33; 2 John 7; Revelation 13:1–18; 14:9–10; 17:1–18; 18:1–24.

> I considered the horns, and, behold, there came up among them another *little horn*, before whom there were *three of the first horns plucked up by the roots:* and, behold, in this horn were *eyes like the eyes of man, and a mouth speaking great things*. (Dan. 7:8)
>
> And of the ten horns that were in his head, and of the other which came up, and before whom three fell; even of that horn that had eyes, and a mouth that spake very great things, whose look was more stout than his fellows. (Dan. 7:20)
>
> And I stood upon the sand of the sea, and saw a beast rise up out of the sea, having seven heads and *ten horns, and upon his horns ten crowns*, and upon his heads the name of blasphemy. And the beast which I saw was like unto a leopard, and his feet were as the feet of a bear, and his mouth as the mouth of a lion: and *the dragon gave him his power, and his seat, and great authority*. (Rev. 13:1, 2)

History tells us that the symbol of the flag of pagan Rome was a fierce red dragon. Revelation says that the dragon, which is Rome, would give the beast its power, seat, and authority. In AD 533, the Emperor Justinian gave the bishop of Rome his power and his authority by making him the ruler in secular and religious matters. Two centuries before, when Constantine moved the capitol of Rome to Constantinople, he left Rome vacant, and the Papacy soon became the most powerful ruler in Rome. Justinian's decree made Rome's rule official in AD 533, and the degree became a reality in 538 AD when the Ostrogoths were driven from Rome, insuring the Roman bishop's rule. The only religious-political power in existence today that existed in AD 538 and that still has its seat, power, and authority is the Roman Church in Italy. "And I saw one of his heads as it were *wounded to death; and his deadly wound was healed: and all the world wondered after the beast*" (Rev. 13:3).

This wounding took place in AD 1798, when the Pope was captured and taken to France where he died in prison.

"He that *leadeth into captivity shall go into captivity:* he that killeth with the sword *must be killed with the sword*. Here is the patience and the faith of the saints" (Rev. 13:10).

"And they worshipped the dragon which gave power unto the beast: and they worshipped the beast, saying, Who is like unto the beast? Who is able to *make war* with him?" (Rev. 13:4).

"And there was given unto him a *mouth speaking great things and blasphemies; and power was given unto him to continue forty and two months*" (Rev. 13:5).

"And he opened his mouth in *blasphemy against God*, to blaspheme his name, and *his tabernacle*, and them that *dwell in heaven*" (Rev. 13:6).

This church set up a false priestly system, encourages its members to pray to saints in heaven, claims to have the power to forgive sins, claims that the pope is "God on Earth," and teaches a false gospel of salvation by works. This false gospel is not just the works of Jesus in the life by the working of the Holy Spirit. It is working to achieve sinless sainthood through a person's own works. Otherwise, a person cannot be saved.

"And it was given unto him to *make war with the saints*, and to overcome them: and power was given him over all kindreds, and tongues, and nations" (Rev. 13:7).

"And the ten horns out of this kingdom are ten kings that shall arise: and another shall rise after them; and he shall be diverse from the first, and he shall subdue three kings" (Dan. 7:24).

Characteristics of the Little Horn

1. The ten horns represent the ten kings on the dragon beast.
2. Three of those horns are "plucked up" or defeated by the little horn.
3. He has the eyes of a man. He too is a king-like power.

4. He is not just a king, but a religious power because he speaks great, pompous, and blasphemous words against God. Blasphemy indicates that someone is offending God or claiming religious authority that he does not possess.
5. He was "more stout" than the other horns. This means, possibly, that he is richer or more resilient. It certainly means that he is different than the other nine horns. They were political kingdoms, but the littler horn, which was stouter than they, was a religious-political power.
6. The little horn makes war against God's people for 1260 years, from AD 538, when the three horns were plucked up, until 1798. In AD 538, the Roman Emperor Justinian gave power and authority to the pope, who warred against the saints until 1798, when Napoleon sent his general Berthier to capture Pope Pius VI and transport him to France where he died in prison. The Roman Church is said to have martyred, tortured, and chased from their homes somewhere between 50 and 68 million people.[44]
7. The deadly wound was healed in 1929 when Mussolini made the Vatican a small but independent nation. Only 500 people live on the grounds of the Vatican today. It is a 112-acre country within a county. Today, every major nation sends an ambassador to the Vatican in Rome.
8. The little horn persecuted God's people *until* the judgment is rendered in favor of the saints and *until* the saints possess the kingdom! In 1844, God began to "judge the dead" and place them forever in His kingdom by blotting out their sins and placing them forever beyond Satan's domain! At about the same time, the judgment on behalf of the dead is rendered, and the little horn stops making war against the saints.

"I beheld, and the same horn *made war with the saints, and prevailed against them; until* the *Ancient of days came*, and *judgment was given to the saints of the* most High; and *the time came* that the *saints possessed the kingdom*" (Dan. 7:21, 22).

One of the reasons the little horn stopped making war against the saints is because he is wounded to death by a burning flame. Notice verse 11: "I beheld then *because of the voice of the great words* which the horn spake: I beheld even till the beast was slain, and his body destroyed, and *given to the burning flame*" (Dan. 7:11). The "burning flame" that destroys the papacy is the Word of God.[45] The Reformation preachers discovered the truths of God's Word and preached them with such power that the influence of the Papacy was destroyed. This is referred to in Revelation, chapter 11: "And I will give power unto my *two witnesses*, and they shall *prophesy a thousand two hundred and threescore days*, clothed in *sackcloth*" (Rev. 11:3).

"These are the two olive trees, and the two candlesticks standing before the God of the earth" (Rev. 11:4).

"And if any man will hurt them, *fire proceedeth out of their mouth, and devoureth their enemies:* and if any man will hurt them, he must in this manner be killed" (Rev. 11:5).

Characteristics of the Judgment in Daniel 7

"I beheld till the *thrones were cast down*, and the *Ancient of days did sit*, whose garment was white as snow, and the hair of his head like the pure wool: his throne was like the fiery flame, and his wheels as burning fire" (Dan. 7:9).

"A fiery stream issued and came forth from before him: thousand thousands ministered unto him, and ten thousand times ten thousand stood before him: *the judgment was set, and the books were opened*" (Dan 7:10).

Notice that, at the end of the 1260 years, something takes place in heaven that should be of interest to every person on earth. The judgment begins and the books are opened. As this takes place, thrones are moved and set up.

"I saw in the night visions, and, behold, *one like the Son of man* came with the clouds of heaven, and *came to the Ancient of days*, and *they brought him near before him*" (Dan. 7:13). Notice that Jesus is brought into God's presence, perhaps on a movable throne. It may be that the angels carry the throne or it has some other form of locomotion. Then the judgment takes place before God's throne.

"And there was *given him* dominion, and glory, and *a kingdom*, that all people, nations, and languages, should serve him: his dominion is an everlasting dominion, which shall not pass away, and his kingdom that which shall not be destroyed" (Dan. 7:14).

"But the *saints of the most High shall take the kingdom, and possess the kingdom* for ever, even for ever and ever" (Dan. 7:18).

1. Shortly after Christ appears before the Father, judgment is given to the saints, and they possess the kingdom.
2. Seventh-day Adventists have interpreted this to mean that, in 1844, when Christ was to cleanse the sanctuary in heaven, He would declare the saints "not guilty," and begin to make up those who would be citizens of the kingdom of God.

> And the seventh angel sounded; and there were great voices in heaven, saying, The kingdoms of this world are become the kingdoms of our Lord, and of his Christ; and he shall reign for ever and ever. And the *four and twenty elders*, which sat *before God on their seats*, fell upon their faces, and worshipped God, saying, We give thee thanks, O Lord God Almighty, which art, and wast, and art to come; because thou hast taken to thee thy great power, and hast reigned. And the *nations were angry*, and thy wrath is come, and the *time of the dead, that they should be judged*, and that thou shouldest *give reward unto thy servants the prophets, and to the saints*, and them that fear thy name, small and great; and shouldest *destroy them which destroy the earth*. And *the temple of God was opened in heaven*, and there was seen *in his temple the ark of his testament:* and there were lightnings, and voices, and thunderings, and an earthquake, and great hail. (Rev. 11:15–19)

Characteristics of the Judgment in Heaven

1. The nations are still raging when the judgment takes place. Christ has not yet returned.
2. The judgment takes place before Jesus comes, and the dead are judged and given their reward.
3. The people who are rewarded have the gift of prophecy in their midst.
4. When the judgment is concluded, God destroys those who are destroying the earth both literally and spiritually.
5. The door into the most holy place is opened before Jesus comes, and the dead are judged, as judgment takes place in the inner room of the sanctuary.
6. The ark is visible in this room, signifying that the ark of the covenant is in heaven. Moses copied the heavenly sanctuary in making the sanctuary for the children of Israel in the wilderness.
7. It is called the ark of *His testament*. Some people have suggested that the Ten Commandments have been done away with, or nailed to the cross. Someone ought to let God the Father know this, shouldn't they? God still claims ownership of His law. It is in heaven, in the ark, and He calls it "His" testament. It is as if God is saying, *The Ten Commandments, which is the testament, are mine! They belong to me. I have them in heaven, and no man can change them!* The only reason men want to do away with them is because they want to do away with God's Sabbath day.

Men want to get rid of only one of God's commandments—the Sabbath. They will allow all the others, but the commandment in which God identified "The Sabbath of the Lord," they want to take away. The very day that God said to "Remember," they tell you to forget. Let me say it as clearly as I can: *The Ten Commandments were not nailed to the cross*. The Sabbath has never been abdicated, abolished, or abandoned. The law of God is just as binding on sinners today as it was when Jesus said, "The son of man"—that's Jesus—"is Lord of the Sabbath" and when He said, "I came not to destroy the law"! Jesus lived a life of perfect love, and love fulfills the law of God!

When the Seventh-day Adventist Church was formed from the remnants of the early Advent believers, they began to study their Bibles and turned their attention to the sanctuary in heaven. They took the rod from the angel and began to measure the altar of incense, and the ark of the covenant. As they studied their Bibles, they read the book of Hebrews and Revelation together, and they learned about Jesus' ministry as the great high priest.

They learned about the judgment going on in heaven right now! They looked in the ark of the testament and saw the law of God, including the seventh-day Sabbath. This truth was discovered through Bible study and prayer. They began to proclaim the message God gave them. They began to share the prophecies of Daniel and Revelation and to proclaim the Bible Sabbath and many other Bible doctrines they discovered. In 1863, the Seventh-day Adventist Church was organized. It became a movement of destiny, proclaiming the coming kingdom of Jesus.

Daniel described this judgment: "But *the judgment shall sit*, and they shall *take away his dominion*, to consume and to destroy it unto the end" (Dan. 7:26).

"And *the kingdom* and dominion, and the greatness of the kingdom under the whole heaven, *shall be given to the people of the saints* of the most High, whose kingdom is an everlasting kingdom, and all dominions shall serve and obey him" (Dan. 7:27).

In 1844, God began judging the dead and will one day come to the living. In 1844, God began putting His saints in His kingdom, never to be removed by sin or Satan. He is now judging the earth in righteousness. He is taking the kingdom away from Satan and giving it to His people who claim salvation through the righteousness of Christ alone. His kingdom is a kingdom of obedience of faith and service to Jesus, and it will be an everlasting kingdom that will never end! Amen and Amen!

CHAPTER 14

THE ARK OF THE COVENANT, A PLACE OF WORSHIP

And after that I looked, and, behold, the temple of the tabernacle of the testimony in heaven was opened.
—*Revelation 15:5*

Nowhere is God's perfect grace revealed more clearly than in the ark of the covenant. In order to understand it more fully, we must first look at the earthly sanctuary system that is described as "the old covenant," "the law of Moses," and "the law contained in ordinances." Paul makes it clear in Hebrews that this system was a "shadow of heavenly things." The old system was a shadow of the plan of redemption, and a shadow of the heavenly. In the heart of both the earthly and heavenly sanctuaries was the "covenant," or "testament," "of the Lord." The Ten Commandment law of God was hidden deep in the heart of God's throne, inside the ark of the covenant. It is interesting that it is referred to as the covenant "of the Lord." It belongs to God. He created it, and He keeps it safely tucked away in His throne, far from the reach of sinful human beings. "For every high priest is ordained to offer gifts and sacrifices: wherefore it is of necessity that this man have somewhat also to offer. For if he were on earth, he should not be a priest, seeing that there are *priests that offer gifts according to the law*" (Heb. 8:3, 4). "Who serve unto the example *and shadow of heavenly things*, as Moses was admonished of God when he was about to make the tabernacle: for, See, saith he, that thou *make all things according to the pattern shewed to thee in the mount*" (Heb. 8:5). "Then verily the first covenant had also ordinances of divine service, and *a worldly sanctuary*" (Heb. 9:1).

Moses constructed the earthly sanctuary and its furniture for the children of Israel according to the "pattern" of the heavenly sanctuary that he was shown by God. God instituted the law of sacrifices and ordinances to teach the people about the coming Lamb of God, in a way that their minds could grasp. The entire system pointed to future redemption and the sacrificial Messiah who would die for the sins of His people and not for Himself. (See Dan. 9:24–27.)

The First Apartment Furniture

The furniture in the apartments of the sanctuary was symbolic representations or types of the throne room in heaven, which Moses saw. Let's look at what Paul describes in Hebrews: "For there was a tabernacle made; the first, wherein was the *candlestick*, and *the table, and the shewbread*; which is called the sanctuary" (Heb. 9:2). It is interesting to note that Paul connected the "golden censer" with the Most Holy Place (Heb. 9:4). The altar and the incense are now a part of the Most Holy Place under the New Covenant.

The Candlestick, or Lampstand

The candlestick, or lampstand, was on the south side of the sanctuary. It was supplied by oil, which has always been used in the Bible to represent the Holy Spirit.[46] The Holy Spirit may not have an actual throne in heaven (does He need one?) but may simply have the lampstand to represent His presence on the south side of the sanctuary. The flame that lights a lamp is symbolic of the light that the Holy Spirit brings into the world. In John 1:9, the Bible teaches that Jesus is the light that shines into the heart of every person who comes into the world. How does Jesus do that? The Bible teaches us that the Holy Spirit convicts the world of sin and leads sinners to repentance. "And out of the throne proceeded lightnings, thunderings, and voices. Seven *lamps of fire were burning before the throne*, which are the seven Spirits of God" (Rev. 4:5, NKJV).

The Table of Shewbread

The table of shewbread was a table that had twelve loaves of bread placed upon it. The bread was like pita bread, and it was baked fresh every Sabbath and placed on this table (Lev. 24:8). The twelve loaves represented the twelve tribes of Israel (which may be why Jesus chose twelve apostles), and the number twelve indicates completeness. Twelve times twelve is 144, and this number is significant in the book of Revelation. The bread represents Christ's body. Jesus is often depicted in the Bible as manna or bread, as in the communion service. The crown around the outside edge of the top of the table upon which the bread sits indicates that the table was a type of the kingly throne upon which Christ sits in heaven. The table was located on the north side of the sanctuary.

The Second Veil

"And after the *second veil*, the tabernacle which is called the *holiest of all*" (Heb. 9:3). So, the curtain between the apartments is called the "second veil." Let's compare this with some other texts in Hebrews.

"Having therefore, brethren, boldness to enter into *the holiest by the blood of Jesus*, by a new and living way, which he hath consecrated for us, *through the veil, that is to say, his flesh*" (Heb. 10:19–20). Exodus 36:8 says that this curtain had cherubim embroidered on it. Thus, the second veil is a curtain of angels, one of which is Michael the great Archangel whom the

Bible indicates is Jesus. The veil is a symbol of Jesus who is the veil of flesh through which we come to the Father. The only way to approach the Father is through the blood of Jesus as He offered His flesh and blood as a sacrifice for sin. It is through His body, blood, and sacrifice that we are brought into the very presence of God. "Which had the *golden censer*, and the *ark of the covenant* overlaid round about with gold, wherein was the golden pot that had manna, and Aaron's rod that budded, and the *tables of the covenant*" (Heb. 9:4).

The only way to approach the Father is through the blood of Jesus as He offered His flesh and blood as a sacrifice for sin.

"And *above it were the cherubim of glory overshadowing the mercy seat*. Of these things we cannot now speak in detail" (Heb. 9:5, NKJV). This text mentions three objects to which I want to call your attention.

The Altar of Incense and the Golden Censer

This censer was to contain hot coals taken from the altar. The priest would place incense on the coals to create smoke with a very strong, sweet aroma. This is symbolic of the prayers of the saints being mixed with the righteousness of the Messiah. The twenty-four elders have censers, and Jesus has a censer. At the close of probation Jesus (called "Michael") throws the censer to the earth, signaling the end of the judgment and the beginning of the last plagues. "And another angel came and stood *at the altar*, having *a golden censer;* and there was given unto him *much incense*, that he should offer it *with the prayers of all saints upon the golden altar which was before the throne*" (Rev. 8:3). "And the *smoke* of the incense, which came *with the prayers of the saints*, ascended up before God out of the angel's hand. And the angel *took the censer*, and filled it with *fire of the altar*, and *cast it into the earth:* and there were voices, and thunderings, and lightnings, and an earthquake" (Rev. 8:4, 5; compare with Rev. 11:19).

The Ark of the Covenant

This was a wooden box overlaid with gold, which had a golden crown around the outside edge of the lid. The lid was called the mercy seat. On top of the lid were two large angels with wings that touched. The blood of the sacrifice was sprinkled on the lid of the ark. God's visible presence was above the seat between the angels. This was symbolic of God the Father's throne in heaven. The mercy seat was located between the Shekinah glory of God's presence and God's law. This meant that, as God looked down upon His law, He viewed it through the mercy that was provided by the blood of Jesus, bringing pardon to God's people from their sins.

The Tables of the Covenant

Also called the tables of His testament, this was the Ten Commandment law. God's moral law was kept *inside* the ark. The law of Moses, the carnal ordinances, the law that was "against us" was kept in a pocket *in the side* of the *ark*. The Ten Commandments are called "the covenant *of the Lord.*" God wrote them in stone. They are not owned by the Jews or by any man. They are a transcript of God's character and are everlasting in nature. The law of Moses was put beside the ark as a witness against the stiff-necked people who would break the commandments that Moses wrote. This is what Paul referred to in Colossians 2:14 as being nailed to the cross. Notice the similarity in language: "And it came to pass, when Moses had made an end of *writing* the words of this law in a book, until they were finished, that Moses commanded the Levites, which bare the ark of the covenant of the LORD, saying, Take this book of the law, and put it in the *side of the ark* of the *covenant of the LORD your God*, that it may be there *for a witness against thee*" (Deut. 31:24–26). "Blotting out the *handwriting of ordinances* that was *against us*, which was contrary to us, and took it out of the way, *nailing it to his cross*" (Col. 2:14).

Colossians 2:14 has confused many over the years, yet it is simple to explain if you let the Bible interpret it for you. When we get to the chapter "Sanctuary Laws for Worship," we will discuss Paul's doctrine of the law in much greater detail and explore this text more deeply. But for our present purposes, just notice what the Bible teaches. What was the "it" that was nailed to the cross? "It" was the "handwriting of ordinances" that was against us. What does Deuteronomy say? It says that Moses wrote the book of the law with his own hand and that he did it as a witness against them. The law that was nailed to the cross was this law, written by Moses and placed in the side of the ark as a witness against the children of Israel.

The law that was nailed to the cross was this law, written by Moses and placed in the side of the ark as a witness against the children of Israel.

"Now when these things were thus ordained, the priests went always into the first tabernacle, accomplishing the service of God. But into the *second* went the high priest *alone once every year, not without blood*, which he offered for himself, and for the errors of the people" (Heb. 9:6, 7).

In the earthly system, the priest would enter the *Most Holy Place* once a year to offer the blood of the covenant for the people and for himself. Some have thought that the curtain was stained with blood and removed. However, there is no evidence in Scripture that the curtain was replaced, and the blood that was sprinkled in the sanctuary was sprinkled "before" the veil (Lev. 4:6, 17). It was also sprinkled upon the mercy seat and the altar of incense. "And the priest was to bring his blood within the veil, and sprinkle it upon the mercy seat and before the mercy seat. The blood was also to be sprinkled upon the altar of incense that was before the veil" (*The Great Controversy*, p. 419). As our high priest, Jesus pleads His blood to answer the law's demands, covers our sins with His righteous life, and mixes His righteousness with our prayers. We are protected from our sins, for God sees His Son's character instead of our lawbreaking and the Spirit interprets our impure prayers through Christ's righteousness, making them acceptable to God.

The sanctuary was cleansed as the blood of the sacrifice was placed upon the scapegoat, which was led out of the camp. This symbolized God's separating the people's sins from them, purifying them, and declaring them not guilty through the blood. "For then must he often have suffered since the foundation of the world: but now *once in the end of the world hath he appeared to put away sin by the sacrifice of himself*" (Heb. 9:26). This verse employs the same sanctuary language. At the end of the world, Jesus has appeared to put away sin by His blood. When the judgment is finished, Christ will come to rescue His people. Sin will not be just forgiven, it will be put away. How? By removing it forever from the universe. The judgment is the legal process through which God accomplishes the removal of sin forever from the earth. He declares his people "not guilty" for all time! "And as it is appointed unto men once to die, *but after this the judgment*" (Heb. 9:27). "So Christ was *once offered* to bear the sins of many; and unto them that look for him shall he appear the second time without sin unto salvation" (Heb. 9:28).

The Sanctuary in Heaven

"A minister of *the sanctuary*, and of the true tabernacle, *which the Lord pitched, and not man*" (Heb. 8:2). "Who serve unto the example and *shadow of heavenly things*, as Moses was admonished of God when he was about to make the tabernacle: for, See, saith he, that thou *make all things according to the pattern shewed to thee in the mount*" (Heb. 8:5). As we now turn our gaze upward to the sanctuary in heaven, we need to talk about God's throne room and what is involved in understanding it. The sanctuary in heaven is the anti-type. It is the original from which all earthly types derived their meaning. We should always remember that, ever since the unseen hand ripped the curtain in the temple in two when Jesus died on the cross, there is no valid earthly sanctuary. As we noticed in Colossians

2:14, the earthly priesthood, sacrifices, and sanctuary all became irrelevant when Jesus died. Many Christians describe their church building as a "sanctuary." This is acceptable in a very limited sense, because the church is more like the outer court of the sanctuary, the "people's court," where the people stood while worship was conducted. There is no true sanctuary on earth now. The throne of God is massive, large enough for the unity of the three divine persons who are represented by the three components of the single huge throne. The ark, the table of shewbread, and the lampstand are all part of the same "throne." The altar of incense is in the "midst of the throne." We read: "And I beheld, and, lo, in the midst of the throne and of the four beasts, and in the midst of the elders stood a lamb as it had been slain having seven horns and seven eyes, which are the seven Spirits of God sent forth unto all the earth" (Rev. 5:6).[47] In order to get a good glimpse of this vast, miraculous place, we need to read Revelation, chapters 4 and 5.

"After this I looked, and, behold, *a door was opened* in heaven: and the first voice which I heard was as it were of a trumpet talking with me; which said, Come up hither, and I will shew thee things which must be hereafter. And immediately I was in the spirit: and, behold, *a throne was set in heaven, and one sat on the throne*" (Rev. 4:1, 2). Notice the similarity of this passage to what we studied in the book of Daniel: "I beheld till the *thrones were cast down, and the Ancient of days did sit*, whose garment was white as snow, and the hair of his head like the pure wool: his throne was like the fiery flame, and his wheels as burning fire. A fiery stream issued and came forth from before him: thousand thousands ministered unto him, and ten thousand times ten thousand stood before him: *the judgment was set, and the books were opened"* (Dan. 7:9, 10).

Notice that sometime shortly after the end of the 1260 years, something takes place in heaven that should be of interest to every person on earth. The problem with the Roman Church that set itself up as the authority in all things religious is that it instituted a creature-centered, man-centered system of worship. This false religious system claims to be the true temple of God, the true sanctuary on earth, the true priesthood, the true authority in all religious matters. In fact, it claims to be the only true church and the authority of God on earth. These preposterous claims, titles, and semi-divine attributes, speak volumes about the idolatrous veneration of the pope, which has been a historical trademark of the *creature-centered* worship of Roman Catholicism. The problem I had when I was a Roman Catholic was that there were always too many people between me and Jesus. These included Mary, saints, popes, cardinals, bishops, and priests. By exalting popes, saints, and Mary to a semi-divine place, *Catholic worship is creature-centered, rather than God-centered*. It obscures the true worship of God. This is an important point to keep in mind when studying the false worship that is promoted by the beast of Revelation 13.[48]

While this false religious system and all the churches that have come out of her, known as Babylon and her daughters, are directing your attention toward human worship and practices, the true church of Christ on earth is directing your attention to the sanctuary system in heaven. The true church in the last days will not be creature centered, but heaven centered. It will be teaching about what our great High Priest is doing in heaven. It will be teaching that there is no earthly system of priesthood besides "the priesthood of *all* believers." All believers are now priests. The church is now heaven centered, cooperating with their great sanctuary priest, Jesus Christ. The Bible teaches that there is one mediator between God and man, Jesus Christ. "For there is one God, and one mediator between God and men, the man Christ Jesus" (1 Tim. 2:5).

While the false religion deceives people by diverting their minds to venerate and pray to saints and the Virgin Mary and to confess their sins to mere men, the true church directs people to Christ and teaches men to go to Him for mediation with God and for forgiveness of sin. The true church does not drink the wine of Babylon's false doctrines. The true church does not teach that dead Christians go right to heaven at death that they might be prayed to. Neither does it teach that the lost are in hell or purgatory when they die. The true church teaches that the dead are in their graves unless they are physically resurrected. The true church rejects the false teachings of the church of confusion. "Babylon is fallen ... be not partakers of her sins" (Rev. 14:8; 18:4). The false religion of the Roman Church and her daughters is contrasted with the pure, primitive, apostolic faith. During the Dark Ages, the true church fled into the wilderness, which included Celtic lands. "And to the woman were given two wings of a great eagle, that she might fly into the wilderness, into her place, where she is nourished for a time, and times, and half a time, from the face of the serpent" (Rev. 12:14). The Church of Ireland, Scotland, and Wales was a church of biblical purity in stark contrast to the continental church of Rome. Just after the beast power ends its 1260-year oppression of God's people, God judges the world, gives His saints their kingdom and crowns, and exalts his Son to His rightful place as ruler of the universe. The judgment is set, and the books are opened. When this judgment begins, thrones are moved and set up. Yes, movable thrones!

While the false religion deceives people by diverting their minds to venerate and pray to saints and the Virgin Mary and to confess their sins to mere men, the true church directs people to Christ and teaches men to go to Him for mediation with God and for forgiveness of sin.

"And he that sat was to look upon like a jasper and a sardine stone: and there was a rainbow round about the throne, in sight like unto an emerald. And round about the throne were *four and twenty seats:* and upon the seats I *saw four and twenty elders sitting*, clothed in white raiment; and they had on their heads *crowns of gold*. When Jesus rose from the dead, he resurrected over twenty people that now make up the twenty-four elders in heaven who are taking part in the judgment of the dead" (Rev. 4:3, 4). "And the graves were opened; and *many bodies of the saints which slept arose, and came out of the graves after his resurrection*, and went into the holy city, and appeared unto many" (Matt. 27:52, 53). They ascended with Jesus to heaven in bodily form. There are no disembodied spirits in heaven. Every human there has a resurrected or translated body. "These are they which were not defiled with women; for they are virgins. These are they which follow the Lamb whithersoever he goeth. *These were redeemed from among men, being the firstfruits unto God and to the Lamb*" (Rev. 14:4). "Wherefore he saith, *when he ascended up on high, he led captivity captive, and gave gifts unto men*" (Eph. 4:8). He led captivity captive! He gave them the gift of eternal life, a new body, a new kingdom, a crown of gold, and the right to sit with Him upon His throne. Jesus arrived in heaven with a group of redeemed saints (possible the twenty-four elders), who are ambassadors of the earth, to participate in the greatest courtroom drama the world has ever seen.

> And out of the throne proceeded lightnings and thunderings and voices: and there were seven lamps of fire burning before the throne, which are the seven Spirits of God. And before the throne there was a sea of glass like unto crystal: and in *the midst of the throne*, and round about the throne, were four beasts full of eyes before and behind. And the first beast was like a lion, and the second beast like a calf, and the third beast had a face as a man, and the fourth beast was like a flying eagle. And the four beasts had each of them six wings about him; and they were full of eyes within: and they rest not day and night, saying, Holy, holy, holy, Lord God Almighty, which was, and is, and is to come. And when those beasts give glory and honour and thanks to him that sat on the throne, who liveth for ever and ever, *The four and twenty elders* fall down before him that sat on the throne, and worship him that liveth for ever and ever, and *cast their crowns* before the throne, saying, Thou art worthy, O Lord, to receive glory and honour and power: for

> thou hast created all things, and for thy pleasure they are and were created. (Rev. 4:5–11)

Notice how the elders worship Jesus for being the Creator God, who takes pleasure in His creatures. The true church is not focused on the creatures as the false religions are. The true church directs attention to the throne room in the heavenly sanctuary. They direct the gaze to the twenty-four elders as they worship the Creator and not the creature. Here we find the Sabbath Commandment reflected. Worship the Creator, keep His day holy, and call the Sabbath a delight and a pleasure. Watch how they bow before Him, casting their crowns at His feet!

> And I saw in the right hand of him that sat on the throne a book written within and on the backside, sealed with seven seals. And I saw a strong angel proclaiming with a loud voice, *Who is worthy* to open the book, and to loose the seals thereof? And *no man in heaven, nor in earth, neither under the earth, was able to open the book, neither to look thereon*. And I wept much, because no man was found worthy to open and to read the book, neither to look thereon. And one of the elders saith unto me, Weep not: behold, the Lion of the tribe of Judah, the Root of David, hath prevailed to open the book, and to loose the seven seals thereof. And I beheld, and, lo, *in the midst of the throne* and of the four beasts, and *in the midst of the elders, stood a Lamb as it had been slain*, having seven horns and seven eyes, which are *the seven Spirits of God* sent forth into all the earth. (Rev. 5:1–6)

Notice that Jesus is standing in the middle of the throne room, in the middle of the throne, in the middle of the elders, and that He looks like a living sacrifice! He looks like a slain Lamb, like the Lamb of Calvary. The middle of the throne is where the altar of incense is. Jesus is the great

Archangel standing before God in the midst of the throne interceding on behalf of His people. He is the great High Priest Paul describes in the epistle to the Hebrews who is ministering on behalf of His people after the order of Melchizedec (Heb. 5:6). There he stands, offering His blood and the incense, mixing His merits in with the prayers of the saints, blotting out their sins in the times of refreshing. This ministry continues until the last case has been decided. The Bible states that God places His seal upon His chosen ones shortly before the close of probation. The close of probation occurs a short time before the second coming of Jesus, and it is the point at which God declares that every human being has had an opportunity to make a decision for Christ. This is the point beyond which no one will be able to reverse his or her decision. How do we know that such an event will occur? According to Revelation 7:1–3, the angels who are holding back the winds of strife in our world will only let them go when all true believers have been sealed. The releasing of the winds of strife is the point beyond which no one else will be sealed. Unless people are sealed by then, they will be lost.

The close of probation occurs a short time before the second coming of Jesus, and it is the point at which God declares that every human being has had an opportunity to make a decision for Christ.

Therefore, when the winds of strife and calamity are let loose by the removal of heaven's restraints upon our world, probation will close. Then it is that heaven's proclamation is made: "Let the evildoer still do evil, and the filthy still be filthy, and the righteous still do right, and the holy still be holy" (Rev. 22:11, ESV). This is the point at which Jesus ceases interceding for our confessed sins in the heavenly sanctuary. Revelation 8:3, 4, symbolically depicts Jesus functioning as our High Priest in the heavenly sanctuary. He mediates for us. He mingles the merits of His intercession with our prayers, and our confessed sins are forgiven. But verse 5, as we mentioned earlier in this study, depicts the end of this intercession. "Then the angel took the censer and filled it with fire from the altar and threw it on the earth; and there were peals of thunder, rumblings, flashes of lightning, and an earthquake." Then the judgment described in Daniel 7:9–14 will be complete. By then the heavenly court will have decided the future of every human being either for life or for death.

"And *at that time* shall Michael stand up, *the great prince which standeth for the children of thy people:* and there shall be a time of trouble, such as never was since there was a nation even to that same time: and *at that time* thy people *shall be delivered*, every one that shall be found *written in the book*" (Dan. 12:1). Notice that the Angel who stands up is called Michael. This is a name used in the Bible to describe Jesus, the ruler of the angels, the Archangel, the One whose voice raises the dead (John 5:27, 28; 1 Thess. 4:16). Notice that he is also called "the Great Prince." Jesus, the Prince of Peace, the Son of God, the great High Priest "stands for the children of the people." At that time—the time of the end—just *before* Jesus comes, He delivers the people by judging them out of that which is written in the book of life. Again, we see a depiction of a pre-Advent judgment. Christ's faithful people will have received the end-time seal of God before the close of probation when universal trouble and calamity take over in our world; Christ's people will be filled with the Spirit, and they will be able to stand true to Him by faith, whatever the circumstances. "And he came and took the book out of the right hand of him that sat upon the throne. And when he had taken the book, the four beasts and *four and twenty elders* fell down before the Lamb, having every one of them harps, and *golden vials full of odours, which are the prayers of saints*" (Rev. 5:7, 8).

The elders each have a golden censer, representing the prayers of God's people. They offer them to Jesus as a sweet aroma, a pleasing offering of praise to Him and His Father, petitioning them for mercy. They are also joining with Jesus, showing their complete agreement and cooperation with His priestly ministry. They stand with Jesus in this work. "And they sung a new song, saying, Thou art worthy to take the book, and to open the seals thereof: for thou wast slain, and hast redeemed us to God by thy blood out of every kindred, and tongue, and people, and nation; and hast made us unto our God *kings and priests:* and we shall *reign* on the earth" (Rev. 5:9, 10).

So these elders are priests, or intercessors, in the sense that they represent their brethren before the throne of God, judging men and angels as Paul suggested in his first letter to the Corinthians: "Know ye not that *we shall judge angels*? How much more things that pertain to this life?" (1 Cor. 6:3). During the millennium, they will have a part in determining the punishment of the wicked and the evil angels. (See Revelation 20.)

> And I beheld, and I heard the voice of many angels *round about the throne* and the beasts and the elders: and the number of them was ten thousand times ten thousand, and thousands of thousands; Saying with a loud voice, Worthy is the Lamb that was slain to receive power, and riches, and wisdom, and strength, and honour, and glory, and blessing. And every creature which is in heaven, and on the earth, and under the earth, and such as are in the sea, and all that are in them, heard I saying, Blessing, and honour, and glory, and power, be unto him that *sitteth* upon the throne, and unto the Lamb for ever and ever. And the four beasts said, Amen. And the *four and twenty elders fell down and worshipped him that liveth for ever and ever*" (Rev. 5:11–14).

Can you see this scene in your mind's eye? There is a circle around the throne of God and the Lamb, the elders and the beasts, and there are millions of angels, all making a sea of praise "round about the throne"! The twenty-four elders are on the floor of the throne room, worshipping Jesus as King of kings and Lord of lords!

Characteristics of God's Throne Room

1. Where God dwells is a huge room. By God, I mean the Father, the Son, and the Holy Spirit. All three are one God, reflected in three personalities that are represented by the three thrones depicted in the sanctuary. The God who sits on all three thrones is a God who is all knowing and all-powerful, and He exists in all places. The single throne contains all three components of the Godhead.
2. The veil that is embroidered with angels in the earthly tabernacle was a symbol, or type, of the angels that fill the most holy place in heaven. Not only was the veil embroidered with hundreds of angels, but so was the ceiling (Exod. 26:31). The embroidered angels were types, or symbols, of the billions of angels in the anti-type. Many different angelic creatures, created for God's pleasure and service, are ministering there. The veil is also a symbol of Christ's flesh, for it is through the veil of His flesh that we approach the Father.
3. God's throne room faces east. The Father's section of the throne is on the west end of the sanctuary. The ark of the covenant faces east. The entire sanctuary on earth was set up so that the worshiper would have their backs to the sun. God's sanctuary ministry has always been in direct opposition to sun worship and the paganism practiced in the world. That is why Satan has sought to inject these false religions into God's church.

The veil is also a symbol of Christ's flesh, for it is through the veil of His flesh that we approach the Father.

4. Jesus' arm of the throne is on the north side of the sanctuary. "Now of the things which we have spoken this is the sum: We have such an high priest, who is *set on the right hand of the throne* of the Majesty in the heavens" (Heb. 8:1). That Jesus' throne is on the north is why Satan declared his intention of sitting on the "sides of the north" (Isa. 14:13). The right side is the north side of the throne room. Satan was jealous of

Jesus and wanted His place in heaven. Satan wanted to "sit" in God's presence. He wanted to "be" Jesus in power but not in character.

5. Some critics of the Investigative Judgment act as if Adventists teach Jesus has been trapped in the holy place for 1800 years. This shows a lack of understanding when it comes to the nature of God and His relationship to time and space. God exists in all places, and Jesus was seated at the right hand of God when He ascended to heaven. He is in the Father and the Father is in Him. He cannot be separated from Him. The doors that the apostle saw in heaven (Rev. 4: 1; 11:19) were symbolically represented in the first and second veils in the earthly sanctuary. A heavenly door must be immense, but it is also symbolic of Jesus, the door through which we approach God. (See John 10:7, 9.)
6. The altar of incense is in the center of the sanctuary, in the middle of the other three thrones. The three arms are part of one whole throne.

   "For the Lamb which is *in the midst of the throne* shall feed them, and shall lead them unto living fountains of waters: and God shall wipe away all tears from their eyes" (Rev. 7:17).

   We just read that Paul connects the "golden censer" with the Most Holy Place (Heb. 9:4).[49] As our heavenly High Priest, Christ presents the prayers of the saints mixed with His righteousness. God's throne room is the place of judgment. Christ is in the midst of the throne, surrounded by a circle of elders, all of whom have censers to intercede for us before God. Jesus is our lawyer, judge, and Savior. The good news of the judgment is that the throne room is a place of perfect grace for every saint, where they are declared "not guilty"!
7. The throne room of God is an incredible place where even the greatest prophets fell down before God as dead men. It is a place of light, power, and the Shekinah glory. It reflects the beauty and light of God's holiness. There the Triune God reigns in all His majesty!
8. One day, God's throne will be on the New Earth. His throne room will be in the midst of an adoring planet. He will make a covenant of peace and no one will violate the everlasting covenant.

9. In those days, Jerusalem will be called the "throne of the Lord," and He will welcome all nations as they gather in the New Jerusalem to worship the Lord from one Sabbath to another for evermore! In the new earth, the Sabbath will be celebrated forever as part of the everlasting covenant!
10. God's throne is a place where God's people are vindicated by His perfect grace! We are free from sin and its consequences! God has ruled in our favor, declaring us righteous still forevermore!

The following Bible verses illustrate the New Covenant promises of glory.

- "Moreover I will make a covenant of peace with them; it shall be an *everlasting covenant* with them: and I will place them, and multiply them, and *will set my sanctuary in the midst of them for evermore*" (Ezek. 37:26)
- "*At that time they shall call Jerusalem the throne of the LORD; and all the nations shall be gathered unto it*, to the name of the LORD, to Jerusalem: neither shall they walk any more after the imagination of their evil heart." (Jer. 3:17)
- "For as the new *heavens and the new earth*, which I will make, shall remain before me, saith the LORD, so shall your seed and your name remain. And it shall come to pass, that from one new moon to another, and from *one Sabbath to another, shall all flesh come to worship before me, saith the LORD*." (Isa. 66:22, 23)

So, Jerusalem will be the location of the throne of the Lord, and all people will gather every Sabbath and every new moon, keeping God's holy Sabbath in the joy and perfection of the New Jerusalem (Isa. 66:23). We are going to have an apartment in the city and a home in the country. When you go up to Jerusalem you can come see Pastor Tom because, wherever there's a musical instrument used to praise the Lord, I'm going to be there! And I just might be one of those "beasts" praising the Lord for twenty-four hours a day, strumming my little harp! Once a week you will come into the great crystal city to worship God and then you will go back home. Now Revelation says that every new moon you are going to come to eat of the tree of life, and every month you are going to eat a different fruit (Rev. 22:2). So we're going to have a big, high celebration once a month, plus, we're going to enjoy the weekly Sabbath. And the Bible says that we are going to gather every week throughout all eternity. Where do these people get the idea that God taught Sabbath observance throughout the Old Testament, and the Sabbath was observed in the days of the apostles, but that, from the time of the apostles until the second coming and the new earth, it has been changed and then it will be changed back when Jesus comes, and we will keep it throughout eternity? I don't think so! The Bible consistently teaches that Saturday, the seventh day of the week, is the only weekly holy day we are commanded to keep.

It has been my hope, in this book, to present God to you in all His glory, seated upon His throne, making us the beneficiaries of His perfect grace as He has made us joint heirs with Christ. The message of the Seventh-day Adventist Church is a message of hope and vindication. The judgment of God is a judgment rendered in your favor by a loving God who has provided perfect grace through Jesus, giving you everything that you need to be saved. When you look upon Jesus, the Author and Finisher of your faith, and when you behold Him as He stands at the altar as the Lamb slain for your sins, know that He is standing there, pleading for your salvation. That is why we have to come to Him today! We have to accept His offer of salvation full and free. We have to choose whether we are going to serve the devil and his earthly pleasures or we are going to serve Christ, whether we are going to feed our minds on worldly things and indulge in worldly pleasures, the lust of the eyes, the pride of life, and the avarice of the world, or we are going to focus on the great heavenly ministry of Jesus, letting Him transform us from the inside out.

We have one mediator, one lawyer, one judge, one priest, one Sabbath, one baptism, one Savior, one faith, one gospel, one way, one truth, one life. It is through our great High Priest, Jesus Christ, who is standing at the altar. At this very time we need to go to Him to seek to become perfect in His righteousness while the door of mercy is swung wide on the hinges of perfect grace so that we can enter the ark of safety. And when the door swings closed, we will already be there, and our name will already be in God's book. If you seek Him now, you won't have to fear when He casts the censer down to the earth. Do it now, before it's too late!

"Behold I come quickly. Blessed is he that keepeth the sayings of the prophecy of this book" (Rev. 22:7). John named the book "Revelation," which means "revealed." Don't listen to those who say you can't understand it. Why would John name a book "revealed" if you are not supposed to understand it? Jesus said that He is going to come quickly. Do you know what He means by that? When He steps out of the sanctuary, it's over, and you will never even know it. You'll be buying a car or taking your kids to school. You'll be going to the grocery store and, just then, the judgment will have closed in heaven, and you will have no idea. I don't know how long the time of trouble and the seven last plagues will be—perhaps a week, two weeks, three weeks, or three months—but all during those plagues no one can be saved, and no one can be lost. By the time you know it, it will be over and it will be too late.

Why would John name a book "revealed" if you are not supposed to understand it?

The hour of His judgment is come. Worship Him who made the heavens, the earth, the sea and all that in them is. Don't worship the beast or his image. Don't accept the antichrist doctrines or the false prophet. "Come out of her, My people, that you be not partakers of her sins." If you are to "come out," you need to have a place to go. God has His true people in many religious organizations and in the world at large. However, the preaching of God's testing truth will someday separate the wheat from the tares. At that time, God's true people will come out and take their stand for the truth of the Bible. There's only one church you can attend if you want to hear *these biblical messages*, and that's the Seventh-day Adventist Church. Will you accept this message? Do you want Jesus to write your name down in the Lamb's book of life and save you when He comes? Is this the message that God wants you to have in the last days? Are you going to follow Christ or antichrist? May you follow Jesus, our great High Priest, into the most holy place, where God's law is in the ark of the covenant. May you see God's Sabbath there in the fourth commandment! May you reflect His mercy to your family, neighbors, and friends. May you show them the loving acceptance of God and teach them to keep the Ten Commandments by faith as only Jesus can teach us. Let us pray.

Father in heaven, Come into our hearts. Forgive us of our sins. We open the door of our heart and invite you in, and we ask that you write our name in the Lamb's book of life. Thank you for being a God who sits high upon your throne! We are so far beneath you! We worship you, O God. Convert us, transform us, and help us to spread this message in a way that will lead others into the true church that keeps the commandments of God and has the faith of Jesus. Thank you, Lord, for loving us and letting us be a part of your family even though we're unworthy and we don't deserve it. Even though we're not worthy, we're still glad that we are a part of your kingdom. Bless us now, we pray, and help us to witness to others about Jesus. May we lead many to you, we pray in Jesus' name, Amen.

Can you see God in all His glory, sitting upon His throne, and Jesus ministering before Him as our great High Priest? The message of Seventh-day Adventism is a message of hope and vindication! The judgment of God is a judgment rendered in our favor by a loving God who provided everything we need to be saved. Look upon Jesus, the Author and Finisher of your faith; behold Him as He stands at the altar as the Lamb slain for your sins! Behold Him there, pleading for your salvation. Come to Him today! Accept His offer of salvation, full and free! "Choose you this day whom ye will serve" (Joshua 24:15)! We have one mediator, one lawyer, one judge, one priest, one Lord, one Savior, one faith, one gospel, and *one* Way, Truth, and Life! It's Jesus Christ! This is present truth! This is the church from which the Reformation continues! This is the church from which God's last day message is proclaimed! The door into the most holy place is open! Come boldly to the throne of grace today!

CHAPTER 15

THE TABERNACLE OF HIS TESTIMONY, A TABERNACLE OF WORSHIP

In this chapter, we are going to study God's perfect grace as it is revealed in what the Bible refers to as the "*tabernacle of the testimony.*" What is "the testimony"? What is the tabernacle? What is the tabernacle of the testimony? What does it mean when God uses this expression, and what does it mean when John the Revelator uses this expression? What is the significance of this term for Seventh-day Adventists today? Let's begin by studying the fifteen verses where this expression is used. "In the *tabernacle* of the congregation without the vail, which is before the *testimony*, Aaron and his sons shall order it from evening to morning before the LORD: it shall be a statute for ever unto their generations on the behalf of the children of Israel" (Exod. 27:21). "And thou shalt anoint the *tabernacle* of the congregation therewith, and the ark of the *testimony*" (Exod. 30:26).

1. **What is "the testimony" referred to in these verses, and what is the ark of the testimony?**

   "And he gave unto Moses, when he had made an end of communing with him upon Mount Sinai, two tables of *testimony*, tables of stone, written with the finger of God" (Exod. 31:18)."And Moses turned, and went down from the mount, and *the two tables of the testimony were in his hand: the tables were written on both their sides*; on the one side and on the other were they written" (Exod. 32:15)."And it came to pass, when Moses came down from mount Sinai with *the two tables of testimony in Moses' hand*, when he came down from the mount, that Moses wist not that the skin of his face shone while he talked with him" (Exod. 34:29). "And he took and put the *testimony* into the ark, and set the staves on the ark, and *put the mercy seat above upon the ark*" (Exod. 40:20). We see from these verses that "the testimony" is the term the Bible uses to describe the two tables of stone that Moses brought down from the mountain where he communed with God. It is the Ten Commandment law that God wrote with His own finger on both sides of the stone tablets. Moses was given the Ten Commandments by the One who identified Himself as "I AM." "And God said unto Moses, I AM THAT I AM: and he said, Thus shalt thou say unto the children of Israel, I AM hath sent me unto you" (Exod. 3:14). So "I AM" wrote the commandments with His own finger. Jesus also identified Himself as "I AM." "Jesus said unto them, Verily, verily, I say unto you, Before Abraham was, I am" (John 8:58). This means that Jesus is the author of the Ten Commandments, a fact that is affirmed by James: "There is one lawgiver, who is able to save and to destroy: who art thou that judgest another?" (James 4:12). So, if there is one lawgiver, that means that God's law is Jesus' law. Let me say it as plainly as I can: The testimony is the law of God contained in the Ten Commandments, which God calls "my testimony" (Ps. 132:12). The "ark of the testimony" is the name that the Bible uses to describe the gold-plated box, with a lid called "the mercy seat," into which Moses placed the Ten Commandments. This gold lid was where the blood of the Lord's goat was sprinkled, making atonement for the sinners who broke the Ten Commandment law contained in the ark of His testimony.

2. **What is the "tabernacle"? And what is the "tabernacle of testimony"?** "And thou shalt beat some of it very small, and put of it before the *testimony* in the *tabernacle of the congregation*, where I will meet with thee: it shall be unto you most holy" (Exod. 30:36). "The *tabernacle of the congregation*, and *the ark of the testimony*, and *the mercy seat that is thereupon*, and all the furniture of the tabernacle" (Exod. 31:7).

   From these verses we learn that the tabernacle of the congregation is the earthly sanctuary that Moses made from the pattern that God showed him on the mountain of the heavenly sanctuary. We know that it was symbolic of the heavenly sanctuary by our next verse: "Who serve unto the example and shadow of heavenly things, as Moses was admonished of God when he was about to make the tabernacle: for, See, saith he, that thou make *all things according to the pattern shewed to thee in the mount*" (Heb. 8:5). Moses made *all things* according to the *pattern* that God showed him of His throne room. Later, we will see that this is true when we get to the book of Revelation. Thus, the earthly tabernacle is a symbolic model of the heavenly sanctuary.

   Let's examine the other verses describing the tabernacle of the testimony.

   "This is the sum of the tabernacle, even of the tabernacle of testimony, *as it* was counted, according to the commandment of Moses, for the service of the Levites, by the hand of Ithamar, son to Aaron the priest" (Exod. 38:21).

   "And thou shalt set the altar of gold for the incense before *the ark of the testimony*, and put the hanging of the door to the tabernacle" (Exod. 40:5).

   "And he brought the *ark into the tabernacle*, and set up the vail of the covering, and *covered the ark of the testimony*; as the LORD commanded Moses" (Exod. 40:21).

   "Without the *veil of the testimony*, in the *tabernacle of the congregation*, shall Aaron order it from the evening unto the morning before the LORD continually: it shall be a statute for ever in your generations" (Lev. 24:3).

"But thou shalt appoint the Levites over the *tabernacle of testimony*, and over all the vessels thereof, and over all things that belong to it: they shall bear the *tabernacle*, and all the vessels thereof; and they shall minister unto it, and shall encamp round about the *tabernacle*" (Num. 1:50).

"But the Levites shall pitch round about the *tabernacle of testimony*, that there be no wrath upon the congregation of the children of Israel: and the Levites shall keep the charge of the *tabernacle of testimony*" (Num. 1:53).

"And when Moses was gone into the *tabernacle of the congregation* to speak with him, then he heard the voice of one speaking unto him from off *the mercy seat* that was *upon the ark of testimony*, from between the two cherubims: and he spake unto him" (Num. 7:89).

"And on the day that the *tabernacle* was reared up the cloud covered the tabernacle, namely, the tent of the testimony: and at even there was upon the *tabernacle* as it were the appearance of fire, until the morning" (Num. 9:15).

"And it came to pass on the twentieth day of the second month, in the second year, that the cloud was taken up from off the *tabernacle of the testimony*" (Num. 10:11).

"And thou shalt lay them up in the *tabernacle of the congregation* before the *testimony*, where I will meet with you" (Num. 17:4).

From these verses we learn that the terms "tabernacle of the congregation" and "tabernacle of the testimony" are used to describe the symbolic earthly sanctuary that Moses built. It is called the "tabernacle of the testimony" because it contained the "*ark* of the testimony," the sacred Ten Commandments of the Lord God.

3. The tabernacle of the testimony today is in the heavenly sanctuary, and God's Ten Commandments are in the ark of the covenant as an everlasting covenant!

"And after that I looked, and, behold, the *temple of the tabernacle of the testimony in heaven* was opened" (Rev. 15:5). The fact that this verse describes the tabernacle of the testimony in heaven just as the seven last plagues are about to be poured out upon a rebellious world shows that God's Ten Commandment law is still the basis of His righteous judgments and that no one can do away with or alter His holy law. The same law that God gave Moses is still in heaven in the very throne of God, and it cannot be reached by sinful, fallen man. All of the Ten Commandments are still binding upon rebellious sinners, including God's fourth commandment. Human beings are to keep holy the seventh day of the week because it was blessed and set aside as holy by God himself, and the Sabbath commandment was written with God's own finger. Notice these key phrases in Revelation 11:19: "And the *temple of God was opened in heaven*, and there was seen *in his temple the ark of his testament:* and there were lightnings, and voices, and thunderings, and an earthquake, and great hail." Here, once again, we see the name, "*the ark of his testament*," and in Revelation 15:5, "*the tabernacle of his testimony*." Notice that John identified the ark as "His testament"—that is, *God's* testament! God is saying in Revelation that the tablets of stone, written on both sides by His finger, belong to Him! They are in heaven, where no human can alter them!

> ***The fact that this verse describes the tabernacle of the testimony in heaven just as the seven last plagues are about to be poured out upon a rebellious world shows that God's Ten Commandment law is still the basis of His righteous judgments and that no one can do away with or alter His holy law.***

4. **God calls His throne room "the temple of the tabernacle of the testimony in heaven."**

By this designation, He is telling the whole universe, "My very throne room, the most holy place in the universe, where I meet with my Son to decide the fate of all humankind, is the temple of the tabernacle of *My law, My mercy seat, and My ark of the everlasting covenant*"!

How dare any human say that God's law has been done away with! How dare any human say that God's Ten Commandments have been made void or altered! How dare any human try to take a chisel and hammer to the Sabbath commandment to try to deface and alter God's stone tablets! Back, I say! Away, I say! You cannot enter God's throne room to do your lawless deeds! You can gain no admittance there!

Now turn with me to the book of Isaiah, chapter 24, and verses 5 and 6:

"The *earth also is defiled* under the inhabitants thereof; because they have *transgressed the laws*, changed the ordinance, *broken the everlasting covenant.* Therefore hath the curse *devoured the earth*, and they that dwell therein are *desolate:* therefore the inhabitants of the earth are burned, and few men left" (Isa. 24:5, 6).

In the epistle to the Ephesians, Paul wrote: "Let no man deceive you with vain words: for because of these things cometh *the wrath of God upon the children of disobedience*" (Eph. 5:6).

The Bible has taught us today that the Ten Commandments of God are still in heaven, in the heart of God's throne room, in His temple, inside the ark of His testament in the tabernacle of His testimony. God has revealed them in the context of the seven last plagues being poured out upon the world because the inhabitants of earth have transgressed God's law and broken the everlasting covenant, which is inside the ark of the covenant. God's wrath will be poured out upon them because they are the "children of disobedience." Paul declares: "Let no man deceive you." Sin is still the transgression of God's law. Repent of your sins! Ask God to sprinkle the blood of Jesus upon the mercy seat for you! Let Jesus give you *His righteousness* as a free gift! Then, if you love Jesus, keep His commandments. Do your best to walk in the *fruit* of the Spirit and not in the lawbreaker's works of the flesh! Do your best to be an obedient child of God, honoring God's commandments, including the one that reminds us of the Sabbath's sanctity, which the world has trampled upon. Do not rest in your own works, but walk in "the obedience of faith" (Rom. 16:26) as a sign that He is the God that "makes you holy" (Exod. 31:13, NLT). The Sabbath that is kept by "resting in the works of Jesus" is yours by faith, making you a perfect Sabbath keeper, for He is our righteousness!

"Behold, I come quickly: blessed is he that keepeth the sayings of the prophecy of this book" (Rev. 22:7).

We walk by faith, saved by perfect grace, transformed by the Spirit, and adopted as the undeserving children of the King, joint heirs with Christ! May you be among those who "keep the commandments of God, and the faith of Jesus" (Rev. 14:12). May you daily commune with the great High Priest of the heavenly tabernacle and be redeemed through His intercession on your behalf. Come quickly, Lord Jesus, *come!* Amen and Amen!

PERFECT GRACE!

PART III
HEAVENLY WORSHIP

Saying with a loud voice, Fear God, and give glory to him; for the hour of his judgment is come: and worship him that made heaven, and earth, and the sea, and the fountains of waters.
—Revelation 14:7

Whenever you talk with people about worship in the church, they usually have strong opinions about what is acceptable in the divine service and are not shy about expressing those opinions. Questions about when to worship, who can conduct worship, what instruments can be played, and what beat can be used when they are played are among the many questions that arise. People may know quite a bit about when to worship God, and they know what musical styles they prefer and even what instruments they think are acceptable, but I am always saddened that many do not know what the Bible actually teaches on the subject. God's perfect grace should be at the very heart of our worship, shouldn't it? Shouldn't we be gracious with our fellow believers regarding the way they choose to express their worship of God? Wouldn't grace cause us not to be unkind or judgmental to young people who may prefer a different form of worship than older church members? Sadly we have often not been gracious at all.

After I had baptized several people of Pentecostal persuasion, a lady church member asked me at a board meeting: "Please make them stop lifting their hands in the air during worship; it's distracting." After I shared several Bible texts with the sister that made it clear that God is pleased and even commands this style of worship, she changed her mind and accepted the practice. She said that she would never feel comfortable doing it herself but that she could accept their expression of faith. This was a courageous and heartfelt attitude change, and I respect her to this day for modifying her views based on the Bible. Another woman told me that the lifting of hands in worship greatly offended her. I said, "Do you realize that the Bible teaches this practice?" She said, "Show me in the Bible where it says that." So I did just that. After six verses that made it crystal clear, she stopped me and said, "Bible or no Bible, I'm not raising my hands." I said, "Well, that settles it then for you, doesn't it!"

This was a courageous and heartfelt attitude change, and I respect her to this day for modifying her views based on the Bible.

Initially, neither of these ladies knew anything about what the Bible actually teaches about worship practices. It is not a subject that is preached about often. Opinions abound on these matters, but serious Bible study is lacking. All these questions are valid and deserve a biblical answer. But just because a person knows *when* to worship God does not mean that he or she knows *how* to worship God. What does the Bible actually teach concerning the *who* and the *how* of worship? In the rest of this book, we will endeavor to mine from God's Word the gold on the subject of worship. We will make the Bible our baseline and judge all other opinions and theories by the Bible. The only true worship *is* biblical and grace oriented! If it isn't both of these, then it isn't worship at all. Only what the Bible teaches concerning worship is *true* worship. Jesus said, "*Thou shalt worship* the Lord thy God, and him only shalt thou serve" (Luke 4:8). Jesus *commands* us to worship God. It isn't optional! Then, in John 4, Jesus says: "But the hour cometh, and now is, when the *true worshippers shall worship the Father in spirit and in truth: for the Father seeketh such to worship him.* God is a Spirit: and *they that worship him must worship him in spirit and in truth*" (John 4:23, 24). We learn several important things here. There are true worshippers, and it is possible to worship God in a way that pleases Him. He wants your worship to be Spirit led and truthful. We learn that God is seeking people who worship Him this way! He is looking for those who are filled with the Spirit and who base their worship experience on the principles taught in His word. We also learn that we *must* worship Him in spirit and in truth.

If we want to please God, worship is not something that we can choose to ignore or simply not participate in. He is seeking a relationship with those who are willing to follow biblical principles of worship and obey His commandment to worship and serve Him only. Why should we worship Him? The reasons are infinite and books abound on why God is worthy of our worship. Churches and ministers alike are not hesitant to tell us what we should do and to reprimand us for not doing it. However, they rarely ever tell us *how* to do it! Because of the contemporary Christian movement that is reaching young people by the millions, some in the traditional church feel very threatened by the changes in style of popular music today. The fear of change and a longing for a simpler time when there was no question or controversy about music are all normal fears and emotions. Churches are infamous for saying the seven last words of a dying church: "We've never done it like that before"! However, just because we find change uncomfortable or a new or different style of music a challenge doesn't give us the right to make our opinions the standard by which to judge others. We are not to hold up our own tastes and opinions as the guide for such questions. The only true standard and guide for the Christian is the Word of God. The Bible and the Bible *only* must be our rule of faith and practice. Churches that used to ban a gospel song track with wonderful lyrics because there is a drum on the track suddenly were being challenged and pressured to allow music that they had always rejected in the past. Suddenly, the popularity and passion of the young people was being brought to bear upon the church in a whole new way. Books have been written about these "worship wars," chronicling the splits and separations that have taken place. It's been very disheartening to see people taking polarizing stands that have only divided the church as those people have imposed their beliefs on those who disagree with them. Can we as a people stop arguing about what "we think" and start putting in the hard work to explore and understand the subject from a biblical perspective? We have already demonstrated that all our worship is imperfect and unacceptable to God except when presented through Christ's righteousness and God's perfect grace. But what does the Bible say our worship should look and sound like?

Can we worship God with passion and awe, like the Roman centurion who accepted Jesus at the cross because of Christ's forgiveness of His enemies? The Centurion was so moved he had to exclaim: "Truly this man was the Son of God" (Mark 15:39).

If we can do this, we will be pleasantly surprised to learn what the Bible has to say about norms for worship. It is my hope that the last section of this book will open a window that lets in more light than heat! We will want to stay locked in like a laser beam upon the Word of God. Once you've prayerfully studied the following chapters and, more importantly, the Bible verses contained therein, I pray that it will encourage you in your quest to worship the Father in spirit and in truth. May it help you to understand the *what* and the *how* of worship, and may it help you find a new and deeper way to the Father who is seeking you to worship Him in spirit and in truth. Worship is only true if it is practiced through God's perfect grace alone. This is my prayer for you today.

CHAPTER 16

HEAVEN-DIRECTED BIBLICAL WORSHIP IN THE DIVINE SERVICE

Sing aloud unto God our strength: make a joyful noise unto the God of Jacob. Take a psalm, and bring hither the timbrel, the pleasant harp with the psaltery.
—David

The Bible teaches that stringed and percussion instruments belong in our worship services, in the house of God, because they were commanded to be used there by God Himself. Consider the following amazing statement from *The Desire of Ages:*

> When He spoke these words, *Jesus was in the court of the temple specially connected with the services of the feast of tabernacles*. In the center of this court rose two lofty standards, supporting *lampstands* of great size. After the evening sacrifice, all the lamps were kindled, shedding their light over Jerusalem. This ceremony was in commemoration of the pillar of light that guided Israel in the desert, and was also regarded as pointing to the coming of the Messiah. At evening when the lamps were lighted, *the court was a scene of great rejoicing*. Gray-haired

> men, the priests of the temple and the rulers of the people, united in the *festive dances to the sound of instrumental music* and the chants of the Levites. (*Desire of Ages*, p. 463)

Now that's quite a picture! Right next to the lampstand in the courts of the tabernacle there was great rejoicing, festive dancing and instrumental music accompanying their chants! And we have just begun! Now let us learn from God's Word *how* to worship! Let me remind you that the *only reason* God accepts our worship at all is because of His perfect grace. Worship without grace isn't worship at all! It's an abomination! All our worship is unacceptable to God, unless purified by the righteousness of Christ (*Selected Messages*, vol. 1, pp. 344, 345). So, now let us take our Bibles and read some verses, letting them speak for themselves. As we read these verses, you will get a sense of what the Bible is trying to teach you about the kind of instruments God wants in His church. They will make His will obvious if we only read what He says.

"After that you shall come to the hill of God where the Philistine garrison is. And it will happen, when you have come there to the city, that you will meet *a group of prophets* coming down from the high place *with a stringed instrument, a tambourine, a flute, and a harp* before them; and they will be prophesying" (1 Sam. 10:5, NKJV).

"Then David spoke to the leaders of the Levites to appoint their brethren to be the singers accompanied by instruments of music, *stringed instruments*, harps, and *cymbals*, by raising the voice with *resounding joy*. The singers, Heman, Asaph, and Ethan, were to sound the cymbals of bronze; ... Thus all Israel brought up the ark of the covenant of the LORD with *shouting and with the sound of the horn, with trumpets and with cymbals, making music with stringed instruments and harps*" (1 Chron. 15:16, 19, 28, NKJV).

"Asaph the chief, and next to him Zechariah, then Jeiel, Shemiramoth, Jehiel, Mattithiah, Eliab, Benaiah, and Obed-Edom: Jeiel with *stringed instruments and harps, but Asaph made music with cymbals*; ... and with them Heman and Jeduthun, to sound aloud with trumpets and cymbals and the musical instruments *of God*. Now the sons of Jeduthun were gatekeepers" (1 Chron. 16:5, 42, NKJV).

Notice that Asaph didn't just mark the rhythm with the cymbals, he "made music" with them. God's prophets also played cymbals, harps, stringed instruments, flutes, and horns, all with resounding joy! These verses describe a joyful God who is pleased when we get enthusiastic in worshipping Him!

"... and the Levites who were the singers, all those of Asaph and Heman and Jeduthun, with their sons and their brethren, stood at the east end *of the altar*, clothed in white linen, having cymbals, stringed instruments and harps, and with them one hundred and twenty priests sounding with trumpets—indeed it came to pass, when the trumpeters and singers were as one, to make one sound to be heard in praising and thanking the Lord, and when they lifted up their voice *with* the trumpets and cymbals *and instruments of music*, and praised the Lord, saying: 'For He is good, for His mercy endures forever,' that the house, the house of the Lord, was filled with a cloud, so that the priests could not continue ministering because of the cloud; for *the glory of the Lord filled the house of God*" (2 Chron. 5:12–14, NKJV).

This passage shows that God was pleased with the cymbals and the music that He had just heard and His response was so glorious that the priests couldn't even continue to minister! In other words, God enjoyed the music! The priests were playing those instruments by the holy altar, and God's glory filled the house of God! If God were displeased with those instruments, He wouldn't have done that. Here is more:

> Now when Athaliah heard the noise of the people running and praising the king, she came to the people *in the temple of the Lord*. When she looked, there was the king standing by his pillar at the entrance; and the leaders and the trumpeters were by the king. All the people of the land were rejoicing and blowing trumpets, also the singers with musical instruments, and those

who led in praise. So Athaliah tore her clothes and said, "Treason! Treason!" (2 Chron. 23:12–13, NKJV)

And the Lord listened to Hezekiah and healed the people. So the children of Israel who were present at Jerusalem kept the Feast of Unleavened Bread seven days with *great gladness*; and the Levites and the priests praised the LORD day by day, singing to the LORD, accompanied by *loud instruments*. Then the whole assembly agreed to keep the feast another seven days, and they kept it another seven days *with gladness*. (2 Chron. 30:20, 21, 23, NKJV)

Now at the dedication of the wall of Jerusalem they sought out the Levites in all their places, to bring them to Jerusalem *to celebrate* the dedication with gladness, both with thanksgivings and singing, with *cymbals and stringed instruments and harps*. also Maaseiah, Shemaiah, Eleazar, Uzzi, Jehohanan, Malchijah, Elam, and Ezer. The singers *sang loudly* with Jezrahiah the director. Also that day they offered great sacrifices, and rejoiced, for *God had made them rejoice with great joy; the women and the children also rejoiced, so that the joy of Jerusalem was heard afar off*. (Neh. 12:27, 42, 43, NKJV)

Let's summarize this section of Scripture. The musicians made music with great gladness using loud instruments within the temple! They sang loudly, using stringed instruments and harps, and they celebrated with gladness and thanksgiving. I think it is wonderful the way it says, "God made them rejoice with great joy"! The whole family rejoiced, and they heard them "afar off"!

They sang loudly, using stringed instruments and harps, and they celebrated with gladness and thanksgiving.

The Use of Percussion Instruments in the Divine Worship Service

Critiques of the newer praise music often make the mistake of comparing the "sanctuary service" of the priests in the Holy Place and Most Holy Place with the church service of today. However, the people themselves never entered the Holy Place or Most Holy Place—only the priests. You cannot compare our present-day church service to the services of the Holy Place and the Most Holy Place. That's comparing apples and oranges—two different categories of worship. The sanctuary in heaven, when compared to the symbolic service of the earthly sanctuary of the Old Testament, is apples to apples. The "house of God" is not an earthly sanctuary in the Old Testament sense. Oranges to oranges would be to compare our church services with the people's court. The court is where the worship services were held. The people were allowed in the outer courts, and that is where they would gather, as well as surrounding the sanctuary compound. It was in this "assembly" that the people would sing the psalms of David.

Leviticus indicates that women were allowed in the sanctuary courtyard except during the prescribed number of days in the month that they were unclean. This was the outer area, not the Holy Place or the Holy of Holies. (See Lev. 12:4.)

During this study, I will reference books by some popular critics of contemporary praise music. In one such book, entitled *Drums, Rock, and Worship*, the author Karl Tsatalbasidis wrote, "Notice that the drum is used only on festive occasions in the Bible, and never in connection with divine service or worship. They also were systematically excluded from the Jerusalem Temple" (p. 44). (The only "drum" that is mentioned in Scripture is the *tof*, which is translated "tabret," "timbrel," or "tamborine," even though the jingling instrument we may think of did not come into existence until the Roman period. The *tof* was the hand-held instrument that Miriam and the other women used in celebrating Israel's deliverance from Pharaoh in Exodus 15:20.) Here the author is referencing another prominent contemporary music critic.[50] Unfortunately, what they are saying is misleading. While, strictly speaking, the word "drum" does not appear in Scripture, there is no scripture or statement of Ellen White that outlaws any percussive instruments. In fact, the Bible specifically states that cymbals, which is a brass percussion instrument just under five inches in diameter, were used "in the house of the Lord," and "in the *service* of the house of the Lord."

Stringed instruments, like the guitar and piano, as well as cymbals, are useable in the service of God's house. (The piano is a stringed instrument that is played by percussion.) God reveals His perfect grace in the way that He accepts musical instruments that some of His followers condemn without justification. The instruments are acceptable. It's the way that they are sometimes played that is not. Praise songs that reveal God's perfect grace and that praise Him with power and reverence are acceptable to God. Let us continue with the next verses.

> Moreover David and the captains of the army separated for the service some of the sons of Asaph, of Heman, and of Jeduthun, who should *prophesy with harps, stringed instruments, and cymbals*. And the number of the skilled men performing their service was: … Of Jeduthun … who *prophesied with a harp* to give thanks and to praise the LORD. All these were under the direction of their father for the music *in the house of the LORD, with cymbals*, stringed instruments, and harps, for *the service of the house of God*. Asaph, Jeduthun, and Heman were under the authority of the king. (1 Chron. 25:1, 3, 6, NKJV)

Notice how cymbals were used: "for the music *in the house of the Lord, with cymbals*, stringed instruments, and harps, for *the service of the house of God*."

It's as if God was making sure that we all would get it—not just *in* the house of the Lord, but "*for the service* of the house of God." Can there be any doubt that God is pleased, when the instruments He commanded are used for the service of His house? There was nothing wrong with using them then, and there is nothing wrong with using them correctly now.

> And he stationed *the Levites in the house of the LORD with cymbals*, with stringed instruments, and with harps, according to the commandment of David, of Gad the king's seer, and of Nathan the prophet; *for thus was the commandment of the LORD* by His prophets. The Levites stood with the instruments of David, and the priests with the trumpets. Then Hezekiah commanded them to offer the burnt offering on the altar. And *when the burnt offering began*, the *song of the LORD also began*, with the trumpets and *with the instruments* of David king of Israel. So they sang praises with gladness, and they bowed their heads *and worshiped*. (2 Chron. 29:25–27, 30, NKJV)

Is it not also clear that these instruments were used to preach or prophesy with and that they were used in connection with the sanctuary? This text shows that, when the priest in the sanctuary service offered the burnt offering, the song of the Lord was played, according to God's commandment, accompanied by cymbals, *in the sanctuary*. There is obviously nothing wrong in using instruments that God commanded to be used, in the way that God allowed. Though they need to be played properly, there is nothing wrong with using them in the house of God.

That is why 2 Chronicles 5:14 says that God's glory filled the house of the Lord with such brilliance that the priests had to leave. God obviously approved of the cymbals they used!

The timbrel was also used in the sanctuary to praise God.

> They have seen Your procession, O God, the procession of my God, my King, *into the sanctuary*. The singers went before, the players on instruments followed after; among them were *the maidens playing timbrels*. (Ps. 68:24, 25, NKJV)

According to this text, the timbrel was played in the sanctuary. Women entered the sanctuary, and played timbrels. It wasn't just "paid musicians," as some suggest. In the New Testament, there is no earthly priesthood. Based on Scripture, we now believe in the priesthood of all believers (Exod. 19:6; 1 Peter 2:9). The ministry of music is open to any musician who has been elected by the church.

If timbrels could be used for worship in the Old Testament, then they are not an evil instrument. What is important is the way that they are played. Notice that timbrels are in the Psalms (68:25), which were written for public worship in the house of God and in the assembly of the saints. We are commanded to praise God in the sanctuary on the timbrel, on the loud cymbals and on the clashing cymbals (Ps. 150:5). We are even instructed to let the children of Zion be joyful and to let them praise him on the timbrel and the harp (Ps. 81:2; 149:3).

> Praise the LORD! *Praise God in His sanctuary*; praise Him in His mighty firmament! Praise Him for His mighty acts; praise Him according to His excellent greatness! Praise Him with the sound of the trumpet; praise Him with the lute and harp! Praise Him with the *timbrel* and dance; praise Him with stringed instruments and flutes! Praise Him with *loud cymbals*; praise Him with *clashing cymbals!* Let everything that has breath praise the Lord. Praise the Lord! (Ps. 150:1–6, NKJV)
>
> Praise the Lord! Sing to the LORD *a new song*, and His praise *in the assembly of saints*. Let Israel rejoice in their Maker; *let the children of Zion be joyful in their King*. Let them praise His name with the dance; *let them sing praises to Him with the timbrel and harp*. (Ps. 149:1–3, NKJV)

We should not forbid that which the Bible does not forbid, nor should we condemn that which the Bible does not condemn. Opponents of the worshipful music played today by our young people need to heed these

Bible verses and stop their "guilt by association" smear tactics of condemnation. All new music is not "rock," and a "trap set" is just a grouping of cymbals and "timbrels." They are similar to biblical musical instruments and can be used to glorify God or not, depending on the way they are played. To say that they can be played separately, but not grouped together to make it easier to play does not make sense. One timbrel or ten, they are approved of, as long as they are played properly. A timbrel is a type of drum. They are both round pieces of wood with a goatskin stretched across the top. Timbrels are often referred to as "hand drums." Can our church members learn to extend God's perfect grace to our youth and encourage them to worship God with enthusiasm and passion, even if it's different than what we have always done before?

It is not good that some writers use the muck they find in the music community to try to smear all Christian contemporary music. Some groups are worldly, and we should not use their music in worship. However, much contemporary praise music is very uplifting. We need to learn to be discriminating in what music we listen to and not just condemn anything that's new. We can use music for a variety of purposes. Some music that we can listen to on the treadmill, jogging five miles, would not be appropriate for worship services and vice versa. We need to have a mature attitude about these cultural issues. Christian freedom in the gospel of Jesus Christ gives us the power of choice, and our musical tastes can be diverse. People are moved in different ways by different music.

You don't need to be a scholar to interpret these texts. Ellen White instructs us to let the Bible interpret itself by using the simple and most obvious meaning. Anyone can understand the texts' meaning. Opponents often use a multitude of words to try to get around and explain away the straightforward meaning of these texts. Don't fall for their tactics. Some are great lawyers, who can argue forever about semantics and language. But when you read these texts prayerfully, you can hear God's voice speaking. A multitude of words does not lesson the power of one "Thus saith the Lord"! We are free to use any of these instruments in a responsible way. Let us love one another in perfect grace!

To the modern church of Israel, the assembly of His saints, God says:

> Sing to the Lord a new song,
> And His praise in the assembly of the saints,
> *Let Israel* rejoice in their Maker.
> Let the children of Zion be joyful in their King....
> *Let them sing praises to Him with the timbrel and harp.*
> (Ps. 149:1–3)

These Bible verses demonstrate that percussion instruments were often used in Jewish worship, both outside the temple and in the house of God, that is, in God's temple, the very sanctuary of God. Remember Ellen White's statement, "At evening when the lamps were lighted, the court was a scene of great rejoicing. Gray-haired men, the priests of the temple and the rulers of the people, united in the festive dances to the sound of instrumental music and the chants of the Levites" (*The Desire of Ages*, p. 463). If Israel's seniors, priests, and rulers could engage in great rejoicing, including dances with accompaniment, shouldn't we be able to encourage enthusiastic worship today? Contrary to what some teach, women played a vital part in that worship. "They have seen thy goings, O God; even the goings of my God, my King, in the sanctuary. The singers went before, the players on instruments followed after; among them were the damsels playing with timbrels" (Ps. 68:24, 25). God received the worship of women playing hand drums in the sanctuary and rejoicing enthusiastically near the Ark of the Covenant. The sheer number of references to these instruments in the Bible shows that it was God's intention that they be used in His worship. They were "commanded by the Lord" and by His prophets. These instruments were used in the very sanctuary of God and in the assembly of the people to bring power and life to their music. This is shown by the references to loud and clashing cymbals. Exuberant praise and worship was something that God had no problem enjoying from His people. He commanded it. Sing a new song, rejoice, be joyful, and praise Him upon the drum and the harp, *in the assembly of the saints!*

So let us worship God with exuberance and joy, not with bedlam, not with noise, not with a din of confusion, but with music played in an uplifting and proper manner. Our music should add to the message and not take away from it. Instruments should enhance the music rather than dominate it. We should not condemn the use of these instruments or "accompaniment tracks" just because there is a cymbal or drum in the background, adding to the power and movement of the song. Can music be done properly? Of course it can. Is it hard for people to change and adjust to new ways? Of course it is. Just remember that "In the Garden" and "How Great Thou Art" were new songs once! Some of the new worship music will be looked at in the same way by the young generation years from now.

Instruments should enhance the music rather than dominate it.

O God, please bless us as we learn to grow and mature as a church, using our freedom of choice in a responsible way and not letting fear and ignorance keep us from showing perfect grace by being supportive and understanding of one another. May modern Israel "let the children" be joyful in their King, and let them sing praises to Him with the cymbal, timbrel, stringed instruments and harp is my prayer in Jesus' name, Amen!

CHAPTER 17

THE SPIRIT OF PROPHECY'S MOST FAMOUS MUSIC STATEMENT

A bedlam of noise shocks the senses and perverts that which if conducted aright might be a blessing.... Satan works amid the din and confusion of such music, which, properly conducted, would be a praise and glory to God.
—Ellen G. White

Ellen White has much to say about music in her writings. Most of what she said has been quoted extensively. However, it has always been implied that she would be against shouting and percussion instruments because of the most widely quoted statements found in the chapter, "Early Fanaticism to be Repeated," in *Selected Messages*, vol. 2, pp. 26–38. Compilations often reflect the opinions of those who do the compiling. The titles and emphasis can be used to characterize something in a negative way. So let's look at this statement, and see if it isn't saying more than the usually emphasized portions would suggest. Here is the statement. The emphasis is mine.

Worship with a Bedlam of Noise

It is impossible to estimate too largely the work that the Lord will accomplish through His proposed vessels in carrying out His mind and purpose. The things you have described as taking place in Indiana, the Lord has shown me would take place just before the close of probation. Every *uncouth* thing will be demonstrated. There will be shouting, with *drums*, music, and dancing. The senses of rational beings will become so confused that they cannot be trusted to make right decisions. And this is called the moving of the Holy Spirit.

The Holy Spirit never reveals itself in such methods, in such a *bedlam of noise*. This is an invention of Satan to cover up his ingenious methods for making of none effect the pure, sincere, elevating, ennobling, sanctifying truth for this time. Better never have the worship of God blended with music than to use musical instruments to do the work which *last January* was represented to me would be brought into our camp meetings. The truth for this time needs nothing of this kind in its work of converting souls. A *bedlam of noise shocks the senses* and perverts *that which if conducted aright might be a blessing*. The powers of satanic agencies blend with the din and noise, to have a carnival, and this is termed the Holy Spirit's working.... No encouragement should be given to *this* kind of worship. The same kind of influence came in after the passing of the time in 1844. The same kind of representations were made. Men became excited, and were worked by a power thought to be the power of God.

History of the Past to Be Repeated

I will not go into all the painful history; it is too much. But last January the Lord showed me that erroneous theories and

> methods would be brought into our camp meetings, and that the history of the past would be repeated. I felt greatly distressed. I was instructed to say that at these demonstrations demons in the form of men are present, working with all the ingenuity that Satan can employ to make the truth disgusting to sensible people; that the enemy was trying to arrange matters so that the camp meetings, which have been the means of bringing the truth of the third angel's message before multitudes, should lose their force and influence.
>
> The third angel's message is to be given in straight lines. It is to be kept free from every thread of the *cheap, miserable inventions* of men's theories, prepared by the father of lies, and disguised as was the brilliant serpent used by Satan as a medium of deceiving our first parents. Thus Satan tries to put his stamp upon the work God would have stand forth in purity.
>
> The Holy Spirit has nothing to do with such a *confusion of noise and multitude of sounds* as passed before me last January. Satan works amid the *din and confusion of such music*, which, *properly conducted, would be a praise and glory to God*. He makes its effect like the poison sting of the serpent.
>
> Those things which have been in the past will be in the future. Satan will make music a snare *by the way in which it is conducted*. God calls upon His people, who have the light before them in the Word and in the Testimonies, to read and consider, and to take heed" (Lt. 132, 1900, in *Selected Messages*, vol. 2, pp. 36–38).

Now let's study the meaning of this passage. What is she speaking against in this passage? Is it the instruments that were used, or was it how the instruments were played? She is not speaking against any musical instrument. She is rebuking the irresponsible use of these instruments to create bedlam and noise. Notice these words: "uncouth," "bedlam of noise," "cheap," "miserable inventions," "confusion of noise, and multitude of sounds," "din," "shocks the senses," "confusion," and "a snare." The music she heard that January was absolute bedlam and would be inappropriate for use in any of God's services.

But notice what she did not say. She did not say that the drums were bedlam. Rather, she said that the music created on them at that meeting was bedlam. This is indicated in her statement, "A *bedlam of noise shocks the senses* and perverts *that which if conducted aright might be a blessing*."

She is talking about the way the music was created. If drums are played "aright," they can be a blessing, according to her statement. She continues: "Satan works amid the *din and confusion of such music*, which, *properly conducted, would be a praise and glory to God*" (*Selected Messages*, bk. 2, p. 37). Here she says that, if the instruments that are creating the din and confusion were properly conducted, they would be a praise and glory to God. Again she says, "Satan will make music a snare *by the way in which it is conducted*."

Here she says that, if the instruments that are creating the din and confusion were properly conducted, they would be a praise and glory to God.

Christian contemporary music that falls into the category of "uncouth, bedlam of noise, cheap, miserable inventions, confusion of noise, and multitude of sounds, din, shocks the senses, confusion, and a snare" should never be introduced into our services. Having said that, the critics of modern worship music rarely draw much distinction between the different types of music found in our churches. They usually just condemn all music containing any use of percussion instruments with a very broad brush. What I am advocating is a more mature approach to the issue of contemporary music of any kind. All music categories are artificial and arbitrary. What is it that makes music "Christian" per se? Isn't it *the lyrics* that make a song "Christian"? Without lyrics, there is no way to tell whether it is Christian or not. Ben Franklin is reported to have said that there is no point in arguing over matters of opinion because one cannot account for taste. There are many "tastes" people have in music. We need to be open to using biblical instruments in a proper, yet enthusiastic way and not try to forbid what God does not forbid. We are not to "add to" His Word.

We should agree to only use music that does not fall into the negative category described, but not to forbid contemporary Christian music that is conducted "aright." The use of cymbals or drums does not make it unfit for worship. It is only when they are played in an improper manner that they are a noisy din. The instrument can be used to create chaos or to glorify God. It is all in the manner in which it is used. So it is clear from this passage that we are not forbidden to use percussion instruments, if we conduct them "aright." It is my prayer that we will be tolerant of others while being careful to not allow the proper use of drums to dominate the music or give the music a sensuous or shocking quality. People on both sides of this issue must pray much and not allow the demagogues to market fear and mistrust of one another. Those who most often feel it is their place to tell others what to listen to and play are often extremely strict people who manifest very little joy or praise in their ministries. Often they are very narrow in their interpretation of issues and give little credibility to anyone who differs with them.

We don't need others trying to force us into compliance with their personal music checklist. Neither do we need them to try to tell us what we have to believe. As Christians we can study the Bible for ourselves, and we can read the Spirit of Prophecy. God will surely help us to come to some reasonable and sound conclusions if we allow the Holy Spirit to guide us into all truth.

CHAPTER 18

BIBLICAL WORSHIP AND EXUBERANT PRAISE

I desire therefore that the men pray everywhere,
lifting up holy hands, without wrath and doubting.
—1 Timothy 2:8, NKJV

Ellen White echoed this biblical exhortation when she wrote: "God is holy, and we must pray, 'lifting up holy hands without wrath or doubting' " (*In Heavenly Places*, p. 71). In addition, God commands us in His sanctuary during the divine service to clap our hands! "*Oh, clap your hands, all you peoples! Shout to God* with the voice of triumph!... Sing praises to God, sing praises! Sing praises to our King, sing praises!" (Ps. 47:1, 6, NKJV). Then in Psalm 63:4, the psalmist proclaims in the sanctuary, "I will *lift up my hands* in your name.... my mouth shall praise you with joyful lips." In Psalm 66:1, he declares, "Make a joyful shout to God, all the earth!" In Psalm 98, we read: "Oh, sing to the Lord a new song! ... Shout joyfully to the LORD, all the earth; break forth in song, rejoice, and sing praises. Sing to the LORD with the harp, with the harp and the sound of a psalm, with trumpets and the sound of a horn; shout joyfully before the LORD, the King" (Ps. 98:1, 4–6, NKJV). Psalm 147 through 149 describe praising God on the harp and with dance, the tambourine, and the harp *"in the assembly of the saints"* (Ps. 149:1, NKJV). Psalm 150 says to praise him *in His sanctuary* with the trumpet, lute, harp, tambourine, dance, stringed instruments, flutes, loud cymbals, and high cymbals. It ends by saying, "Let everything that has breath praise the LORD. Praise the LORD!"

Ellen G. White on Joy and Praise

Some think of the prophetess as a cold, sour-faced person who was always telling young people to stop having fun! Nothing could be further from the truth! Let's look at a side of her that you may never have had the opportunity to examine.

"As Christians we ought to praise God more than we do.... The melody of praise is the atmosphere of heaven: Let there be singing in the home, of songs that are sweet and pure, fewer words of censure and more of cheerfulness and hope and joy.... catch the themes of praise and thanksgiving from the heavenly choir round about the throne ... what joy the angels would look down from heaven upon us if we were *all* praising God ... begin to sing the song of praise and rejoicing here below.... Let your *lips* be tuned to praise God.... Angels in heaven are praising God *all the time* and ... mortals ... offer no song of praise.... If you sit in heavenly places with Christ, you cannot refrain from praising God. Begin to educate *your tongues to praise Him* and *train* your hearts to make melody to God; and when the evil one begins to settle his gloom about you sing praise to God.... Satan will leave you.... We need to offer praise and thanksgiving to God, not only in the congregation but in the home.... We need to *praise God much more than we do. We are to show that we have cause for rejoicing.... By our failure*

***Begin to educate your tongues to praise Him** and **train** your hearts to make melody to God; and when the evil one begins to settle his gloom about you sing praise to God.*

to express gratitude we are dishonoring our Maker" (*Heavenly Places*, pp. 94–96, 101).

"Make a joyful shout to the LORD all you lands" (Ps. 100:1).

"Sunday the power of God came upon us like a mighty rushing wind. *All* arose upon their feet and praised God with a *loud voice*; it was something as it was when the foundation of the house of God was laid. *The voice of weeping could not be told from the voice of shouting*. It was a triumphant time; all were strengthened and refreshed. I never witnessed such a powerful time before" (Lt. 28, 1850, to the church in Brother Hastings' home, November 7, 1850). "Our last conference was one of deep interest. Two were dug from beneath the rubbish. The present truth was presented in its clear light and it found way to the hearts of the erring. Before the meeting closed all were upon their knees, some were crying for mercy that had been cold-hearted and indifferent, others were begging for a closer walk with God and for salvation. It was a powerful time as I ever witnessed; the slaying power of God was in our midst. *Shouts of victory filled the dwelling*. The saints here seem to be rising and growing in grace and the knowledge of the truth" (Lt. 30, 1850, to Brother and Sister Loveland, December 13, 1850).

"*Singing, I saw, often drove away the enemy and shouting would beat him back*. I saw that pride had crept in among you, and there was not childlike simplicity among you. The fear of man, I saw, must all go" (Ms. 5a, 1850, "To the Church in Your Place," July, 1850). "I saw we must be daily rising and [must] keep the ascendancy above the powers of darkness. I saw singing to the glory of God often drove the enemy away and shouting *would beat him back and give us the victory*. I saw that there was too little glorifying God, too little childlike simplicity among the remnant" (Ms. 5, 1850, "A Vision the Lord Gave Me at Oswego," July 29, 1850).

"The glory of the Lord shone about us, and we all rejoiced and triumphed in God for His unbounded goodness to us. *All* in the room were blest and *shouted the praise of God*" (Lt. 9, 1853, to Sister Kellogg, December 5, 1853).

"Father's face was lighted up with the glory of God. Sister Ings felt His power as never before. *We all shouted the praise of God*. It was *weeping for joy and blessing of God with gladness of heart*. Everyone in the room was blessed" (Lt. 11, 1877).

"We returned to rest, but we could not sleep. We were too happy for sleep. *We praised our Saviour nearly all night*. There was not much sleeping done in the house that night. God had come with His holy presence into the house, and His sanctifying presence was too highly prized to sleep over the hours to us so precious. We have been very happy ever since. Peace and joy have flowed in upon our souls like a river. There has been uninterrupted peace and rest in the dear Saviour. Such an assurance as we are having is worth more than riches or gold, honor or worldly glory. I prize it! I prize it! *The praise of God has been in our hearts, and upon our lips continually since that good evening*. My peace is like a river and the righteousness thereof like the waves of the sea." Letter 11, 1877, pp. 1, 2. (To "Dear Children," August 31, 1877.)

"Therefore by Him let us continually offer the sacrifice of praise to God, that is, the fruit of our lips, giving thanks to His name" (Heb. 13:15, NKJV).

Isn't it interesting that sometimes we can push Satan back and obtain the victory by "shouting praise to God"? Are you ready to do that—to not just sit quietly, "thinking" your praise, but to shout it out loud, with all the passion you possess? As I have fellowshipped with our people, I have found that the more moved they are by some spiritual truth, the quieter they get! Our members are deeply reverent toward God. But it is often more akin to Roman Catholic reverence that teaches the people to be silent, rather than a biblical reverence that encourages God's people to praise Him in a loud and enthusiastic way. Our churches need to be safe places where we can feel free to exuberantly praise the Lord. So what am I encouraging here? You may be a shy person who finds this kind of worship difficult to participate in. That's fine. God also says, "Be still and know that I am God" (Psalm 46:10). There is a place for quietly communing with the Spirit. What I am encouraging is that those members be tolerant of others who are not so inhibited. Someone once uncharitably characterized my wife's raising of her hands during the doxology as "channeling evil spirits." When people obey God and praise Him, they should not be the victim of such condemnation. God commands us to lift up our hands in His sanctuary in praise to Him. God encourages His people to shout His praises with uplifted hands. Can we not be as tolerant of those who actually do what He commands?

My conviction is that we have lost our first love. Praise and worship can revive our first love and give us strength to overcome. These statements impress me with the necessity of praising God all the time, softly and loudly, in church, at home, and everywhere! God expects "all" to praise Him. Not showing gratitude to God "dishonors our Maker." Let us exalt the God of heaven and praise His holy name! Let us love one another in a spirit of perfect grace, tolerance and understanding. We are all different in worship. Let us dwell on our precious Savior who has "set us free" to worship Him in spirit and in truth.

CHAPTER 19

BIBLICAL WORSHIP WITH APPLAUSE AND UPLIFTED HANDS

And Solomon stood before the altar of the LORD in the presence of all the congregation of Israel, and spread forth his hands toward heaven: … What prayer and supplication soever be made by any man, or by all thy people Israel, which shall know every man the plague of his own heart, and spread forth his hands toward this house: … And it was so, that when Solomon had made an end of praying all this prayer and supplication unto the LORD, he arose from before the altar of the LORD, from kneeling on his knees with his hands spread up to heaven.
—*1 Kings 8:22, 38, 54*

Solomon lifted his hands in worship. Even if we are personally uncomfortable praising God by clapping or uplifting our hands, should we not be willing to acknowledge what the Bible teaches on the subject and extend perfect grace to our brothers and sisters who do? The Bible is amazingly forthright. Notice in the next biblical section the obvious meanings. They clapped their hands in the sanctuary by the altar. It wasn't just a few of them either, it was *all the congregation!* In his prayer, Solomon even instructed "everyone" to pray with uplifted hands toward the temple.

> And the guard stood, every man with his weapons in his hand, round about the king, from the right corner *of the temple* to the left corner of the temple, along *by the altar and the temple*. And he brought forth the king's son, and put the crown upon him, and gave him the testimony; and they made him king, and anointed him; and *they clapped their hands*, and said, God save the king. (2 Kings 11:11, 12)

Even if we are personally uncomfortable praising God by clapping or uplifting our hands, should we not be willing to acknowledge what the Bible teaches on the subject and extend perfect grace to our brothers and sisters who do?

> And he *stood before the altar* of the LORD in the presence of *all the congregation* of Israel, and spread forth *his hands:* … For Solomon had made a brazen scaffold, of five cubits long, and five cubits broad, and three cubits high, and had set it in the midst of the court: and upon it he stood, and kneeled down *upon his knees* before *all the congregation* of Israel, and spread forth *his hands toward heaven*, … Then what prayer or what supplication soever shall be made of any man, or of all thy people Israel, when every one shall know his own sore and his own grief, and shall spread forth *his hands in this house*. (2 Chron. 6:12, 13, 29)

> And Ezra *blessed the LORD*, the great God. And *all the people* answered, Amen, Amen, with *lifting up their hands:* and they

> bowed their heads, and *worshipped the LORD* with their faces to the ground.... So they read in the book in the law of God distinctly, and gave the sense, and caused them to understand the reading. And Nehemiah, which is the Tirshatha, and Ezra the priest the scribe, and the Levites that taught the people, said unto all the people, This day is holy unto the LORD your God; mourn not, nor weep. For all the people wept, when they heard the words of the law. Then he said unto them, Go your way, eat the fat, and drink the sweet, and send portions unto them for whom nothing is prepared: for this day is holy unto our Lord: neither be ye sorry; for *the joy* of the LORD is your strength. (Neh. 8:6, 8–10)
>
> Hear the voice of my supplications, when I cry unto thee, when *I lift up my hands* toward thy holy oracle. (Ps. 28:2)
>
> To the chief Musician, A Psalm for the sons of Korah. O *clap your hands, all ye people; shout* unto God with the voice of triumph. For the LORD most high is terrible; he is a great King over all the earth. (Ps. 47:1, 2)

The people of God were weeping and lifting up their hands as they were bowing down to worship God. David lifted his hands to God in prayer. God instructs us through His prophet to clap our hands in the sanctuary when we praise Him. These psalms were for public worship in the people's court of the temple. They were told to shout and were admonished to remember that the joy of the Lord is our strength. Be joyful! Let it out and—shout!

> God is gone up *with a shout*, the LORD with the sound of a trumpet. Sing praises to God, sing praises: sing praises unto our King, sing praises. For God is the King of all the earth: sing ye praises with understanding. (Ps. 47:5–7)

O God, thou art my God; early will I seek thee: my soul thirsteth for thee, my flesh longeth for thee in a dry and thirsty land, where no water is; to see thy power and thy glory, so *as I have seen thee in the sanctuary*. Because thy lovingkindness is better than life, *my lips* shall praise thee. Thus will *I bless thee* while I live: *I will lift up my hands in thy name*. (Ps. 63:1–4)

To the chief Musician, A Song or Psalm. Make a *joyful* noise unto God, all ye lands: Sing forth the honour of his name: make his *praise glorious*. (Ps. 66:1, 2)

Mine eye mourneth by reason of affliction: LORD, I have called daily upon thee, I have stretched out *my hands unto thee*. (Ps. 88:9)

O sing unto the LORD *a new song*; for he hath done marvellous things: his right hand, and his holy arm, hath gotten him the victory. ... Make a joyful noise unto the LORD, all the earth: make a *loud noise*, and *rejoice*, *and sing praise*. Sing unto the LORD with the harp; with the harp, and the voice of a psalm. With trumpets and sound of cornet make a *joyful noise before the LORD*, the King. ... Let the floods *clap their hands:* let the hills *be joyful* together. (Ps. 98:1, 4–6, 8)

My *hands also will I lift up* unto thy commandments, which I have loved; and I will meditate in thy statutes. (Ps. 119:48)

I will praise thee with my *whole heart*. (Ps. 138:1)

Let my prayer be set forth before thee as incense; and *the lifting up of my hands* as the *evening sacrifice*. (Ps. 141:2)

I stretch forth *my hands* unto thee: my soul thirsteth after thee, as a thirsty land. Selah. (Ps. 143:6)

For ye shall go out with joy, and be led forth with peace: the mountains and the hills shall break forth before you into singing, and *all the trees of the field shall clap their hands*. (Isa. 55:12)

> Arise, cry out in the night: in the beginning of the watches *pour out thine heart* like water before the face of the Lord: *lift up thy hands toward him* for the life of thy young children, that faint for hunger in the top of every street. (Lam. 2:19)
>
> Let us lift up *our heart with our hands* unto God in the heavens. (Lam. 3:41)
>
> I will therefore that men pray *every where, lifting up holy hands*, without wrath and doubting. (1 Tim. 2:8)
>
> By him therefore let us offer the *sacrifice of praise to God continually*, that is, the fruit of our *lips* giving thanks to his name. (Heb. 13:15)

They even applaud in heaven!

"The command to Abraham demanded the most agonizing sacrifice. All heaven beheld with wonder and admiration Abraham's unfaltering obedience. *All heaven applauded his fidelity*" (*Patriarchs and Prophets*, p. 155).

CHAPTER 20

PROCLAIMING THE GOSPEL, THE JUDGMENT HOUR AND HEAVEN-DIRECTED WORSHIP IN A BIBLICAL WAY!

All scripture is given by inspiration of God,
and is profitable for doctrine, for reproof,
for correction, for instruction in righteousness.
—2 Timothy 3:16

God's perfect grace needs no improvements from us! His perfect grace is sufficient! His plan of salvation needs no additions from us in any way! His gospel, judgment and worship provide us with perfect grace unbounding, and truly amazing! Are we getting it? Are we representing God's last-day message as perfect grace, sufficient, and all about what God has done for us? As we look to sum up the areas in which we have missed the true proclamation of the first angel's message, it is important to remember that we should never judge the

God's perfect grace needs no improvements from us!

intentions of those who have shared their biblical understanding, even if we now believe it is incorrect. We need to remember that most of the theories and myths of Adventism were taught to our people by well-meaning and dedicated ministers who were doing the best they could. However, if the people can learn something that has been shown to be biblically incorrect, they can unlearn it too. It's important to remember our motto, "The Bible Only," and to not get tied to traditional beliefs that have been shown to be inadequate. The Seventh-day Adventist Church's doctrinal positions as stated in the list of our twenty-eight fundamentals of faith is absolutely correct on the subjects of the gospel, perfection, and the sanctuary. That being said, a sizable group of church members have no idea what the church's official position is on these subjects, and they may hold theories that contradict both the Bible and the church's position. Many confuse the subjects of sanctification and glorification and actually believe that a person can achieve sinless perfection before Jesus returns. This contradicts the Bible, Ellen White, and the church's official position. Yet, they believe it nonetheless. Many also believe that, when Jesus steps out of the most holy place and probation closes that all will be lost if they are not living in sinless perfection. This makes a mockery of the gospel, instills fear in the believer's heart, and nullifies any assurance of salvation. In many churches and conferences, these ideas are branded as "conservative" doctrines, and anyone not accepting them is deemed "liberal." Harvest theology that teaches we must achieve sinless perfection before Christ comes is not "conservative"—it is heretical, and it stands in the Catholic gospel tradition of salvation by works. It is not "liberal" to teach that sinless glorification only occurs after Jesus comes and not before. The true gospel

It's important to remember our motto, "The Bible Only," and to not get tied to traditional beliefs that have been shown to be inadequate.

accounts us perfect, even while we are being sanctified. Our people need to be set free from such labels of condemnation.

In the area of worship and music, there is little biblical understanding on what the Bible actually teaches. The church has not addressed the subject in the twenty-eight fundamentals as it has the gospel and the sanctuary. While our church has taken strong positions regarding which day we should worship on, official sources have been far less clear on *how* to worship in our churches. If my assertions in this book are correct, there are large groups of Adventists who attend church but who, having missed the gospel, are emphasizing fear rather than hope concerning the conclusion of Jesus' ministry as High Priest and are condemning worship practices that the Bible encourages and even commands. How can a concerned Seventh-day Adventist help the situation and become a part of the answer and not part of the problem?

As you have read this book, and learned what the Bible teaches on the gospel, the sanctuary, and worship, you may have encountered a different point of view than your own on many things. The "traditional" view differs from church to church in Adventism. Some conferences are very gospel oriented, Christ-centered, and encouraging of biblical worship. Others are legalistic, fear oriented, and are very critical of any types of worship besides what is considered traditional as defined by their culture. And there are those that are in between. The same could be said of the churches around the world.

My reason for writing this book has been to encourage Seventh-day Adventists everywhere to be part of the answer and not part of the problem by no longer preaching a gospel of achievement and a sanctuary message of fear in the time of trouble, to encourage Adventist to stop criticizing biblical worship practices and embrace a Christocentric, hope-filled sanctuary message that encourages Adventists to worship God in biblical ways that may not be culturally traditional but that are theologically correct and commanded in God's Word.

CONCLUSION

As we have studied the first angel's message, we have learned that God's perfect grace is sufficient for our salvation. We have learned that the gospel is about what God has done for humankind, rather than about what humankind does for God. We have learned that no one is perfect but Jesus Christ. We have discovered that the everlasting gospel is about receiving righteousness rather than achieving righteousness. We have learned that all our righteousnesses are as filthy rags and that Isaiah's appraisal of the same is referring to the good works we do and not just our sins. We have discovered the meaning of the sanctuary service in the tabernacle of the Jewish people and in the heavenly sanctuary.

Jesus, our great High Priest, presents His character in place of our character, and God looks at us as if we had never sinned. Rather than achieving a perfect character, we receive credit for Christ's perfect character when we appropriate His righteousness as we are being justified by faith. As Seventh-day Adventists, we need to acknowledge the unworthiness of our own characters and that our only hope of a righteous character is to have it credited to us by faith in Christ. We also need to preach the sanctuary message and the judgment in such a way that it teaches the triumph of the sinner by being declared sinless and holy in Christ and being placed forever beyond the reach of sin and Satan. By being declared righteous, God will pronounce us righteous still, and we will be saved completely for all eternity from that moment forward. We must proclaim the message that, after the close of probation, we no longer need a mediator because Christ has successfully mediated in our behalf. We will never be without a Savior because Christ will always be with us, even during the time of trouble and after the close of probation. We cannot be lost from that point on because all our sins have been paid for by Christ on Calvary and mediated by our great High Priest before probation had closed, placing us forever beyond the reach of Satan. All of our sins are fully paid for from the moment of our birth to the moment of our death or translation; they have all been paid in full by the blood of the Lamb and accounted for in the judgment, and we have been declared "*not guilty*"!

We will never be without a Savior because Christ will always be with us, even during the time of trouble and after the close of probation.

We have learned that, while we are down here on earth, we can rejoice in the fact that we are under God's perfect grace and not under the condemnation of the law! We can worship God with exuberance and joy. We are not being irreverent when we show God our love with passion! We can clap our hands, lift our hands heavenward, and praise Him with an enthusiasm that reflects our deep spiritual connection with our Savior. Once we *rediscover* the first angel's message of God's perfect grace, we will never again look at the gospel, the judgment, or worship in the same way! God has revealed to us that He has provided salvation for us that is full, perfect, and free and that we are saved by what He has done for us and not by what we do for Him! We have learned that only Jesus' Sabbath observance and Jesus' law keeping saves us and not our own! We have learned that the sanctuary in heaven is a wonderful place where we can go for help and grace in time of need! We have learned that God inhabits the praise of His people and that we are to worship Him in the heavenly sanctuary with reverence and passion! The sanctuary has revealed to us that Jesus gives us perfect grace to save us, to advocate for us, and to enable us to worship

Him in spirit and in truth. We have learned that this message is all about *Jesus! He gives us His perfect grace as our Savior, our priest, and the center of all our worship!*

> And I saw another angel fly in the midst of heaven, having the everlasting gospel to preach unto them that dwell on the earth, and to every nation, and kindred, and tongue, and people, saying with a loud voice, Fear God, and give glory to him; for the hour of his judgment is come: and worship him that made heaven, and earth, and the sea, and the fountains of waters. (Rev. 14:6, 7)

As we go forth boldly proclaiming God's perfect grace to the world, we are to let them know that Jesus has provided all they need to be saved by His perfect, amazing grace. We are to tell them that the judgment is going on in heaven to render a "not guilty" verdict on our behalf, and that they have a great High Priest who is ministering as our advocate even now, offering up His White Robe of Righteousness for all who will receive it. We can rejoice in those blessings by worshiping God in Spirit and in truth, and as we share this message filled with joy and hope in the Lord Jesus Christ, it will change the world!

Pastor Tom Hughes has been a Christian for forty-nine years and a Seventh-day Adventist pastor for over forty years. He currently serves his church in pastoral ministry, is the speaker of the "Bible Biker" Radio broadcast, and has a motorcycle ministry you can learn more about on his websites:

www.BibleBiker.com and www.PastorTomHughes.com

Feel free to contact Pastor Hughes if he can be of service to you. Contact information can be found on the websites.

Pastor Tom Hughes, MA

KEY PASSAGES IN CHAPTER 1

Revelation 5—And I saw in the right *hand* of Him who sat on the throne a scroll written inside and on the back, sealed with seven seals. Then I saw a strong angel proclaiming with a loud voice, "Who is worthy to open the scroll and to loose its seals?" And no one in heaven or on the earth or under the earth was able to open the scroll, or to look at it. So I wept much, because no one was found worthy to open and read the scroll, or to look at it. But one of the elders said to me, "Do not weep. Behold, the Lion of the tribe of Judah, the Root of David, has prevailed to open the scroll and to loose its seven seals." And I looked, and behold, in the midst of the throne and of the four living creatures, and in the midst of the elders, stood a Lamb as though it had been slain, having seven horns and seven eyes, which are the seven Spirits of God sent out into all the earth. Then He came and took the scroll out of the right hand of Him who sat on the throne. Now when He had taken the scroll, the four living creatures and the twenty-four elders fell down before the Lamb, each having a harp, and golden bowls full of incense, which are the prayers of the saints. And they sang a new song, saying: "You are worthy to take the scroll, And to open its seals; For You were slain, And have redeemed us to God by Your blood Out of every tribe and tongue and people and nation, And have made us kings and priests to our God; And we shall reign on the earth." Then I looked, and I heard the voice of many angels around the throne, the living creatures, and the elders; and the number of them was ten thousand times ten thousand, and thousands of thousands, saying with a loud voice: "Worthy is the Lamb who was slain To receive power and riches and wisdom, And strength and honor and glory and blessing!" And every creature which is in heaven and on the earth and under the earth and such as are in the sea, and all that are in them, I heard saying: "Blessing and honor and glory and power *Be* to Him who sits on the throne, And to the Lamb, forever and ever!" Then the four living creatures said, "Amen!" And the twenty-four elders fell down and worshiped Him who lives forever and ever.

> **The divine beauty of the character of Christ, of whom the noblest and most gentle among men are but a faint reflection;** of whom Solomon by the Spirit of inspiration wrote, He is "the chiefest among ten thousand, ... yea, He is altogether lovely" (Song of Solomon 5:10–16); of whom David, seeing Him in prophetic vision, said, "Thou art fairer than the children of men" (Psalm 45:2); Jesus, the express image of the Father's person, the effulgence of His glory; the self-denying Redeemer, throughout His pilgrimage of love on earth, was a living representation of the character of the law of God. In His life it is made manifest that heaven-born love, Christlike principles, underlie the laws of eternal rectitude.
>
> "Till heaven and earth pass," said Jesus, "one jot or one tittle shall in nowise pass from the law, till all be fulfilled." By His own obedience to the law, Christ testified to its immutable character and proved that *through His grace* it could be perfectly obeyed by every son and daughter of Adam. On the mount He declared that not the smallest iota should pass from the law till all things should be accomplished—all things that concern the human race, all that relates to the plan of redemption. He does not teach that the law is ever to be abrogated, but He fixes the eye upon the utmost verge of man's horizon and assures us that until this point is reached the law will retain

> its authority so that none may suppose it was His mission to abolish the precepts of the law. So long as heaven and earth continue, the holy principles of God's law will remain. His righteousness, "like the great mountains" (Psalm 36:6), will continue, a source of blessing, sending forth streams to refresh the earth. (E. G. White, *Thoughts from the Mount of Blessing*, pp. 49, 50, emphasis added)

When you read that, through God's grace, His law could be "perfectly obeyed" by every descendant of Adam, she is not asserting that sinners with a carnal nature can achieve sinless perfection. She is asserting that Adam could have maintained his sinless perfection *before* he became carnal in nature and that, through God's grace, sinful human beings can have Christ's perfect character credited to theirs and, by faith, be accounted as having a perfect character (*Steps to Christ*, p. 62). The law has never been done away with. Jesus magnified it by being the *only* person to ever perfectly obey it. Remember, "Nobody is perfect but Jesus" (*That I May Know Him*, p. 136).

ENDNOTES

1. We will later consider the statement upon which "harvest theology" is based: "**When the character of Christ shall be perfectly reproduced in His people, then He will come to claim them as His own**" (*Christ's Object Lessons*, p. 69). She is referring to God's people collectively and not individually. She did not teach sinless perfectionism. Rather, she taught: "Nobody is perfect but Jesus" (*That I May Know Him*, p. 136).

   "It is the privilege of every Christian not only to look for but to **hasten the coming of our Lord Jesus Christ**, (2 Peter 3:12, margin). Were all who profess His name bearing fruit to His glory, how quickly the whole world would be sown with the seed of the gospel. Quickly the last great harvest would be ripened, and Christ would come to gather the precious grain" (*Christ's Object Lessons*, p. 69). The fruit is from the gospel tree. Once we appropriate the righteousness of Christ, we will want to witness and share the gospel with others. Her statement is not talking about the fruit of sinless perfection through character development.
2. "Pray, pray earnestly and without ceasing, but do not forget to praise. It becomes every child of God to **vindicate His character**. You can magnify the Lord; you can show the power of sustaining grace. There are multitudes who do not appreciate the great love of God nor the divine compassion of Jesus. Thousands even regard with disdain the matchless grace shown in the plan of redemption. All who are partakers of this great salvation are not clear in this matter. They do not cultivate grateful hearts. But the theme of redemption is one that the angels desire to look into; it will be the science and the song of the ransomed throughout the ceaseless ages of eternity. Is it not worthy of careful thought and study now? Should we not praise God with heart and soul and voice 'for His wonderful works to the children of men'?" (*Testimonies for the Church*, vol. 5, p. 317–318). When Ellen White states that God's people "vindicate the character of God" she is not talking about them "achieving" a sinless character. She is talking about "*sustaining grace*". She refers in the same statement to "*the matchless grace shown in the plan of redemption.*" She states this in the context of "great salvation" for God's people. She is encouraging us to praise God for his redeeming, saving

grace, and "vindicate" him by revealing his grace in our lives BY FAITH. She says this to encourage us to study the science of gospel salvation now, and to praise God with our whole heart and soul.

She does not mean that we must achieve sinless perfection so we can "vindicate" God's character. She is encouraging God's people to be faithful, and by their example strive to be found faithful to the gospel by bearing the fruit of praise, gratitude and the obedience of faith. She is not teaching Harvest Theology because our characters are "as filthy rags," our good works are sinful, and we can hardly vindicate even ourselves by our sinful characters, let alone vindicate God. She is simply encouraging us to take God's side in the great controversy, and to demonstrate our faith by our works, imperfect though they may be. Walking by faith, trusting only in Christ's righteousness is the only way our characters are an affirmation of God's character. Since the noblest and gentlest among men are but a faint reflection of the character of Christ, no human other than Jesus Christ vindicates God's character in the fullest sense.

In our limited sphere, doing our best, we can imitate the pattern, never equaling it. In this relative sense we can vindicate God's point of view. However, if we define vindicating God's character as achieving sinless perfection, we are mis-characterizing the meaning of her statement. Her statement was an admonishment to accept and study the gospel of Jesus Christ and by grace through faith alone, vindicate God by taking his side, accepting his redemption and walking in the obedience of faith, receiving a righteous character, NOT achieving it.

3. "Sacred silence also, as part of the celebration, is to be observed at the designated times." Number 45 of the General Instruction of the Roman Missal (Third and Emended Typical Edition, 2008) Paragraph 30 of the Liturgy Constitution, Sacrosanctum Concilium, likewise prescribes: "And at the proper times all should observe a reverent silence."

Number 56 of the General Instruction specifies better the importance of silence within the Liturgy of the Word, while number 78 makes the same clear for the Liturgy of the Eucharist: "The Eucharistic Prayer demands that all listen to it with reverence and in silence." Number 84 then underscores the importance of the observance of silence as a means of good preparation for the reception of Holy Communion: "The priest prepares himself by a prayer, said quietly, that he may fruitfully receive Christ's Body and Blood. The faithful do the same, praying silently … Consequently, the observance of the moments of silence envisioned by the liturgy is of great importance. These moments of silence are as much an integral part of the ars celebrandi (art of celebrating) of the ministers as is participatio actuosa (active participation) on the part of the faithful. Silence in the liturgy is the moment in which one listens with greater attention to the voice of God and internalizes His word, so that it bears the fruit of sanctity in daily life." Available at http://1ref.us/n0, accessed 02/28/18.

4. "Singing, I saw, often drove away the enemy and *shouting would beat him back*. I saw that pride had crept in among you, and there was not childlike simplicity among you. The fear of man, I saw must all go" ("To the Church in Your Place," Ms 5a, July 1850, pp. 1, 2).

   "I saw singing to the glory of God often drove the enemy, and *praising God would beat him back and give us the victory*. I saw that there was too little glorifying God, too little childlike simplicity among the remnant" ("A Vision the Lord Gave Me at Oswego," Ms 5, July 1850, pp. 1, 2).
5. See James R. Nix, "Another Look at Israel Damon," p. 5. Available at http://1ref.us/n1, accessed 02/28/18.
6. Of course Christ *does* add grace after grace to meet all our needs as we submit to Him. (See James 4:6 and Heb. 4:16.) When we are saved by grace through faith, God works in us both to will and to do of His good pleasure, and we walk in Christ's good works by the obedience of faith, renouncing our own works as sinful and inadequate (Phil. 2:13; Eph. 2:10).
7. This basis for this view is a statement of Ellen White that does not say what people have taken it to mean, "Among those who are waiting for the coming of the Lord, meat eating will eventually be done away; flesh will cease to form a part of their diet. We should ever keep this end in view, and endeavor to work steadily toward it. I cannot think that in the practice of flesh eating we are in harmony with the light which God has been pleased to give us" (*Christian Temperance and Bible Hygiene*, p. 119). She is presenting vegetarianism as a goal to be worked toward, not an ultimatum. It is truly the healthiest way to live, and she is encouraging God's people to get back to Adam's original diet.
8. *The Sanctuary Service*, Chapter 21, pp. 299–321.
9. *The Sanctuary Service*, Chapter 21, pp. 299–303, 315–318, 321.
10. Larry Kirkpatrick, *Last Generation Theology in 14 Points*, 5 and 14.
11. *Catholic Catechism of the Catholic Church*, article 2, "Grace and Justification"; The Council of Trent (1547) DS 1528, Cannons IX and XXVI.
12. R. Larry Shelton (ThD, Fuller Theological Seminary), "Perfection, Perfectionism," *Evangelical Dictionary of Theology*, 2nd ed., Paternoster Press, 2001, p. 906. For John Wesley's explanation of how Christians are not and are perfect, see "Christian Perfection," available at http://1ref.us/nc, accessed 03/01/18).
13. William Liversidge, *Victory in Jesus*, pp. 56–64; *The Sanctuary Service*, Chapter 21, pp. 303.
14. See *Seventh-day Adventists Believe*, pp. 133–147.
15. http://1ref.us/n2 (accessed 02/28/18).
16. http://1ref.us/n3 (accessed 02/28/18).
17. "Speaking of the law, Jesus said, 'I am not come to destroy, but to fulfill.' He here used the word 'fulfill' in the same sense as when He declared to John the Baptist His

purpose to 'fulfill all righteousness' (Matthew 3:15); that is, to fill up the measure of the law's requirement, to give an example of perfect conformity to the will of God.

His mission was to 'magnify the law, and make it honorable.' Isaiah 42:21. He was to show the spiritual nature of the law, to present its far-reaching principles, and to make plain its eternal obligation.

The divine beauty of the character of Christ, of whom the noblest and most gentle among men are but a faint reflection; of whom Solomon by the Spirit of inspiration wrote, He is 'the chiefest among ten thousand, ... yea, He is altogether lovely' (Song of Solomon 5:10–16); of whom David, seeing Him in prophetic vision, said, 'Thou art fairer than the children of men' (Psalm 45:2); Jesus, the express image of the Father's person, the effulgence of His glory; the self-denying Redeemer, throughout His pilgrimage of love on earth, was a living representation of the character of the law of God. In His life it is made manifest that heaven-born love, Christlike principles, underlie the laws of eternal rectitude. 'Till heaven and earth pass; said Jesus, 'one jot or one tittle shall in nowise pass from the law, till all be fulfilled.' By His own obedience to the law, Christ testified to its immutable character and proved that through His grace it could be perfectly obeyed by every son and daughter of Adam. On the mount He declared that not the smallest iota should pass from the law till all things should be accomplished—all things that concern the human race, all that relates to the plan of redemption. He does not teach that the law is ever to be abrogated, but He fixes the eye upon the utmost verge of man's horizon and assures us that until this point is reached the law will retain its authority so that none may suppose it was His mission to abolish the precepts of the law. So long as heaven and earth continue, the holy principles of God's law will remain. His righteousness, 'like the great mountains' (Psalm 36:6), will continue, a source of blessing, sending forth streams to refresh the earth" (E. G. White, *Thoughts from the Mount of Blessing*, p. 49, 1896).

18. The commandment itself is simple, "Remember the sabbath day, to keep it holy. Six days shalt thou labour, and do all thy work: But the seventh day is the sabbath of the LORD thy God: in it thou shalt not do any work, thou, nor thy son, nor thy daughter, thy manservant, nor thy maidservant, nor thy cattle, nor thy stranger that is within thy gates: For in six days the LORD made heaven and earth, the sea, and all that in them is, and rested the seventh day: wherefore the LORD blessed the sabbath day, and hallowed it" (Exod. 20:8–11).
19. This is derived from, "When the character of Christ shall be perfectly reproduced in His people, then He will come to claim them as His own" (*Christ's Object Lessons*, p. 69). Here she is not talking about their achieving a sinless, perfect character equal to Christ's. She is talking about God's people collectively reflecting His character, not individually. No one but Jesus has a perfect character (*Thoughts from the Mount of Blessing*, p. 49).

20. Background on how these books were brought together from Ellen White's writings can be found in Robert W. Olson, "How *The Desire of Ages* Was Written," available at http://1ref.us/n4, accessed 02/28/18.
21. This is the author's view of the thrust of *Messages to Young People* (1930). The book was compiled in a different era by the General Conference Missionary Volunteer Department. It is largely from Ellen White's articles in the *Youth's Instructor*, but also including material from *Review and Herald* and *Signs of the Times*, "pertaining to young people and young people's problems" (*North Pacific Union Gleaner*, May 27, 1930, p. 4; May 20, 1930, p. 10; see also *Atlantic Union Gleaner*, May 21, 1930, p. 4).
22. Here the word for "rest" is *anapausis*.
23. See study on "There remaineth therefore a rest" in "Sabbatimos in Hebrews," available at http://1ref.us/n5, accessed 02/28/18.
24. *That I May Know Him*, p. 182, emphasis added.
25. Strong's has several definitions for *teleios:* (1) brought to its end, finished, (2) wanting nothing necessary to completeness, (3) perfect, (4) that which is perfect, consummate human integrity and virtue, of men, full grown, adult, of full age, mature.
26. Spirit of Prophecy Quotations:

"God declares, 'There is none righteous, no, not one; (Rom 3:10). ***All*** **have the same** ***sinful*** **nature.** All are liable to make mistakes. ***No one is perfect.*** The Lord Jesus died for the erring that they might be forgiven. It is not our work to condemn. Christ did not come to condemn, but to save" (*In Heavenly Places*, p. 292).

[God's law] "Could not justify man because ***in his sinful nature he could not keep the law***" (*Patriarchs and Prophets*, p. 373). "The religious services, the *prayers, the praise*, the *penitent confession of sin ascend from true believers* as incense to the heavenly sanctuary, but passing through the *corrupt channels of humanity*, they are so defiled that unless purified by blood, they can *never* be of value with God. They ascend not in spotless purity, and unless the Intercessor, who is at God's right hand, presents and purifies all *by His righteousness, it is not acceptable to God*. All incense from earthly tabernacles must be moist with the cleansing drops of the blood of Christ. He holds before the Father the censer of His own merits, in which there is no taint of earthly corruption. He gathers into this censer the prayers, the praise, and the confessions of His people, and with these He puts *His own spotless righteousness*. Then, perfumed with the merits of Christ's propitiation, the incense comes up before God *wholly and entirely acceptable*. Then gracious answers are returned... Oh, that all may see that *everything in obedience*, in penitence, in praise and thanksgiving, must he placed upon the glowing fire of the *righteousness of Christ*" (*Selected Messages*, vol. 1, pp. 344, 345).

"We do not understand *our perverse natures*; and often when we are gratifying self, following our own inclinations, we flatter ourselves that we are carrying out the mind of God" (*Testimonies to Ministers*, p. 503). "The divine beauty of the *character of*

Christ, of whom the noblest and most gentle among men are but a faint reflection... Jesus, the express image of the Father's person, the effulgence of His glory; the self-denying Redeemer, throughout His pilgrimage of love on earth, was a living representation of the character of the law of God" (*Thoughts from the Mount of Blessing*, p. 49).

"Those who know that *they cannot possibly save themselves, or of themselves do any righteous action*, are the ones who appreciate the help that Christ can bestow. They are the poor in spirit, whom He declares to be blessed...Those whose hearts have been moved by the convicting Spirit of God see that *there is nothing good in themselves*. They see that *all they have ever done is mingled with self and sin*. Like the poor publican, they stand afar off, not daring to lift up so much as their eyes to heaven, and cry, 'God, be merciful to me the sinner.' Luke 18:13, R.V., margin. And they are blessed" (*Thoughts from the Mount of Blessing*, pp. 7, 8).

"I ask, How can I present this matter as it is? The Lord Jesus imparts all the powers, all the grace, all the penitence, all the inclination, all the pardon of sins, in presenting His righteousness for man to grasp by living faith—which is also the gift of God. *If you would gather together everything that is good and holy and noble and lovely in man and then present the subject to the angels of God as acting a part in the salvation of the human soul or in merit, the proposition would be rejected as treason*" (*Faith and Works*, p. 24).

"*There is not a point that needs to be dwelt upon more earnestly, repeated more frequently, or established more firmly in the minds of all than the impossibility of fallen man meriting anything by his own best good works. Salvation is through faith in Jesus Christ alone*... Let the subject be made distinct and plain that it is not possible to *effect anything* in our standing before God or in the gift of God to us *through creature merit*. ... If any man can merit salvation *by anything he may do, then he is in the same position as the Catholic* to do penance for his sins. Salvation, then, is partly of debt, that may be earned as wages. *If man cannot, by any of his good works, merit salvation, then it must be wholly of grace,* received by man as a sinner because he receives and believes in Jesus. It is wholly a free gift. *Justification by faith is placed beyond controversy*. And all this controversy is ended, as soon as *the matter is settled that the merits of fallen man in his good works can never procure eternal life for him*" (*Faith and Works*, pp. 18–20).

"Some seem to feel that they must be on probation and must prove to the Lord that they are reformed, before they can claim His blessing. But these dear souls may claim the blessing even now. They must have His grace, the Spirit of Christ, to help their infirmities, or they cannot form a Christian character. Jesus loves to have us come to Him, just as we are—*sinful, helpless, dependent.... We can do nothing, absolutely nothing, to commend ourselves to divine favor*. We must not trust at all to ourselves or to our good works; but when as *erring, sinful beings* we come to Christ, we may find rest in His love. *God will accept every one that comes to Him trusting wholly in the merits of a crucified Saviour*. Love springs up in the heart. There may be no ecstasy of feeling, but there is an abiding, peaceful trust. Every burden is light; for the yoke which Christ imposes is easy. Duty becomes a delight, and sacrifice a pleasure. The path that before seemed shrouded in darkness becomes bright with beams from the Sun of Righteousness. This is walking in the light as Christ is in the light" (*Faith and Works*, p. 38).

"*Neither Joseph, Daniel, nor any of the apostles claimed to be without sin.* Men who have lived nearest to God, men who would sacrifice life itself rather than to knowingly sin against Him, men whom God has honored with divine light and power, have *acknowledged themselves to be sinners*, unworthy of His great favors. They have felt their weakness and, sorrowful for their sins, have tried to copy the pattern Jesus Christ" (*Faith and Works*, p. 43).

"Christ looks at the spirit, and when He sees us carrying our burden with faith, *His perfect holiness atones for our shortcomings. When we do our best, He becomes our righteousness*. It takes every ray of light that God sends to us to make us the light of the world" (Letter 22, 1889; *Faith and Works*, p. 102).

"There are those who have known the pardoning love of Christ and who really desire to be children of God, yet they realize that *their character is imperfect, their life faulty*, and they are ready to doubt whether their hearts have been *renewed by the Holy Spirit*. To such I would say, Do not draw back in despair. We shall often have to bow down and weep at the feet of Jesus because of our *shortcomings and mistakes*, but we are not to be discouraged. *Even if we are overcome by the enemy, we are not cast off, not forsaken and rejected of God*. No; Christ is at the right hand of God, who also maketh intercession for us. Said the beloved John, 'These things write I unto you, that ye sin not. And *if any man sin*, we have an advocate with the Father, *Jesus Christ the righteous*.' 1 John 2:1. And do not forget the words of Christ, 'The Father Himself loveth you.' John 16:27. He desires to restore you to Himself, to see His own purity and holiness *reflected in you*. And if you will but yield yourself to Him, *He that hath begun a good work in you will carry it forward to the day of Jesus Christ.* Pray more fervently; believe more fully. As we come to distrust our own power, let us trust the power of our Redeemer, and we shall praise Him who is the health of our countenance. *The closer you come to Jesus, the more faulty you will appear in your own eyes; for your vision will be clearer, and your imperfections will be seen in broad and distinct contrast to His perfect nature.* This is evidence that Satan's delusions have lost their power; that the vivifying influence of the Spirit of God is arousing you" (*Steps to Christ*, pp. 64, 65).

"*No deep-seated love for Jesus can dwell in the heart that does not realize its own sinfulness*. The soul that is transformed by the grace of Christ will admire *His divine character; but if we do not see our own moral deformity, it is unmistakable evidence that we have not had a view of the beauty and excellence of Christ.* The less we see to esteem in ourselves, the more we shall see to esteem in the *infinite purity and loveliness of our Saviour*. A view of *our sinfulness* drives us to Him who can pardon; and when the soul, realizing its helplessness, reaches out after Christ, He will *reveal Himself in power*. The more our sense of need drives us to Him and to the word of God, the more exalted views we shall have of *His character*, and the more fully we shall *reflect His image*" (*Steps to Christ*, pp. 64, 65).

"*While we cannot do anything to change our hearts or to bring ourselves into harmony with God; while we must not trust at all to ourselves or our good works,* our lives will reveal whether the *grace of God* is dwelling within us. *A change will be seen in the character*, the habits, the pursuits. The contrast will be clear and decided between what they have been and what they are. *The character is revealed, not by occasional good deeds and occasional misdeeds, but by the tendency of the habitual words and acts*" (*Steps to Christ*, p. 57).

"It is true that there may be an outward correctness of deportment without the renewing power of Christ. The love of influence and the desire for the esteem of others may produce *a well-ordered life*. Self-respect may lead us to *avoid the appearance of evil. A selfish heart may perform generous actions.* By what means, then, shall we determine whose side we are on? *Who has the heart? With whom are our thoughts?* Of whom do we love to converse? Who has our warmest affections and our best energies? If we are Christ's, our thoughts are with Him, and *our sweetest thoughts are of Him.* All we have and are is consecrated to Him. We long to bear His image, breathe His spirit, do His will, and *please Him in all things*" (*Steps to Christ*, p. 58).

"Those who are true to God will be menaced, denounced, proscribed. They will be 'betrayed both by parents, and brethren, and kinsfolks, and friends,' even unto death. Luke 21:16. *Their only hope is in the mercy of God; their only defense will be prayer.* As Joshua pleaded before the Angel, *so the remnant church*, with brokenness of heart and *unfaltering faith*, will plead for pardon and deliverance through Jesus, their Advocate. They are *fully conscious of the sinfulness of their lives*, they see their *weakness and unworthiness*; and they are ready to despair…" (*Prophets and Kings*, p. 588).

"But while the followers of Christ *have sinned*, they have not given themselves up *to be controlled* by the satanic agencies. They have *repented of their sins* and have sought the Lord in humility and contrition, and the divine Advocate pleads in their behalf. He who has been most abused by their ingratitude, who knows their sin and also their penitence, declares: *'The Lord rebuke thee, O Satan. I gave My life for these souls*. They are graven upon the palms of My hands. *They may have imperfections of character; they may have failed in their endeavors; but they have repented, and I have forgiven and accepted them*'" (*Prophets and Kings*, p. 589).

"As the people of God afflict their souls before Him, pleading for purity of heart, the command is given, *'Take away the filthy garments*,' and the encouraging words are spoken, 'Behold, *I have caused* thine iniquity to pass from thee, and I will clothe thee with change of raiment.' Zechariah 3:4. *The spotless robe of Christ's righteousness* is placed upon the tried, tempted, faithful children of God. The despised remnant are clothed in glorious apparel, *nevermore to be defiled by the corruptions of the world*. Their names are retained in the Lamb's book of life, enrolled among the faithful of all ages. They have resisted the wiles of the deceiver; they have not been turned from their loyalty by the dragon's roar. *Now they are* ***eternally secure*** *from the tempter's devices*" (*Prophets and Kings*, p. 591).

"The religion of Christ never degrades the receiver. *It never makes him coarse or rough, discourteous or self-important, passionate or hardhearted*. On the contrary, it refines the taste, sanctifies the judgment, and purifies and ennobles the thoughts, bringing them into captivity to Jesus Christ...*God's ideal for His children is higher than the highest human thought can reach*. The living God has given in His holy law a transcript of His character. The greatest Teacher the world has ever known is Jesus Christ; and what is the standard He has given for all who believe in Him? 'Be ye therefore perfect, even as you're Father which is in heaven is perfect.' Matthew 5:48. As God is perfect in His *high sphere* of action, so man may be perfect *in his human sphere... The ideal of Christian character is Christlikeness*. There is opened before us a path of continual advancement. We have an object to reach, a standard to gain, which includes everything good and pure and noble and elevated. There should be continual striving and constant progress onward and upward *toward perfection of character....*" (*Counsels to Parents and Teachers*, p. 365).

"To man is allotted a part in this great struggle for everlasting life—he must respond to the working of the Holy Spirit. It will require a struggle to break through the powers of darkness, and the Spirit works in him to accomplish this. But man is no passive being, to be saved in indolence. He is called upon *to strain every muscle and exercise every faculty* in the struggle for immortality, yet it is *God that supplies the efficiency. No human being can be saved in indolence*. The Lord bids us, 'Strive to enter in at the strait gate: for many, I say unto you, will seek to enter in, and shall not be able.' Luke 13:24. 'Wide is the gate, and broad is the way, that leadeth to destruction, and many there be which go in thereat: because strait is the gate, and narrow the way, which leadeth unto life, and few there be that find it.' Matthew 7:13, 14" (*Counsels to Parents and Teachers*, p. 366).

"While Jesus is pleading for the subjects of His grace, Satan accuses them before God *as transgressors*. The great deceiver has sought to lead them into skepticism, to cause them to lose confidence in God, to separate themselves from His love, and to break His law. Now he points to the record of their lives, to *the defects of character, the unlikeness to Christ*, which has dishonored their Redeemer, to all the sins that he has tempted them to commit, and because of these he claims them as his subjects. *Jesus does not excuse their sins, but shows their penitence and faith, and, claiming for them forgiveness, He lifts His wounded hands before the Father* and the holy angels, saying: I know them by name. I have graven them on the palms of My hands. 'The sacrifices of God are a broken spirit: a broken and a contrite heart, O God, Thou wilt not despise.' Psalm 51:17. And to the accuser of His people He declares: 'The Lord rebuke thee, O Satan; even the Lord that hath chosen Jerusalem rebuke thee: is not this a brand plucked out of the fire?' Zechariah 3:2. *Christ will clothe His faithful ones with His own righteousness,* that He may present them to His Father 'a glorious church, *not having spot, or wrinkle, or any such thing.*' Ephesians 5:27. Their names stand enrolled in the book of life, and concerning them it is written: 'They shall walk with Me in white: for *they are worthy.*' Revelation 3:4" (*The Great Controversy*, p. 484).

"*No man can look within himself and find anything in his character* that will recommend him to God, or make his acceptance sure. It is *only through Jesus*, whom the Father gave for the life of the world, that the sinner may find access to God. *Jesus alone is our Redeemer*, our Advocate and Mediator; in Him is *our only hope for pardon, peace, and righteousness*. It is by virtue of the blood of Christ that the sin-stricken soul can be restored to soundness.... *Apart from Christ we have no merit, no righteousness. Our sinfulness, our weakness, our human imperfection make it impossible that we should appear before God unless we are clothed in Christ's spotless righteousness....* When you respond to *the drawing of Christ*, and join yourself to Him, you manifest *saving faith....* Faith familiarizes the soul with the existence and presence of God, and, living with an eye single to the glory of God, more and more we discern *the beauty of His character, the excellence of His grace*" (*God's Amazing Grace*, p. 183).

27. There are some Spirit of Prophecy quotations that seem to be at odds with righteousness by faith. However if you take a deeper look, you'll discover they are not.
28. See http://1ref.us/na (accessed 02/28/18).
29. See *Review and Herald*, Feb. 9, 1897.
30. The Greek has ἡγιασμένοι ἐσμὲν, which literally means, "the ones having been sanctified we are."
31. *Seventh-day Adventist Bible Commentary,* vol. 7A, 450.3.
32. Talking about the events predicted in Revelation 10.
33. "The methods used by Gregory VII were equal to the general corruption: He claimed the right to interfere in any secular or spiritual affair of any country in Europe.... Gregory 'deposed' Henry IV—a new power based on another Papal forgery—and forced Henry to kneel in the snow outside the gates of the Castle of Cannossa and beg absolution on 28 January 1077" (Ronald Bruce Meyer, "Pope Gregory VII 'Hildebrand' [d. 1085], available at http://1ref.us/nb, accessed 03/01/18).
34. "After the French Revolution, Pius rejected the 'Constitution civile du clergé' on 13 March 1791, suspended the priests that accepted it, provided as well as he could

for the banished clergy and protested against the execution of Louis XVI. France retaliated by annexing the small papal territories of Avignon and Venaissin. The pope's co-operation with the Allies against the French Republic, and the murder of the French attaché, Basseville, at Rome, brought on by his own fault, led to Napoleon's attack on the Papal States. At the Truce of Bologna (25 June 1796) Napoleon dictated the terms: twenty-one million francs, the release of all political criminals, free access of French ships into the papal harbours, the occupation of the Romagna by French troops etc. At the Peace of Tolentino (19 February 1797) Pius VI was compelled to surrender Avignon, Venaissin, Ferrara, Bologna, and the Romagna; and to pay fifteen million francs and give up numerous costly works of art and manuscripts.... At the end of March 1799, though seriously ill, he was hurried to Parma, Piacenza, Turin, then over the Alps to Briançon and Grenoble, and finally to Valence, where he succumbed to his sufferings before he could be brought further. He was first buried at Valence, but the remains were transferred to St. Peter's in Rome on 17 February 1802 (see Napoleon I). His statue in a kneeling position by Canova was placed in the Basilica of St. Peter before the crypt of the Prince of the Apostles" (Giovanni Angelico Braschi, "Pope Pius VI," *Catholic Encyclopedia*, vol. 12, 1913, p. 132).

35. George R. Knight, A Brief History of Seventh-day Adventists, p. 18–19.
36. "Our fondest hopes and expectations were blasted and such a spirit of weeping came over us as I never experienced before. It seemed that the loss of all earthly friends could have been no comparison. We wept and wept until the day dawned! And I began to feel that there might be light and help for us in our present distress." And he goes on to talk about it. But you can see the bitterness of it—they wept and wept" (Excerpt from sermon, "The Prophecy That Failed," by J. R. Hoffman, quoting from Hiram Edson manuscript).
37. "And we entered into the granary. We shut the doors about us and we bowed down before the Lord. And we prayed earnestly, for we felt our necessity. We continued in earnest prayer until the witness of the Spirit was given that our prayers were accepted, and that light would be given and our disappointment would be explained and made clear and satisfactory. After breakfast, I said to my brethren, 'Let us go and see" and encouraged some of our other brethren. And so we started. And while passing through a large field, I was stopped ..." The man's name is Hiram Edson. "... I was stopped about mid-way of the field. Heaven seemed to open to my view and I saw, distinctly and clearly, that instead of our Lord coming through the open skies, that our Lord was working in the heavenly temple" (Excerpt from the sermon "The Prophecy That Failed" by J. R. Hoffman).
38. No sinner will ever even come close to equaling Christ's accomplishments. Only one perfection is possible, God's! You *alone* are holy! (Rev. 15:4). "The divine beauty of

the character of Christ, of whom the noblest and gentlest among men are but a faint reflection...was a living representation of the character of the law of God" (*Thoughts from the Mount of Blessing*, p. 49).

39. "Now, while our great High Priest is making the atonement for us, we should seek to become perfect in Christ. Not even by a thought could our Saviour be brought to yield to the power of temptation. Satan finds in human hearts some point where he can gain a foothold; some sinful desire is *cherished*, by means of which his temptations assert their power. But Christ declared of Himself: 'The prince of this world cometh, and hath nothing in Me.' John 14:30. Satan could find nothing in the Son of God that would enable him to gain the victory. He had kept His Father's commandments, and there was no sin in Him that Satan could use to his advantage. This is the condition in which those must be found who shall stand in the time of trouble" (*The Great Controversy*, p. 623, emphasis added).

    "It is in this life that we are to separate sin from us, through faith in the atoning blood of Christ. Our precious Saviour invites us to join ourselves to Him, to unite our weakness to His strength, our ignorance to His wisdom, our unworthiness to His merits. God's providence is the school in which we are to learn the meekness and lowliness of Jesus. The Lord is ever setting before us, not the way we would choose, which seems easier and pleasanter to us, but the true aims of life. It rests with us to co-operate with the agencies which Heaven employs in the work of conforming our characters to the divine model. None can neglect or defer this work but at the most fearful peril to their souls" (*The Great Controversy*, p. 623).

    "The apostle John in vision heard a loud voice in heaven exclaiming: 'Woe to the inhabiters of the earth and of the sea! for the devil is come down unto you, having great wrath, because he knoweth that he hath but a short time.' Revelation 12:12. Fearful are the scenes which call forth this exclamation from the heavenly voice. The wrath of Satan increases as his time grows short, and his work of deceit and destruction will reach its culmination in the time of trouble" (*The Great Controversy*, p. 623).

40. Some have pointed to the fact, that, when Martin Luther died, he was working on his commentaries on the books of Moses. Many Lutherans are surprised when they read what Luther wrote about Adam and the Sabbath. "...from the beginning of the world the Sabbath was intended for the worship of God." "Unspoiled human nature would have proclaimed the glory and the kindnesses of God in this way: on the Sabbath day men would have conversed about the immeasurable goodness of the Creator; they would have sacrificed; they would have prayed, etc. For this is the meaning of the verb 'to sanctify.'" "On the Sabbath day he would have taught his children; through public preaching he would have bestowed honor on God with the praises which He deserved; and through reflection on the works of God he would have incited himself and others to expressions of thanks. On the other days he would have worked, either tilling his

field or hunting" (*Luther's Works*, volume 1, Lectures on Genesis, Chapters 1–5, Saint Louis: Concordia Publishing House, 1958, translated by George V. Schick, edited by Jaroslav Pelikan, pp. 80, 82).

41. See http://1ref.us/nd (accessed 03/01/18).
42. Hymn No. 626, "In A Little While, We're Going Home." *Seventh-day Adventist Hymnal*, Review and Herald Publishing Association (1991).
43. The disciples had thought the temple would stand forever, but Jesus had told them, "See ye not all these things? verily I say unto you, There shall not be left here one stone upon another, that shall not be thrown down" (Matt. 24:2). When Titus leveled the city, he did not destroy the temple. Yet, the Jesus' prophecy came true. "Angels of God were sent to do the work of destruction, so that one stone was not left one upon another that was not thrown down" (Ms. 35, 1906, in *Seventh-day Adventist Bible Commentary*, vol. 5, p. 1099).
44. "Alexander Campbell, well known religions leader of the nineteenth century, stated in debate with John B. Purcell, Bishop of Cincinnati, in 1837 that the records of historians and martyrologists show that it may be reasonable to estimate that from fifty to sixty-eight millions of human beings died, suffered torture, lost their possessions, or were otherwise devoured by the Roman Catholic Church during the awful years of the Inquisition. Bishop Purcell made little effort to refute these figures" (citing *A Debate on the Roman Catholic Religion*, Christian Publishing Co., 1837, p. 327; John B. Wilder, *The Shadow of Rome*, Zondervan Publishing Co., 1960, p. 87).
45. The flame may also refer to the final destruction (Rev. 20:10).
46. (Luke 4:18). The Holy Spirit has anointed Jesus with anointing oil symbolizing the baptism of the Spirit and healing power.
47. The RSV simply renders this as, "And *between* the throne and the four living creatures and among the elders ..." I am conceptualizing the throne as the whole region occupied by God the Father, the Son, and the Holy Spirit.
48. Samuele Bacchiocchi, Seventh-day Adventist author.
49. The word *thumiatērion* is translated "censer" in the KJV. The two places this Greek word is used in the Septuagint Old Testament (2 Chron. 26:19; Ezek. 8:11) are clearly referring to censers. The altar of incense was in the Holy Place.
50. John W. Kleining, *The Lord's Song: The Basis, Function and Significance of Choral Music in Chronicles* (Sheffield, England, 1993), pp. 82, 83.

TEACH Services, Inc.
PUBLISHING
www.TEACHServices.com • (800) 367-1844

CPSIA information can be obtained
at www.ICGtesting.com
Printed in the USA
JSHW030147170323
38917JS00001B/3